BILL - A cartoon

RON - HOW MANY SEXES ARE THERE?

BILL - 3. the male sex, the female sex + insects

RON - WHERE DO BAD GIRLS GO?

BILL - Most everywhere.

RON - WHAT CAUSES MOST ACCIDENTS?

BILL - The nut that holds the wheel.

RON - SO ONCE AGAIN WE COME TO THE CRUCIAL QUESTION.

BILL - Before you give me the question I want to say one thing. My wife's name is Armentrude G. Diddle biddle

RON - DIDDLE BIDDLE?

BILL - Diddle biddle

RON - I SEE.

BILL - I thought you would.

RON - THEN HERE'S THE 5ᵗʰ + FINAL QUESTION. WHO INVENTED THE STEAM ENGINE?

BILL - what?

RON - THAT'S ABSOLUTELY CORRECT! JAMES WATT. NOW THAT YOU HAVE WON THE GRAND PRIZE HOW DO YOU FEEL? CALM - COOL - COLLECTED?

BILL - I'm calm, I'm cool but I doubt if I'll ever

Suits Me

Walt Whitman and Wallace Stevens

Worlds into Words: Understanding Modern Poems

Gin Considered as a Demon (poems)

Coming to Light: American Women Poets in the 20th Century
(edited with Marilyn Yalom)

Selected Poems of Anne Sexton
(edited with Diana Hume George)

Anne Sexton: A Biography

Suits Me: The Double Life of Billy Tipton

Suits Me

THE DOUBLE LIFE OF
BILLY TIPTON

Diane Wood Middlebrook

A *Virago* Book

Published by Virago Press 1998

First published in the United States by
Houghton Mifflin Company, New York 1998

Copyright © Diane Wood Middlebrook 1998

The author is grateful for permission to quote lines from the following: "How Little It
Matters, How Little We Know," music by Philip Springer, lyric by Carolyn Leigh,
reprinted by permission of Tamir Music and EMI Music Inc.; "My Wubba Dolly," by Kay
Werner and Sue Werner, reprinted by permission of EMI Music Inc.; "The Nearness
of You," by Ned Washington and Haogy Carmichael, copyright © 1937 and 1940 by
Famous Music Corporation, copyright renewed 1964 and 1967 by Famous Music
Corporation; "It's Only a Paper Moon," lyric by Billy Rose and E. Y. Harburg, music by
Harold Arlen, copyright © 1933 (renewed) by Chappell & Co., Glocca Morra Music, and
S. A. Music Co., all rights reserved.

The moral right of the author has been asserted

A CIP catalogue record for this book
is available from the British Library

ISBN 1 85381 658 2

Printed and bound in Great Britain by
Clays Ltd, St Ives plc

Virago Press
A Division of
Little, Brown and Company (UK)
Brettenham House
Lancaster Place
London WC2E 7EN

To the memory of my mother,

HELEN DOWNEY WOOD

Born 13 June 1919, Aramo, Idaho
Died 29 October 1991, Spokane, Washington

Contents

LIST OF ILLUSTRATIONS

BILLY TIPTON'S FAMILY TREE

PATERNAL
THOMAS TIPTON (1848–1917)
m. Deco Ella Bywater (1854–1916)

    1. Julia Lee (1877–1920)

    2. John H. (1880–1909)

    3. Dorothy (Dove) (1882–1942)

    4. Beatrice (Bess) (1886–1961)

    5. GEORGE WILLIAM (1892–1975)

MATERNAL
MATTIE CHATWELL (1864-ca. 1956)
m. Jefferson Bryant Lindsay

    1. Maude
    2. Rosa
    3. Claude
    4. Cora
       a. Madeline (1915–)
       b. Eilene (1918–)
       c. John (1930–)

m. Tom Parks
    1. REGINALD LOIS (1896–1971)

m. (Daddy) Wallace Fleming

GEORGE WILLIAM TIPTON   m.   REGINALD LOIS PARKS
  m. Marie   m. Charles Herr
  m. Irene   m. Lynn M. Fullenwider
    1. James Paul Tipton (1935–)

DOROTHY LUCILLE   William Thomas Tipton (1921–)
  (1914–1989)

  w. Non Earl, 1934

  w. June, 1943

  w. Betty, 1946

  w. Maryann, 1954

  w. Stella Marie ("Kitty") Flaherty, 1962
    1. John Thomas (1963–)
    2. Scott Lee (1963–)
    3. William Alan (1969–)

PREFACE

This is the story of a female jazz musician named Billy Tipton, who lived as a man from the time she was nineteen until "he" died at age seventy-four and was discovered to be female. Billy Tipton's death in the provincial western city of Spokane, Washington, made news all over the world, not because Billy was a well-known musician but because the scale of the deception and the scarcity of explanations endowed the skimpy available facts with the aura of myth.

Though Billy Tipton wrote no account of his motivations, he did leave a legal will that named his former wife Kitty Tipton Oakes as executor of his estate. She and the three sons that she and Billy adopted were among the numerous people—including several other Mrs. Tiptons—who had been unaware during Billy's lifetime that Billy was female. Depression-era Oklahoma gave a *Grapes of Wrath* background to Billy's story, and playing jazz in a swing band seemed to have been the original purpose of her ploy. But how had she pulled it off, and why had she...well, kept it up? Mrs. Oakes decided to look for a writer who would research Billy Tipton's life and discover answers.

In the late summer of 1991, when I went to Spokane to give a talk about my newly published biography of the poet Anne Sexton, Mrs. Oakes approached me as a writer who was also a local girl (Spokane had been my home town until I finished high school). We discussed the issues involved in permitting an outsider to conduct research into private family matters. Mrs. Oakes, hoping for a book that might eventually become the basis of a film about Billy Tipton, agreed to make available everything she had found in Billy's office, along with the family papers and photographs in her own possession, and to grant me complete editorial autonomy in using these materials.

The most urgent research priority was to find, before it was too late, the people who had known Billy Tipton. Eventually I located most of the key witnesses, with the help of a number of professional journalists. My first guide to the territory was Bob Lee, a columnist at the *Daily Oklahoman*, without whose help this tale could not have been told. I also thank James Risser, director of the Knight Journalism Fellows Program at Stanford University, who provided me annually with a fresh supply of experts. Gerry Everding, a veteran investigative journalist and senior news editor at Washington University in St. Louis, served as a resourceful and judicious research assistant. Other significant research was performed by Robert Basil, Charles Boeckman, William F. Clark, Mary Ellen Foley, Mark Hollars, Lawrence Jackson, Gerald Johnson, Nova A. Lemons, Adam Mars-Jones, Leah Middlebrook, and Ron Turner.

Billy Tipton led the itinerant life of a professional musician. Because very few people saved the letters Billy wrote on the road, I was dependent for information on the recollections of other musicians who had lived the life. For showing me how it was, I acknowledge first and foremost the late Norma Teagarden, a jazz pianist who knew Billy Tipton at the very outset of her career as a cross-dressing musician in Oklahoma City. Other musicians who traveled and performed with Billy and generously shared their memories were Wayne Benson, Clarence Cagle, Russ Carlyle, the late Don Eagle, Paul Jensen, Ron Kilde, Dick O'Neil, Tommy Perkins, Bill Pierson, Kyle Pugh, Lewis Raines, Kenny and Dolly Richards, Marvin Richter, Ben Tessensohn, Jerry Seaton, Bonnie Spencer, Walter "Son" Wallin, and Bill Watson. Additional thanks are due to Dave Sobol, Billy's business partner, for his unfailing helpfulness. And my gratitude goes to the pianist Jeri Brown, to the drummer Roberta Ellis Brower, to the vocalist Marigold Hill (formerly Mrs. George Mayer), and to Lillian Murphy, a.k.a. Sara, who played banjo with the Oklahoma City Arkansawyers. Each of these artists gave me a woman's angle on Billy's way of life.

Two former Mrs. Tiptons who provided indispensable insight into the private Billy Tipton were Betty Cox and the late Maryann Cattanach. I thank them for their warmth toward me, for their sense of the ridiculous, and for not flinching before the subject of sex. To Stormé DeLarverié, Jamison Green, Jay Prosser, and Rupert Raj-Gauthier, I am grateful for views from inside the transgendered life.

Some of the most expressive sources of information about Billy Tipton came from two specifically twentieth-century forms of documentation, photographs and audiotapes. In this biography, where words from the subject are in short supply, pictures provide the most eloquent testimony to the way life felt and looked. I thank Dorothy Tipton's brother and sister-in-law, W. T. and Doris Tipton, for sharing not only their memories but the legacy of Tipton family photographs and papers in their stewardship, and for their gracious hospitality during my visits to them. Dorothy's cousins, who are given pseudonyms in this book at their request, thoughtfully provided photographs, a written memoir, and abundant highly quotable accounts of Dorothy's mother's side of the family. Kitty Tipton Oakes's collection of photograph albums covered every year of her married life with Billy, and both she and her son William Alan Tipton provided invaluable recollections.

The audiotapes that capture Billy's work as a musician are few in number but full of information about the music business of the swing era. For assistance in understanding how much these threads of polyester could reveal, I owe much to archivists of recorded sound: Larry Appelbaum, studio engineer and jazz film curator at the Library of Congress; Chuck Haddix, of the Marr Sound Archive at the University of Missouri–Kansas City; and Barbara Sawka, of the Stanford University Libraries. Madeline Matz, film and television research librarian at the Library of Congress, also provided important leads. For assistance with print materials, special thanks to Robert Blackburn, assistant curator of the Oklahoma State Historical Society, the staff of the Cheney-Cowles Museum in Spokane, the staff of the Lesbian Herstory Educational Foundation in New York, and William McPheron, curator of English and American Literature Collections at the Stanford University Libraries. The staff of the Oklahoma Air and Space Museum provided rare photographs of Billy Tipton's father.

The task of reconstructing Billy's life required contributions from many people, and each name listed here represents an episode for which formal acknowledgment is small recompense. My thanks go to Paula Backscheider, Don Ball, Tony Bamonte, J. Birney Blair, Jeff Bloomgarden, Agnes Cowles Bourne, Joann and Michael Brandon, Hadda Brooks, L. W. James Brooks (a.k.a. Doebelly), Mary Lee Brueshof, Doug Brock, Kathrean Cagle, Terry Castle, Helen Chickering, Doug Clark, the late Carrie Flaherty Collins, Butch Colyear, Hazel Craddock, Caroline Crawford, Loretta Crews, Patty Cunningham, Glenn Davis, the late Terry Dea, Dorothy Dreher, Elizabeth Drorbaugh, Roger Felice, Roy Ferguson, Doug Foster, Renee Fox, Madeleine Ginsburg, Kathleen Mayer Grandmain, Al Good, Lionel and Barbara Greenwood, Harry Guinn, Ellie and Thomas Hamburger, Non Earl Hancock, Shannon Handler, Clint Harrison, Phyllis Stalick Holmes, Alvin Hooper, Margaret Shepard Hoy, Juanita Jama, Christine Stewart Jones, Grant Joos, Eulah Keene, Paul and Louise Keesee, Gilbert Keithly, Pauline Lane, Dorothy LaPlante, Shirley Lent, George R. Lindholm, Verda Lippitt, Lela Lowell, Ming Quia Ma, Jack Mallett, Larry Martin, Greg and Marian Mason, Lee McKee, the late Lula Mae Meier, Bernie Mitchell, Shannon Moffatt, Bill Murray, Jimmy B. Nixon, Jerry, Bev, and Denise Numbers, Robert Oakes, Frank Parman, Mary Helen Parsons, Virgil Phillips, the Honorable Justin L. Quackenbush, Don Reynolds, the late Helen P. Rhoden, Lucille Rice, John Riley, Elaine Ronconi, Robert L. Rotchford, Jr., Joan Salathiel, Grover Sales, Jacob Samara, William Savage, Dorothy Sessions, Pauline Shipley, Clark Stewart, Barron Stringfellow, Pat Swan, Marilyn Swan-Dyer, Beverly Talbott, Kathleen Tanksley, Fred Teagarden, Nadine Myers Thiel, James C. Thomas, Jr., James Tolbert, Hazel Turner, Harry Quinn, George Weldon, J. L. and Thelma Whitt, Hal Wilder, Norm Wilson, Terry Wilson, Bryan Willis, Lewis Wolpert, Kate Wright, and Susan Zlomke.

For their warm hospitality during these years of research travel, I thank my father, Thomas Wood, and his wife, Arene, and my sister Colleen Dea and her family, in Spokane; Jerry McLoud, in Tulsa; and Kurt and Marilyn Metzl, in Kansas City.

For opportunities to present work in progress, I thank Professors Marjorie Garber and Henry Louis Gates, Jr., of Harvard University, organizers of the conference "Life Likenesses: The Seductions of Biography" in October 1993; Tom Goldstein, former dean of the School of Journalism at the University of California at Berkeley and organizer of the conference "Whose Life Is It, Anyway?" in March 1995; Professor Jeremy Treglown of the University of Warwick, organizer of the conference "Literary Journalism and Literary Scholarship," and Jay Dempster, who prepared a CD-ROM version of "The Biographer as Investigative Journalist" for my use at that conference in November 1995; Professor Mariamne Whatley, chair of women's studies at the University of Wisconsin, Madison, for the invitation to present a talk titled "Biography in the Age of Hypermedia" in March 1996; Professor Iris Litt, for the opportunity to discuss "What Pronoun Do You Choose for a Cross-Dresser?" with the Associates of the Stanford University Institute for Research on Women and Gender in January 1997; and Catherine Muther, of the Three Guineas Foundation, for the invitation to present the slide lecture "Portrait of the Artist as a Brave Little Girl," in conjunction with the exhibition "Brave Little Girls" at the San Francisco Public Library in October 1997.

For careful readings of manuscript drafts, I am greatly indebted to the jazz specialists who tuned my instrument: Don Asher, Robert Basil, Jim Merod, Sheldon Meyer, and Grover Sales. Additional helpful readings were provided by members of the Biographers' Seminar at Stanford University and by Richard Almond, Mary Ellen Foley, Estelle Freedman, Mortimer Herzstein, Ann Hogle, Alex and Tabitha Kessler, Kevin Kopelson, Norma Miller, and Ron Turner.

Throughout the development of this project I benefited from the shrewd good sense of my agent, Georges Borchardt, and from the friendship, advocacy, and judgment of my editor, Peter Davison. At the very end, Liz Duvall's mastery of the craft of manuscript editing made all the difference.

The eagle eye of Carl Djerassi looked longest at work in progress. For his companionship and forbearance during these years of research and writing, I cannot thank him enough.

The dedication of this book to my mother expresses gratitude to the first person from whom I ever heard the words that form a refrain in Billy's story: "To understand, you'd have to have lived through the Depression." She had, and now I have too.

DIANE WOOD MIDDLEBROOK
London and San Francisco,
September 1997

AUTHOR'S NOTE

Billy Tipton's success in passing as a man creates a problem for anyone writing about this person's life: should Billy be called "he" or "she"? My account uses both pronouns. "He" and "his" are used to refer to Billy's professional persona and to the relationships he conducted with people who thought he was a man. Billy is "she" in early life and in professional life when the people around her know she is cross-dressing. I also use the female pronouns "she" and "her" when I attribute motives and skills to Billy as the producer of the illusion of masculinity, both onstage and off.

PART I

Beginnings

1889–1932

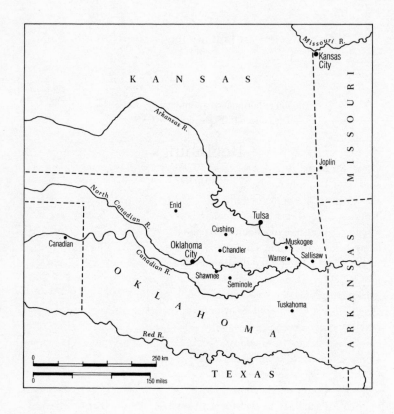

Born Naked

≡≡≡≡≡

21 January 1989

You're born naked and the rest is drag.
— Drag queen RuPaul, *Lettin' It All Hang Out*

ONE SATURDAY MORNING in January 1989, an emergency call summoned paramedics to a trailer park on the outskirts of Spokane, Washington, the home of Billy Tipton, an aging white jazz musician. Tipton had been very ill, too weak to leave his bed, but had resisted all attempts to get him to a doctor. His adopted teenage son, William, had been looking after him. That morning, after carrying Billy to the bathroom, William had closed the door and, out of earshot, telephoned his mother, Kitty. They hadn't spoken for nearly a year. Divorce had dispersed the family almost a decade earlier, and Kitty had remarried, but she could still be counted on in a crisis. She advised William to dial 911 and have Billy moved to a hospital. William made the call, then went to carry his father to the breakfast table. Billy Tipton gave a deep sigh and slumped against his son, unconscious.

That sigh was a secret escaping. The medics arrived almost immediately, lay Tipton on the floor of the trailer, squatted over him, and opened his pajamas to feel for a heartbeat. One of them turned to William and asked, "Son, did your father have a sex change?" William stepped forward and caught a glimpse of his father's upper body, then stumbled back against the screen door and down the trailer's steps. What had he seen? "I was in awe. I had no thoughts — just looked up at the sky, thinking it was some hallucination from drugs. If my father had lived as a woman, she would have had big breasts."

Nobody but Billy had seen that nude torso for about forty years, not even the women who had lived with him as wives. Billy was a very private person, they explained later. He invariably locked the bathroom, where he washed and dressed. People who knew his habits knew that he always wore binding on his chest to support the ribs that had been fractured when the front end of a Buick had plowed into his body — or so he said.

And many, many people knew Billy Tipton. Spokane had been one of the regular stops on his trio's circuit in the early 1950s, during the brief heyday of legal gambling in private clubs in Washington State, when a band could make a good living backing strippers, magicians, jugglers, tap dancers, any sort of variety act that would draw customers into the clubs to drink and play the slot machines. In 1958, Billy settled in Spokane, and the Billy Tipton Trio became the house band at a downtown nightclub called Allen's Tin Pan Alley. Billy bought a house in the Spokane Valley and started earning a second income as an agent in the Dave Sobol Theatrical Agency, booking the musicians.

In Spokane, out of professional respect, Billy Tipton was referred to as a jazz musician. He referred to himself as an entertainer, for he had long before given up trying to make a living at jazz, though he smuggled it into floorshows he worked up with other members of his trio, playing a repertory of swing standards on saxophone and piano. Oklahoman by birth, he was attuned to the stingy provincial audiences he had to please in Spokane, and he had a flair for showmanship. As an emcee, he adopted the gregarious style of the businessmen who were regular customers at the clubs, and female fans were attracted by his boyish good looks and his meticulous style of dress.

After Billy married Kitty in 1962, they adopted three sons and involved themselves in the PTA and the Boy Scouts. In his work life too Billy was an exemplary citizen. If a charity wanted to hold a dance or a fellow musician was down on his luck, Billy Tipton was the one who would organize a benefit. He led an active public life in the community for thirty years.

But by the time of his death, Billy was almost destitute. Not much business walked through the doors of the booking agency, where he still worked on commission. He showed up in a fresh shirt every morning nonetheless, with a joke on the tip of his tongue to greet anyone who dropped by the seedy little office. He was a heavy smoker and chronically short of breath, and often quipped that ulcers and hemorrhoids were occupational hazards in the music business, but he brushed off questions about his health. Untreated, hemorrhaging ulcers finally killed him.

Billy Lee Tipton was pronounced dead in the emergency room of Valley General Hospital that Saturday, never having regained consciousness, leaving a mystery as his most substantial legacy. *He* was dead. But who was *she*?

A buzz began after the autopsy on the Monday afternoon following Billy's death. The autopsy report, written by a pathologist aware of Billy's history, established that the body was that of a normal biological female past menopause. The coroner signed the pathologist's report, then placed a call to a local journalist offering a scoop. "Get hold of Billy Tipton's death certificate," he told the journalist. Billy had been a prominent figure in the entertainment business in Spokane. Didn't the public have a right to know?

One person who didn't think so was Billy's former wife Kitty, now Mrs. Robert Oakes. She contacted a funeral director, swore him and his staff to secrecy, and arranged for cremation of the body. When she learned that the local newspaper was planning to publish the discovery of Billy's hidden identity, she paid a visit to the managing editor and demanded privacy for the family. But one of Billy's sons had already granted an interview, and this constituted sufficient family permission to override Kitty's objections. The editor compromised by holding the story until after Billy's memorial service the following Monday, and by keeping it off the front page. "Jazz Musician Spent Life Concealing Fantastic Secret" was published Tuesday morning, 31 January, in the newspaper's regional section.

The wire services picked up the story at once. Even the *New York Times* carried a respectful, faintly marveling obituary for Billy Tipton. Media companies followed with proposals for feature films and made-for-TV movies, and Kitty and the three Tipton sons were greatly in demand for talk-show appearances.

The spotlights revealed a family at war, with the two older sons, John and Scott, allied against William, the youngest, and Kitty. A tabloid published a story called "My Husband Was a Woman and I Never Knew," in which Kitty said she believed that she and Billy had been legally married and legally divorced and that she had never been physically intimate with Billy because of her own poor health. The two older sons claimed that they had not known Billy's sex — "He'll always be

Dad to me," said John — though before Billy's death, both had begun using the family names of their biological mothers as aliases. But John and Scott did not believe Kitty's claim to ignorance about Billy's identity. Calling Kitty "a fake," they assigned the rights to their story to a film company. The enmity between the two camps was poignantly expressed after Billy's cremation by a division of his ashes into two boxes, one entrusted to John and Scott and the other to William. As a journalist observed, "Even now, ironically, there are two Billy Tiptons."

As many of the articles written about Billy Tipton pointed out, Billy was not unique in solving an economic problem or seizing a tempting opportunity just by donning trousers. Throughout history, women had been putting on men's work clothes in order to perform work reserved for men. Some went to sea, like the Pirate Jenny of Kurt Weill's song, who had a number of real-life counterparts. Some went to war; a nurse who served during the American Civil War estimated that she had observed as many as four hundred cross-dressing women in the Union Army alone. Some wrote their memoirs. Among the most colorful on record is a Spanish nun named Catalina de Erauso, born in 1592, who fled the convent to become a soldier in Panama and, after disclosing her sex, received papal dispensation to continue wearing men's clothes. In old age, she wrote a tell-all autobiography that was adapted for the stage. The French writers George Sand, in the nineteenth century, and Colette, in the twentieth, also cross-dressed and told. But some of the cross-dressers we know about were exposed, like Billy Tipton, only after their death. James Miranda Stuart Barry (1795–1863), for example, served as a physician and surgeon for forty-six years in the Medical Department of the British Army, where he rose to the rank of inspector general. The attendant who laid out the body for burial discovered Barry's sex, but the information was suppressed in order to preserve the dignity of the army. Dr. Barry is credited with performing the first successful cesarean delivery in the British Empire and is now recognized as the first British woman physician, but of course conducted this medical career entirely in the guise of a man.

But Billy Tipton was not history, Billy was *today*, and with no credible explanation for his motivations coming from anyone close to the source, the world was free to make of Billy Tipton what it would. The world was ready. During the years in which Billy's style of music had been going out of fashion in the entertainment business, gender had come into its own as a theme in art and politics. The very term "gender" was now a marker on the grave of venerable assumptions about the importance of sex difference. Billy Tipton literally became a poster boy for raising consciousness about the confusion of sex (biological) and gender (culturally meaningful physical and social attributes) when, shortly after his death, his image appeared in San Francisco on the cover of a how-to book addressed to cross-dressers and transsexuals. Artists, too, appropriated Billy as a symbol. A group of avant-garde female jazz musicians from Seattle dubbed themselves the Billy Tipton Memorial Saxophone Quartet; Billy's obituary provided the story line for an opera titled *Billy*, produced in Olympia, the capital of Washington State. Thinly disguised versions of Billy's story also formed the plots of several plays that received wide critical attention. One, titled *Stevie*, by Eduardo Machado, was staged at the Mark Taper Forum in Los Angeles by the British actor and producer Simon Callow. Another, *The Slow Drag*, by Carson Kreitzer, was produced Off Broadway in New York and as cabaret theater in London. Academic researchers immediately took an interest in explaining Billy, while on the Internet, Billy's name became shorthand for a whole host of issues among groups with list names across a range of identifications from "sappho" (lesbians) to "boychicks" and "f2mlist" (female-to-male transgenderists).

Generalizations and symbols will take us only so far in thinking about an individual life, however. What could be learned about *Billy's* reasons for adopting men's clothing and a masculine identity? Billy, it turned out, had left plenty of clues, beginning with a legal will. Early in their marriage, Billy and Kitty Tipton had owned a certain amount of property. With a lawyer's assistance, Billy had drawn up a will in 1965, after the adoption of their first child; updated it in 1971, after the adoption of their youngest son; and updated it again in 1982, after he and Kitty separated. In every version of the will, Kitty was named executor of the estate. By the time Billy died, his estate consisted mainly of debts, plus the alto and soprano saxophones he had never pawned and the diamond ring he had always worn while playing the piano. Those relics of his career in show business went to William. The older sons, John and Scott, were acknowledged with one dollar each.

The other documents found in Billy's files revealed mainly how shrewd he had been in avoiding the attention of officialdom. He had a social security number but lived in poverty during his last years rather than claim benefits. No marriage or divorce was ever recorded for the William L. or Billy Lee Tipton in question, though, as would later be discovered, a sequence of women had called themselves Mrs. Tipton on their driver's licenses. Wisely, Billy had generated few medical records, since the intention to pass as a man would have been diagnosed as pathological during most of his lifetime. Not much evidence of Billy's inner life was to be found, either. There was no personal journal among his papers, and only a few letters survive from among the hundreds written to family members during the years Billy spent on the road, traveling with various bands.

Nor had much of Billy Tipton's art been recorded for posterity: a couple of demo tapes from the 1940s, a couple of LPs on generic labels produced during the late 1950s. Billy had not made a serious effort to become a recording star and had mainly earned his living playing dance music of the kind popularized by small jazz ensembles in the 1930s and 1940s. At his best, he sounded as much as possible like Benny Goodman's piano player Teddy Wilson. If Billy Tipton possessed a measure of Teddy Wilson's talent, however, he did not strive for Teddy Wilson's visibility. On the occasions when success approached, Billy retreated.

Yes, Billy had covered his tracks. Yet a collection of personal letters found among his professional memorabilia suggests that at the end, Billy decided to let her accomplishments be known. She had been in contact with two affectionate women cousins, whom Kitty had never even heard about before Billy's death. The cousins, it turned out, had been actively corresponding with Billy for years and knew all about Billy's family life: the marriage to Kitty, the adoption of the children, the divorce. For the past several years, they had been trying to persuade Billy to join them in the Midwest and take up life as a woman again — the woman they still called Dorothy. Why had Billy turned down the opportunity to slip away once her sons were grown? Wasn't it because she wanted to take a posthumous bow? The young musicians Billy booked at the Sobol agency recalled Billy's stories about the old days in the music business, traveling with the likes of Jack Teagarden, Bernie Cummins, Russ Carlyle, Scott Cameron. The stories were not always true, but they show us that Billy hoped to be remembered as belonging to a legendary era in American music, even though her participation required a lifelong disguise. The dramatic way she surrendered her secret at the time of her death suggests that she wanted the disguise to become part of the record too.

Billy Tipton had come of age as a musician at the same time that technology was inventing ways to separate the musician's body from the musician's sound. Take the case of Teddy Wilson, Billy's idol, one of the first black men to play with a prominent group of predominately white artists. Benny Goodman's integrated orchestra reached its huge audiences over the radio and on records. The music flowed right into the bodies of white listeners without rousing antipathy toward this kind of intimacy with the black man. Billy Tipton probably made the acquaintance of Teddy Wilson's elegant piano style in 1936, listening on a car radio to *Camel Caravan*, broadcast over CBS from New York. Billy studied Wilson's recordings until he could imitate Wilson's style, and later, when he had a small group of his own, adopted the Goodman quartet's "Flying Home" as a theme song. For Billy, the title of this song was loaded with private meanings that reached back into her childhood as Dorothy and evoked her relationship with her father, an aviator. But the Billy Tipton Trio's imitation of the Goodman group's "Flying Home" was purely practical, for bands like Billy's succeeded best when they most closely reproduced the recorded sound of jazz celebrities. At the peak of Billy's career, every successful small-time musician was to some extent a skilled impersonator. For instance, Billy's trio often performed "Exactly Like You," made famous by Louis Armstrong. Billy caught the multiple meanings of this clever title early in her career as a musician, and improvised on it for the rest of her life, in undetected drag.

Undoing Billy's disguise raises intriguing questions. Billy worked almost exclusively with men, in close quarters, for years at a stretch. Happily, the plot of Billy's story lets us watch one woman's bold solution to gaining a certain amount of recognition in what was largely a man's world. But how did she compensate for being raised as a girl and trained to play music as a girl? Would a professional career have been possible if Billy had lived openly as a woman? After all those years of playing a man, *was* Billy a woman, or just female?

Other questions rise in the wake of what can be learned about Billy's sexual practices. His former wife Kitty assumed that because there was no sex in their marriage, there was no sex in Billy's story. "Everybody wants to know the wrong thing," she often said in response to intrusive questions about their private life. But Kitty was only the last woman in Billy's life to be called Mrs. Tipton — the last of at least five. At least one of these women knew that Billy was a woman; at least two of them made love with Billy for years thinking that Billy was a man. What is really the "wrong" thing in Billy's story, then — deceitfulness? Gaining erotic satisfaction from women who would not have permitted the same intimacies if they had known Billy's sex? And what did Billy want? What was in it for her when she chose not only to adopt the role of a man but to play it in every scene, including those we think of as the most confiding?

Precisely because we can gain so little access to Billy's thoughts and feelings, to answer such questions we have to direct our gaze toward Billy's skills as an artist. The most important of these was a gift for mimicry. Billy deployed well-worn vaudeville traditions of impersonation in the nightclub skits he wrote. He parodied Elvis Presley and Liberace, and he played rubes ("Goofus," "Cindy") and kids ("Little Playmate," "All I Want for Christmas Is My Two Front Teeth"). Billy never impersonated adult women, but he frequently donned a sunbonnet to play the role of little girl in acts such as "My Wubba Dolly" and "Little Nell." Hidden under the broad comedy of these standard routines was an actor's talent for adopting and using the body language of another person. Billy was both acting the role and acting the actor who played it.

Billy's near-lifelong stint of male impersonation seems on first impression akin to the overt use of drag by contemporary performance artists, such as David Bowie's androgynous persona Ziggy Stardust. Or transvestite supermodel RuPaul's how-to interviews on his personification of a glamour queen. Or Madonna's impersonation of Michael Jackson. Or Laurie Anderson's cool, technologically assisted, sporadic appropriations of masculinity onstage. All of these artists make visible the stylizations by which gender is communicated as "natural."

But Billy is different. A perpetual improviser, never out of character, Billy drew her material from the gender fundamentalism of everyday life: the general belief that gender difference arises from anatomical sex difference in human beings and that gendered behavior is the natural outcome of sex difference. Playing a sequence of roles historically reserved for the "opposite" sex, Billy demonstrated by her accomplishment that gender, unlike sex, is in large part a performance: *she* was the actor, *he* was the role. And if her first act of cross-dressing was a brilliant, problem-solving prank, Billy quickly found that being taken for a man provided access to almost everything she wanted — music, travel, the love of adventurous and caretaking women.

Inevitably, death ended the act and exposed the actor. Billy was prepared. An adept illusionist to the end, she had done away with her sex-concealing gear, for the trailer was empty of the jockstrap and bindings familiar to Billy's wives and sons. Billy had prepared to emerge from behind his screen like the Wizard of Oz, to dissolve the magic into wisdom, revealing by her nakedness in death that the "difference" between men and women has little to do with biology. And locked away in Billy's office closet, along with the carefully worded and updated will, was the record of a lifetime's achievements: clippings and photographs documenting the transformation of Billy from *she* to *he* and the annotated routines, musical arrangements, and program notes in which Billy makes eye contact with posterity. These professional files show how, night after night, Billy scattered clues and riddles about the drag she wore, including risqué gags about homosexuality and jokes that called attention to the costume. Some have been placed at the heads of chapters and on the endpapers of this book, as though they were Billy's own comments on the story, for her handwritten versions convey an artist's pride in craft and discipline. They suggest that Billy was anticipating our admiration of her skill, our curiosity about her strategies, and, yes, our pursuit of her secrets.

But Who Was *She?*

1889–1928

BILLY TIPTON: From now on, my motto is "Wine,
women, and *so long!*"
— "Drunk," circa 1955

DOROTHY LUCILLE TIPTON was born in Oklahoma City on 29
December 1914 and reborn as Billy Lee Tipton in the summer of 1933.
This transformation deprived Billy of a background. Passing as a man,
Billy rarely talked about his folks or his childhood home, even to his
closest companions. A slip of the tongue could prove dangerous.

Yet it was to a pair of glamorous, exhibitionistic, neglectful parents
that Dorothy owed her skills as a musician and quite possibly her
vocation as an actor. Dorothy adored them, and Billy found a clever
way to hang on to them by subterfuge, writing them into the nightclub
routines he adapted from vaudeville handbooks. Replacing stock
phrases with details from his own past, Billy could bring right onto the
stage with him the parents and the little brother who were too ashamed
of his act to admire his performance. Most telling was his sendup of a
radio quiz show, "Gee Quiz."

STRAIGHT MAN: Where were you born?
BILLY TIPTON: Oklahoma. I wanted to be near my mother. But
she was disappointed when I was born.
STRAIGHT MAN: Why? Did she want a girl?
BILLY TIPTON: No — a divorce.

BILLY TIPTON: My father was an inventor. If it wasn't for one of
my father's discoveries, I wouldn't be here now.
STRAIGHT MAN: What was it?

BILLY TIPTON: My mother! She worked in a dance hall and
   raised five children at the same time.
STRAIGHT MAN: How could she do that?
BILLY TIPTON: Long intermissions.

The disappointed mother in Billy's life was Reggie Parks. Her disap-
pointments set in early, for she was raised as an orphan. Her mother, a
beauty named Mattie, was a widow with three daughters, a son, and no
money when she married a wastrel named Tom Parks. Mattie's fifth
child, Reggie, was born in 1896, in Fort Smith, Arkansas. Reggie barely
knew her father. When she was three years old, Mattie, fearing Tom
Parks's violence, fled to New Orleans with the five children. For safe-
keeping, she put her four girls into the House of the Good Shepherd,
originally a workhouse set up for prostitutes but now an orphanage
managed by nuns.

Mattie Parks took her son upriver with her to Natchez, where she
hid out in a black neighborhood for a while. She then opened a bawdy
house in Yazoo City and later married one of the wealthy customers. By
the mid-1920s, she was a prosperous woman, owning with her husband
a beautiful home in Jackson, Mississippi, and a handful of other businesses, including a cotton plantation called Little Bonanza.

Meanwhile, Mattie's female children lived with the nuns, knowing
little about their mother's activities. The nuns were strict and extremely frugal, not given to pampering what they called the "inmates."
They taught the girls to sew and cook and clean house, expecting them
to enter domestic service when they left the orphanage at age sixteen.
But Reggie, the youngest and prettiest child in the orphanage, was
treated differently from the other girls. The nuns made her their pet.
Reggie loved to sing and dance, and the nuns permitted her to put on
little shows for the other children. Pictures show her with long blond
curls that careful fingers had whirled into ringlets.

One consequence of being abandoned to the care of strangers was
that Reggie had only the vaguest notion of where she came from, how
old she was, and even what her real name was. Before entering the
House of the Good Shepherd, she was called Bossy, and her mother
registered her and her half-sisters under a false name to protect them
from Parks. The nuns named her Regina Lois, and she acquired the
nickname Reggie as a kid. Once married, she assigned herself the

dignified and manly name Reginald, adding Mae as a little feminine flourish, displacing Lois on some official records. But on her marriage license, on Dorothy's birth certificate, and on her tombstone, she is just plain Reggie.

When her closest sister, Cora, was sixteen and Reggie was twelve, the two of them left the House of the Good Shepherd to live with one of their older sisters. Both girls went to high school in the small town of Chandler, just east of Oklahoma City.

Reggie took to secular life as if she had been raised under the influence of her worldly mother. Growing up in an institution where luxuries were withheld on principle, she had developed powerful hungers, along with a conviction that she could get almost anything she wanted by looking pretty. "My face is my fortune," she often said, an attitude that sticks in the memory of those who watched her pass through a lot of hard times. As a young teenager she began experimenting with makeup in order to look older, outlining her mouth in a fashionable cupid's bow with brilliant lipstick and plucking her eyebrows into thin half-moons to emphasize her best feature, wideset eyes under a high smooth forehead, from which her naturally blond hair flowed back in waves. She was flirty with her eyes, had a coy way of looking up sideways. Later, people remarked on her striking resemblance to the actress Barbara Bel Geddes (best known for her stage role in *The Moon Is Blue* and for her part in the film *Vertigo*). She also had a distinctive way of filing her fingernails into sharp points and painting them bright red, achieving an effect both sexy and scary. According to family stories, Reggie played the piano for local dances when she was just a teenager, nimbly displaying those red fingernails.

And this is how Reggie was discovered — as Billy Tipton's quiz show sketch later put the case — by the inventor who was to become Dorothy/Billy's father. George William Tipton was nineteen years old when he fell in love with the little blonde who played ragtime for the high school dances. (He was Billie to his family, but since Billy Tipton's story is populated by an abundance of people with the same name, he will be called G.W.) He had gone to high school in Chandler but was now working as a machinist in Oklahoma City, where he repaired and built and raced motor cars. G.W. was from a family of "mechanical-minded" men, as one of them put it. If a Tipton was doing something to an engine, "he was concentrating on that and everything else could go to hell." But young G.W. was also something of a playboy. Once he discovered Reggie Parks, he began making regular afternoon trips to Chandler on the first motorcycle the town had ever seen. At the schoolyard, he would sit astride the cycle, waiting for Reggie. The littlest kids in town, already let out from the grade school, would gang around to admire the fabulous machine. One afternoon G.W. offered a ride to his seven-year-old cousin Bonnie Spencer. Clinging to G.W.'s back, speeding along at thirty-five miles an hour, Bonnie got so excited he wrapped his legs around the engine. "I carry the burn scars to this day," he says, lifting a trouser leg proudly. "I *wanted* to be related to him, he was so popular!"

G.W.'s parents, Thomas and Deco Bywater Tipton, had moved from Missouri to Chandler at the turn of the century, when Oklahoma was still Indian territory. G.W.'s father owned a livery stable, and his brother worked for the railroad. Everyone in the Tipton family was literate, according to the census. And everyone in the family was musical. The Tiptons owned a piano — a luxury. The sisters — Julia, Bess, and Dove — were given piano lessons and enjoyed classical music. G.W. played popular music. Bonnie Spencer, who went on to become a bandleader in Oklahoma City, remembers that G.W. taught him Scott Joplin's "Maple Leaf Rag," his first music lesson. Bonnie had been given his unusual name by his mother, who wanted a daughter. In those days toddlers of both sexes wore long hair and skirts, so his mother's fantasy lasted until he was about six years old. He recalls that his mother cried and cried when he put on his first short pants and became a boy.

In 1909 the Tipton family moved from Chandler to Oklahoma City, where there were great opportunities for mechanical-minded men. Chandler was still a cattle town, but Oklahoma City was already a model midwestern metropolis, its wide avenues shuttled by trolley lines and its main streets illuminated by electric lamps. On the roof of the electric company, a sign bragged LIGHT & POWER in hundreds of bulbs, visible for miles over the open prairie at night. G.W. went to work as a machinist and within a couple of years became service manager at the agency for Dodge and Hudson cars.

G.W. also built and drove stripped-down racing cars, always assigning them his lucky number, 4. A photo from the era shows a raffish young man in a leather helmet and rolled shirtsleeves, seated in a

Reggie and G.W. on a fishing trip, 1913

homemade racer with a Hudson Super Six engine, a big 4 painted on the cowl. G.W. is wearing the happiest expression that any camera ever captured.

By 1913, when G.W. met Reggie Parks, he was earning enough to support a wife. They got married in a fever, and G.W. took his young bride home to Oklahoma City, where they moved into a little apartment of their own. He had just turned twenty-one; she was sixteen, and madly in love. Reggie sent a snapshot back to the folks in Chandler, inscribed "Reggie and Bill on a fishing trip. The happiest man and wife on earth." They are posed against a roadster, displaying their shiny wedding rings. In another photo, taken at Pike's Peak later that spring, Reggie in her

trousseau finery poses with handsome G.W. on the running board of a
big touring car, flanked by her sisters-in-law and their rich husbands.
The orphanage with its deliberate deprivations was far behind this
pretty young bride.

Dorothy Lucille Tipton was born a year and a half later, in Oklahoma
City, to which she returned in 1933 to be reborn as Billy, a self-made
man. Many of the citizens of Oklahoma City had changed their names,
fudged their ages, invented educations, and covered their tracks. In
her daring act of self-invention, Billy Tipton was to do all of that plus a
little more, and the place was most suitable, for Oklahoma City too had
been created in one day: 22 April 1889, between noon and sunset.

This is how it came about. Early in 1889, the United States Congress
announced a series of land runs, the first to take place in April. Three
days in advance of the rush, people began streaming through Kansas,
Missouri, Arkansas, and Texas — twenty thousand people, by estimate, gathering in the Indian lands that formed the boundaries of the
first territory to be claimed. People ganged along the borders in every
sort of vehicle from prairie schooner to bicycle. Thousands prepared to
board trains specially scheduled by the Santa Fe Railroad. Cavalry
were dispatched along the lines to keep the peace and to fire the
starting guns.

At the stroke of noon on 22 April, banners fell, shots rang out, bells
tolled, and the hordes began pouring in. Many rushed to stake out
homesteads for farming, others to seize locations in town sites. All of
the lots in what would soon be called Oklahoma City were claimed
immediately, at least once, during that first afternoon. By sunset, the
place had been transformed from a railroad platform on a riverbank to
a surprisingly orderly tent encampment of twelve thousand souls.

The foundations of the distinctively divided culture of Oklahoma
City, the culture that shaped Billy Tipton's early career, were laid immediately in this newly established settlement by the rivalry between
two township societies. The Seminole Land and Improvement Company claimed lots in the choice northern area of the small township. Its
members had entered illegally, concealed themselves until noon on 22
April, then emerged with their surveyor to stake claims. Another company pitched its tents southward and won the nickname "kickers" in
those early days; eventually its members rechristened themselves
"Kickapoos." Mass meetings were called to sort out a form of city

government. Seminole Company leaders won the first election. The Kickapoos had already elected their own government, which they hung on to for a year. Each company laid out streets in areas where it had clear majority rule. The surveyors worked with different points of reference, and when the different sections of town were joined, some of the streets didn't quite meet and were different widths. The doglegs stayed. Motorists in downtown Oklahoma City still navigate dramatic jogs in a couple of the main thoroughfares, monuments to the old rivalry.

Just as North Town and South Town were established in the local psyche immediately after the land run of '89, so liberal applications of money determined the difference, not much later, of west and east. The Santa Fe Railroad tracks formed a straight edge running north to south right through the middle of town, dividing west from east. West was best — northwest, that is. The other main coordinate was Reno Street, boundary of the original town site, which was laid out perpendicular to the Santa Fe tracks. These geometries became the basis of an enduring class system in Oklahoma City. North of Reno and west of the Santa Fe tracks would stand the banks, the insurance companies, the telephone and telegraph offices, the government buildings, the nicer dry-goods stores, and the classy hotels. Further northwest would rise the mansions of the few who achieved every homesteader's dream of wealth and luxury.

An address in the southeast part of town, where Dorothy Tipton's working-class grandparents bought a house in 1909, had another sort of lineage. On land-run day, tents were raised on Second Street, and shortly afterward they were replaced by multistory bawdy houses. (These were, incidentally, the first jazz clubs in Oklahoma City.) The gamblers and the bootleggers set up shop nearby. Soon a business-woman from the mining camps of Colorado, "Big Anne" Wynn, took charge of prostitution in Oklahoma City. She rapidly became an influence in city politics, successfully negotiating the survival on Second Street of dancing, sex, and whiskey. Though Oklahoma had established Prohibition when it achieved statehood, in 1907, thirteen years ahead of the rest of the country, drink could always be found in Oklahoma City. Even today people joke that the legalization of alcohol in 1959 destroyed the efficient home-delivery services that the bootleggers had provided. To this day, Oklahoma Citians identify themselves as either North Town or South Town, Southies still carrying on the legacy of the kickers.

Billy Tipton's family were Southies, and the site of what was to become Dorothy Tipton's transformation into Billy was historically the refuge of people willing to shed one identity and don another in the interest of getting ahead. They parceled the city into spaces with well-understood boundaries, and they developed an ethos of grudging tolerance toward almost any way of life, a tolerance maintained by adopting the view that one person's private doings were none of anybody else's damn business. And jazz was the first art that flourished in this place.

The year after Dorothy's birth, Reggie and G.W. moved into G.W.'s big family home, where there was space and welcome for a baby, the only grandchild. But the young family had not been part of the household for much more than a year when G.W.'s mother was killed in a horrible accident — the car she was riding in was hit by a train. She was sixty-two years old. Her shocked relatives saved her bloody garments in an heirloom trunk, as though they couldn't bear to part with the evidence of what had been snatched away from them.

G.W. was driving the car in which his mother died. Baby Dorothy, sixteen months old, was in the car too and suffered severe injuries, including many lacerations, a broken arm, and what insurance reports describe as a "contusion of the abdominal wall." Thomas Tipton initiated a suit against the railroad engineer for negligence, claiming $10,000, and so did G.W., on behalf of Dorothy, but after a long investigation both claims were settled out of court for much, much less money than they sought. A question about G.W.'s culpability lingers around the memory of this accident, for he was a risk-taking man.

Little Dorothy recovered completely from the accident. But throughout adult life Billy Tipton explained that he wore bindings around his midsection because of an old injury. He claimed that his ribs had been broken in a car accident and were still sensitive to pressure, still needed the support of wide elastic bandages. The autopsy performed on Billy Tipton seventy-three years after this childhood trauma revealed no evidence of scarring or fracture. But Dorothy's attachment to her father was wound into those bindings. Once she began to dress as a man, G.W. disowned her. Yet he was the source and model of much that would later be perceived as masculine in her conduct, including her daring.

G.W. Tipton was not drafted when the United States entered the war in Europe in 1917, because he was a married man with dependents.

During the war he worked for McClelland Gentry Motor Company, a glamorous job in the days when automobiles were still exciting toys for the rich. He rose from mechanic to machinist to service manager. In a commemorative photograph posed alongside a partly disassembled Hudson luxury road car, he wears a three-piece suit and tie and a fedora, while the mechanics stand around in caps and greasy white overalls.

At the war's end, G.W. shared the benefits that flowed into civilian life by purchasing a war-surplus airplane. In 1918 the army owned a large inventory of Curtiss JN4 biplanes that had been used for training pilots, who nicknamed them Jennies. In the spring of 1919, G.W. heard that Jennies were for sale cheap in Houston, Texas, still in their original crates. He had never flown a plane, let alone put one together, but he persuaded his pal Bennett "Hun" Griffin, a recently discharged bomber pilot, to accompany him to Houston, where they assembled and tested one of the planes. Then G.W. received an hour and forty-five minutes of instruction in the open cockpit, on the flight back to Oklahoma City. This was the sum total of his training, ever.

G.W. and Hun landed in a pasture outside the city, and from that moment G.W. was in the aircraft business. An airport for Oklahoma City was already on the drawing boards by 1919 but was slow to materialize. Meanwhile, planes could land on any open field. G.W. bought a meadow on the outskirts of town and set up a repair station where he salvaged wrecked planes, rebuilt them, and traded in them. He also piloted the first airmail routes in Oklahoma City. He learned to design and build airplanes, and he built the engines to lift them. Eventually a number of models bore his name. At the time of his death, in 1975, G.W. was remembered as one of the major contributors to the early days of aviation in Oklahoma. "This man who had cut his teeth on racing automobiles and gasoline engines felt, in common with much of the nation's youth, the urge to fly," said his eulogist. "He became an aircraft designer and builder in an era when the air age was new, a time when aviators were swaggering, leather-helmeted daredevils and the ambition of every boy was to become a Lindbergh."

Aviation was an expensive hobby. To attract attention to the repair business that supported his passion, G.W. began offering passenger flights on Sundays. Customers would pay as much as three dollars apiece for the thrill of spending fifteen minutes in the air. G.W. also took up stunt flying. He had the temperament for show business — people remember him as a tease, full of pranks and jokes, and a mimic, wonderfully funny and mean. As a stunt flyer, he specialized in wing-walking. Another pilot would fly the plane while G.W. clambered onto the top wing and balanced there, or walked around, in the powerfully gusting Oklahoma wind.

On at least one occasion G.W. amazed the town by taking Dorothy up with him. One Oklahoma City citizen remembers this very well, because like Dorothy, she was just six years old. "There was a big pasture outside the Oklahoma City limits, about a mile square," she said. "My brothers and I would climb a stile to get into the pasture and watch the little fabric-covered sprucewood planes. About once a month one of them would crash, and people would race out in their cars to try to get hold of a piece of the wreckage. Well, one of the stuntmen was Tipton. One time he took his little six-year-old daughter up there with him, set her out on the wing with him, on the top wing. I remember how it scared me, that little girl up there with the wind blowing on her."

Dorothy was an only child at this time, and the only grandchild in the whole Tipton family. She had been named after G.W.'s sister Dove, whose real name was Dorothy — a name very common in the Midwest in those days, partly because of the success of *The Wonderful Wizard of Oz*. G.W. seems to have felt rather possessive of her and took a hand in raising her. One of Dorothy's cousins recalled that she was "a sturdy, healthy child," a tomboy. "My dad once saw Dorothy fighting with some boys and asked her dad, 'Aren't you afraid those boys will hurt that little girl?' Her dad said no, Dorothy could hold her own." When Dorothy was eight years old, G.W. built her a car with a real combustion engine in it and taught her to drive, making her into a real Tipton. But, the cousin recalled, Reggie wanted a "dainty" daughter and tried to encourage feminine tastes in her little girl. For example, when Reggie decided to bob her beautiful long blond hair, she had the cuttings made into a wig for a doll that she gave to Dorothy for Christmas.

Family albums illustrate these crosscurrents. A professional studio photograph shows Dorothy at around age three wearing a frilly lace cap and a dress of pale voile. Her feet are crossed primly at the ankle, and on her arm shines a bracelet that might be gold. Here is Reggie's dainty daughter. Other photographs show that different notions of womanli-

Reggie's dainty daughter, about age three

ness prevailed on the Tipton side of the family. In one snapshot, little Dorothy races a tricycle alongside an expensive automobile while Aunt Dove looks down from the driver's seat. (Reggie never learned to drive.) Other pictures show Dorothy in the cockpit of the Jenny, posed in the pilot's seat — another revealing referent of the Tipton Trio's theme song, "Flying Home."

The high-flying Tiptons entered the Roaring Twenties with their lean years behind them. Their second child, a son, was born on 28 December 1921, the day before Dorothy's seventh birthday, and was named William Thomas Tipton, after his father and his grandfather. By then the Tiptons were well-off enough to buy the large house adjacent to the family home on East Second, with a garage at the rear that G.W. turned into a machine shop for his new business.

As owner of Billie Tipton Piston Parts, G.W. was in a position to profit from the postwar boom, and photographs suggest that he did, at least for a while. The baby son enters the album posed in a fancy goatcart, a prop that accompanied a traveling photographer. Another photo from the era shows G.W. in a leather helmet at the controls of one of his biplanes, accompanied by Aunt Bess in a fur coat. Reggie rode around town with G.W. in a new Nash convertible with a rumble seat and bought expensive clothes at Oklahoma City's fanciest department stores.

During this period, Reggie's sister Cora moved briefly to Oklahoma City with her family. As in their girlhood at the orphanage, Reggie was lucky where Cora was not. Cora too had married a machinist, but unlike G.W., he was often out of work. His two daughters, Madeline and Eilene, today remember wistfully the one year during their childhood that the family had enough to eat. It was the year they lived with

G.W. at the controls, Bess in a fur coat

their grandmother Mattie in her plantation home on the Yazoo River in Mississippi. Mattie, having by then married the affluent planter, was sympathetic to Cora and took in the whole family.

Cora and her family went to Oklahoma City in 1923, drawn by the example of the Tiptons' prosperity. Madeline and Eilene enrolled in the same school as Dorothy and retained vivid memories of the year they spent together as children. "Dorothy was a happy child, always play-acting. Acting was what she liked," Madeline recalled. "And musical ability ran in the family on both sides. I remember Aunt Reggie and our uncle taking turns playing 'Tiger Rag,' 'Nola,' 'Kitten on the Keys,' 'Twelfth Street Rag' — they just pounded it out." Said Eilene, "Both of them could make a piano get up and walk!"

Dorothy and her little brother Bill, about 1924

Reggie, who gave Dorothy her first piano lessons, played music to have fun, and she played by ear rather than "by note," as the Oklahomans say. And she taught Dorothy how to rag. Ragtime was not jazz — it was not improvised — but it required skills that would transfer to jazz, such as syncopating the melody while keeping a regular rhythm going in the accompaniment. Later Dorothy would learn to read music, acquire correct fingering techniques, and master the intricacies of arranging. In childhood she learned to play what she heard, like a child learning a language. Piano music was one of her mother tongues.

What music did the Tiptons hear? Often it was recorded or broadcast music, which was rapidly replacing the live music played in family homes. What the Tiptons liked best — ragtime, cakewalk, blues — was "race music," written and popularized by black musicians. It usually reached white families like the Tiptons indirectly, on the crisp pages of sheet music or in the sound of invisible black fingers pressing the keys of player pianos. The cover drawing of Reggie's sheet music for "Nigger War Bride Blues" conveys the racial schizophrenia of the music business in the twenties, showing black soldiers marching to war with a black bride looking on, hankie in hand; inset at the center of the drawing is a publicity portrait of a white male singer, captioned "Featured by Billie O'Brien."

Oklahoma City was as racially segregated as any city in the South. The law confined Negroes to a grid of blocks south of Second Street and east of the Santa Fe Railroad tracks, which meant that the spacious house the Tiptons owned on East Second Street stood on the very boundary that separated the races. Though Oklahoma City never experienced anything as apocalyptic as the riots that devastated the Negro section of Tulsa in 1921, ugly behavior by whites was promoted by the enforcement of severe Jim Crow laws throughout the state. An early map of Oklahoma City marks off a "No Trespass" zone where these laws were enforced. As a man who still lives on East Second put it, "If you were black, you didn't go north of Second Street without a job or a reason."

Despite these conditions, Oklahoma City had a large black middle class, with East Second Street, nicknamed Deep Deuce, forming its main commercial district. The G.W. Tiptons lived in the 100 block of East Second. Deep Deuce began in the 300 block, and a lively black entrepreneurial community flourished there. Lining the street were professional offices, hotels, pharmacies, furniture stores, funeral homes, a famous performing arts and movie theater (Aldridge's), a famous dance hall (Slaughter's), and the offices of a newspaper outspoken in the cause of racial justice (*Black Dispatch*).

Deep Deuce was also host to some of the best jazz musicians in the world. As one music historian has observed, blacks migrating from New Orleans toward Kansas City, Chicago, and points east passed through Oklahoma, bringing ragtime and jazz and making the state a major musical crossroads. During the winter months, Oklahoma City's Ritz Ballroom was the first home base of Walter Page's Blue Devils, one of the Midwest's most famous jazz bands, featuring soloists such as William Basie (before he acquired the nickname Count) and the Oklahoma City–born Jimmy Rushing.

During Dorothy Tipton's childhood, the young Ralph Ellison lived about six blocks away. Born the same year as Dorothy, Ellison would go on to become an eminent writer, celebrating the life of East Second Street in his memoir *Shadow and Act*. One of his vignettes puts the saxophone player Lester Young in a shoeshine parlor on Deep Deuce, "jamming in a shine chair, his head thrown back, . . . his feet working on the footrests." Sometimes the black musicians would stroll into the white middle-class sections of town, instruments in hand, playing requests. Ellison remembered that the jazz guitarist Charlie Christian made money that way as a young boy, accompanied by his talented brothers and his blind father. After closing time in the white parts of town, white musicians (men only) would sometimes slip across the color line and head for the strip of nightspots that began in the 300 block of East Second, to sit in on a black jam session. One white musician active in the 1930s remembered, "You know, back then we never thought anything about going over to East Second Street and walking in there and playing. When they found out you were a musician, no problem. Because we had some guys who played pretty good." Until desegregation, such musicians were among the few Oklahomans who ever experienced the advantages of a racially mixed society.

The amber of family memory embeds G.W. and Reggie in a Roaring Twenties glow. They were a matched pair: good-looking, fun-loving, hot-tempered, sexy, ambitious. But after a dozen years of marriage, they began to turn against each other. When G.W. was mad at Reggie, he would take up one of his airplanes and buzz the house to torment her. Sometimes Reggie called the police, who laughed at the idea of trying to arrest him. That was a glamorous kind of row. A cargo of less amusing grievances piled up as well, and the marriage finally crashed and burned in 1927.

It was G.W. who filed the petition for a divorce, seeking custody of the children. He claimed that Reggie had been openly conducting a love affair with a man named Jack Ramsey and repeatedly telling him that she did not love him anymore. On the first of March, she had told G.W. that she was leaving him.

It seems that G.W. set a private detective on Reggie's heels to gather evidence of adultery. He found that Jack Ramsey had wired Reggie twenty dollars to be used as railroad fare to Canadian, Texas, and that Reggie had collected the money at an Oklahoma City bank under the name Dorothy Ramsey, then purchased a ticket and boarded the Santa Fe train at 3:45 P.M. When she arrived the following day at 2:30 A.M., "she was met by the said Jack Ramsey and they embraced each other fondly and kissed a number of times." The couple went to the Lone Star Hotel and "retired together," remaining in their room until 11:30 A.M., "occupying the same bed." When they emerged, Jack Ramsey began introducing Reggie around town as his wife. Meanwhile, the children were "being kept in school and cared for properly by this plaintiff," G.W., who argued that it would be "very detrimental to their interest" to be in Reggie's care.

Not four days after departing for Texas as Dorothy Ramsey, Reggie was back in Oklahoma City in a lawyer's office. Waving aside all the charges against her and claiming that she had never given G.W. "any provocation whatsoever" and had "at all times demeaned herself properly as a faithful and dutiful wife," Reggie zeroed in on what was, to her, the big issue: community property.

Reggie stated that at the time she wed G.W. she was fourteen years of age and that the couple had "no money or property whatsoever," that for a number of years she was forced to live with his sisters, and that her living conditions and arrangements were "almost unbearable." She received no money for her clothing but "was forced to wear the cast-off clothing of plaintiff's sisters" and serve as "the family drudge." Reggie also maintained that G.W.'s business success had been a joint effort.

By adhering to "strict rules of economy," the couple had been able to buy a home and then build a small machine shop. For a number of years Reggie had served as bookkeeper and kept all the accounts. With her assistance, Reggie asserted, the business had flourished and was by 1927 worth approximately $20,000. They owned other valuable property as well: three airplanes, a Dodge automobile, an Essex Coach, and a third, unspecified car.

As Reggie told it in her cross-petition, success had gone to G.W.'s head and made him mean. "After plaintiff began to prosper he began to indulge himself in wild parties and to drink and carouse around, and remained away from home for several days at a time . . . in the company of lewd women and immoral men; would come home drunk and abuse the defendant . . . Beat and whipped and wounded her in the presence of others; had friends take her out of the house so he could bring women home." Reggie believed herself entitled to an equitable share of the property, and because she had no means independent of G.W., she requested court costs, child support, and alimony.

This cross-petition set the scene for a contentious divorce. Much like the one between Charlie Chaplin and his wife, which was currently running in the local papers, it was a battle over money. (In a front-page story in the *Daily Oklahoman*, Mrs. Chaplin was quoted as saying, in regard to the $1500 monthly alimony payment she sought, "When my husband began giving other persons diamond bracelets, it was time for me to stop making my own clothes and buy some.") G.W. claimed he could not pay fifty dollars a week for Reggie's support, because he was heavily in debt. He also claimed that this was Reggie's fault. He would have been able to support his family "had it not been for the faults of the defendant in neglecting her duties." The court, he argued, "should not permit her on top of all these counts to rob plaintiff of such means as he has for the support and care of his children in order that she might have money to support another man."

As usual, the children became pawns in the game of taking sides. Days after G.W. filed for divorce, his sisters Bess and Dove packed up Dorothy and her little brother and took them to Kansas City. Through her lawyer, Reggie asserted the claims of mother-right. G.W.'s lawyer was ready with an explanation. G.W. had been "very much humiliated on account of this trouble and very anxious that the real facts in the actions of their mother not become known to the said children and especially to the little girl who is twelve years of age . . . it would be detrimental to the said daughter that she be forced to endure the jeers and jests of her peers with reference to her mother."

Mother-right settled the argument in Reggie's favor. The court ordered G.W. to return the children to Oklahoma City and placed them in Reggie's custody at the end of March. Meanwhile, the romantic Jack Ramsey faded from view. But Reggie had shown her hand. By claiming her getaway money under the alias Dorothy, she had waved a red flag at her snooty sister-in-law Dorothy. Never mind that it was her daughter's name as well. Reggie's callousness toward young Dorothy's feelings is memorialized in Billy's routine "Gee Quiz," where it gives an edge to the joke about being born in Oklahoma "because I wanted to be close to my mother." Dorothy was learning that Reggie didn't want a daughter, she wanted a divorce.

The children stayed with Reggie throughout the proceedings, while the parents blasted away at each other. The trial began in April and continued through August. At intervals, G.W. was arrested for failing to pay temporary alimony and child support and was enjoined to stop "harassing and molesting" the defendant. Meanwhile, numerous witnesses were summoned for depositions, and charges of misconduct mounted on both sides.

The final hearing took place on 23 August 1927. Reggie was granted custody of the children, title to the remaining equity in the house, first lien on the machine shop, a lump sum of $2500 in alimony, $50 per month for child support, and attorney's fees and court costs. In short, she got everything she asked for, despite the proof of adultery which gave G.W. his strongest legal claim against her. Perhaps the court took a serious view of Reggie's countercharges that G.W. was not only an adulterer himself but a wife-beater as well.

G.W. was outraged. His attorney served notice of his intention to appeal to the Supreme Court of the State of Oklahoma. This appeal was granted, and the plaintiff was given thirty days to make and serve his case. He applied for monthly extensions throughout the rest of the year and for much of the following year.

Meanwhile, Reggie rented a house and started looking for work. Her son, who was only six years old when the family broke up, remembered that she took a job at one of the big department stores in Oklahoma City. Reflecting back on his mother's situation, he felt a pang of commiseration. "Mother had been a housewife all her life. She was a good cook, made the best apple pie you ever put in your mouth. But she had no formal education, no way to support herself."

Then, out of the blue — or so it appears in the thinly plotted script written into court documents — a new turn of events redirected the action. In October 1928, more than a year and a half after Reggie Tipton bolted, G.W. Tipton suddenly dropped his appeal of the divorce decree. In exchange for an additional $1500 cash, Reggie relinquished claim to everything she had won in the divorce, including custody of the children. They would be sent to Kansas City to live with their aunt Bess.

Why did Reggie change her mind? Because she had found another man. This was Charlie Herr, who had been a boyhood friend of G.W.'s back in Chandler and had subsequently become an engineer with the State Department of Highways. Herr and his wife had been summoned as character witnesses on behalf of G.W. in the divorce proceedings. But Charlie Herr had also known Reggie back in her high school days. The divorce decree in the case of *Tipton* v. *Tipton* became final and binding on 27 October 1928, and a week later, free of all impediments, the former Reggie Tipton married the newly divorced Charlie Herr. Full-time motherhood had been a long intermission in Reggie's life, and it was over.

· 3 ·

Kansas City

1929–1932

> Took a lot of fortitude to be as happy as she was.
> — Cousin Madeline, reflecting on
> Dorothy's life, 1993

DOROTHY HAD JUST TURNED fourteen when she and her little brother, Bill, seven, boarded the train for Kansas City early in January 1929. Dressing them for the journey, their mother sobbed aloud, Bill recalled. "I was Mother's baby, you know. She was awfully sad to see us go." Well, why *did* she send the children to Kansas City, to be raised by their aunts? "I speculate that she thought it would be hard on us to move around with Charlie Herr's work," he answered, a little defensively. "But I missed my mother quite a bit, and resented not having her."

Whatever Reggie's motives were, once she decided to surrender custody, there was no question of who would fill her place. G.W.'s older sisters Bess and Dove, now in their mid-forties, had prospered in every way, but they were both childless. They had always taken a great interest in G.W.'s children, though, and were ready to welcome them.

Bess and Dove were not only sisters but close friends, with the complementary personalities signaled by their nicknames. Dove (for Dorothy) was mild-mannered and warm, with a comforting large bosom. Bess (for Beatrice) was bossy and venturesome, like the famous English queen. In her youth, she had been named "police queen" in a beauty contest staged by the Oklahoma City Police Department. A studio portrait of Bess in her twenties shows solid, corseted good looks, quite unlike Reggie's coy flirtatiousness, and if Bess's face was her fortune too, she had shown better sense than to invest it in a playboy.

Dove, in white, and Bess, in black

Bess had married a man of property named George Coffey and moved with him to Kansas City.

William Least Heat-Moon once wrote that the western boundaries of Minnesota, Iowa, Missouri, Arkansas, and Louisiana form a nearly straight line that bisects the United States both geographically and culturally. "When you stand east of those states you're in the East; cross over and you're in the West. It's simple and clear," he asserts. "Kansas City, Missouri, is the last Eastern city." Reversing the direction of immigration her Missouri-born parents had undertaken at the turn of the century, Bess had moved east, where the new frontier was urban. She and her husband set about investing in real estate and racehorses. By 1929 they owned several income-producing commercial properties and a farm and were renting a spacious apartment in the Rockhill district on Kansas City's south side. After the children's arrival, they bought a home in the country club district, yet further south. In Kansas City, south meant away from the stockyards, whose stench was almost inescapable in the humid river air. The country club district was a residential community of one thousand acres laid out as an upscale complex of houses, schools, recreational areas, and shops. It was also a community constrained by deed restrictions that limited the use of the land and the ability of the title holder to sell it. Catholics and Jews were explicitly denied access, along with Negroes, who were segregated by state laws. Social types who flourished in this environment are caricatured in the novels *Mrs. Bridge* and *Mr. Bridge,* by Evan Connell, who grew up in the country club district. (A screen adaptation of his novels was filmed on location there.) Street names in the community convey this rigorous social planning. Bess and George Coffey's handsome house was at 415 Sixty-second Street West Terrace — an engineer's poetry of grids and numbers, uneuphoniously rational.

Bess and George Coffey were not Social Register, but their tastes and views made for prosperity in a town ruled by the notorious Democratic party boss Tom Pendergast from the mid-1920s until World War II. Citizens like the Coffeys tolerated the open racketeering and graft fostered by machine politics as the social cost of an apparently healthy business environment. The Coffeys personally appreciated the liberal reinterpretation of the gambling laws that restored horse-racing to Kansas City, and threw themselves into raising, training, and racing thoroughbreds shortly after Riverside Race Track opened, in 1928. George Coffey became known around town as a sportsman. Bess bred Persian cats, and the house was full of her prizes. She proudly displayed other trophies of their prosperity too, including a ring with big matching diamonds "like the headlights on a car" and a pair of earrings, one carat for each ear. Bess had more diamonds than she could keep track of. When traveling, she carried her jewelry in tobacco pouches, and one day she walked off and left a little sackful of diamonds in a restroom.

Aunt Dove had also married well. Her husband, Logan Jaques, was a wealthy cattleman from Arizona. In the mid-1920s they apparently suffered some financial losses, so they moved to Kansas City and bought a brick apartment building on Warwick Boulevard, in the center of town, and Dove became active in ward politics. The move reunited Bess and Dove. From then on, though they lived in separate residences, they were a team.

When Dorothy and her brother arrived in Kansas City, the winter school term was just beginning. The transition was not well timed for either one of them. At fourteen, Dorothy was in her last semester of elementary school, entering a class of affluent and cliquish adolescents. Bill was entering the first grade for the second time that year. He recalled being miserable, homesick for his mother and father. He and Dorothy enrolled in the same school and turned to each other for comfort despite the difference in their ages, and Dorothy served as his protector while they settled into the new neighborhood. As he recalled, "Some of the kids picked on me, and Dorothy would whip their rear end."

And what about their father? Now that the children were resettled with his sisters, did he take an interest in raising them? The answer is no. By 1930, G.W. had become superintendent of the Ranger Aircraft Company in Oklahoma City and was too preoccupied with business to visit them. A couple of years later, when he took over the management of the old Richards Airport in Kansas City, he moved to the apartment building owned by Dove and her husband, but he continued to leave the child-rearing to his sisters. "Dad set me up a place in the basement there to build model airplanes," said Bill. "We'd sometimes take them out to Seward Park to fly them. But he was always so busy working, you know. He didn't have a lot of time for a kid."

Dorothy and Bill were well looked after by Aunt Bess, however. They had rooms of their own in the big house on West Terrace and spent most weekends with both aunts and their husbands at the Coffeys' farm in the country east of town, on Blue Ridge Boulevard. "It's in the middle of Kansas City now but was farmland then," Bill recalled, "an acreage with goats, chickens, a lake at the back of the house, and a caretaker that looked after it." The Coffeys were squires rather than farmers. "We'd go out in Uncle Logan Jaques's big old open-air Cadillac touring car," Bill said. "We'd spend the day, picnic, fish a little bit. They all kidded me because I walked up to a goat and said, 'My name is Billy, goat!'"

While Dorothy lived with her Aunt Bess, Bess tried to make her into a lady. A photograph taken when Dorothy was about fifteen suggests what the struggle may have felt like to both of them. Squeezed into an unbecoming flounced dress, she is posed in a garden against a background of trailing clematis. A dainty wrist corsage draws attention to a powerful, adult-looking hand. Dorothy is well into puberty, and has inherited the body type of her big-bosomed, big-hipped aunts. She radiates self-conscious discomfort at being displayed in such a getup.

Dorothy, about age fifteen

Yet Bess was a goodhearted woman who believed she was looking out for Dorothy's best interests, and Dorothy's subsequent history as Billy proved her right. Bess held strong views about proper speech and dress and other forms of polite conduct. The lasting imprint of her tutelage gave Billy's persona a magical touch of class, permitting him to draw a little apart from others and demand respect for his privacy.

It was also to Bess that Dorothy owed her excellent training as a musician, and Bess was proud of Dorothy's achievements. Indeed, that photograph of Dorothy in a fussy dress may well commemorate one of her piano recitals. Music was taken very seriously in Bess's household, Bill recalled: "Aunt Bess had a baby grand in the living room, a Knabe. She was extremely strict about our practicing. I was only seven, and I'd try to sneak out and play if she left the house. An incident I still remember: in the grade school I attended, they wouldn't let you leave the classroom except in a dire emergency. I filled my britches one day and had to walk home in them. Aunt Bess made me sit down to practice as soon as I got home. No exceptions. There I sat in my messy knickers till she said, 'What's that I smell?' Oh, she made me go through a lot. She was the same with Dorothy."

Both Dorothy and Bill were enrolled at the Gertrude Concannon School of Music, where Dorothy studied piano, violin, and saxophone. Quite a few of her music books have survived, showing the lessons set by Miss Concannon over a period of years, some with pencil annotations by Dorothy. Dorothy made little progress on the violin, though after Billy Tipton was established in the music business, he claimed to have been a prodigy who gave a violin recital at age seven. But she excelled at classical piano. A printed program from a recital in which she took part lists her as playing Rachmaninoff's Op. 3, No. 4, "Polichinelle," on a Steinway grand, and at other recitals she performed standards by Liszt and Chopin. "Let the melody sing," she reminded herself in a note on an arrangement of "*Simple Aveu* (Simple Confession)," by Francis Thomé. "Bring out left hand," she prompted on the Rachmaninoff prelude she was learning. Apparently she learned that lesson well, since Billy's deftness with the left hand was a hallmark of his professional piano style.

Bess imposed the discipline of strict routines on the children, but they quickly learned that she had unconventional notions of mothering. "On Saturdays when I was in the first grade, Aunt Bess would load me in the car, occasionally Dorothy too, and we'd go to the stables where she had the horses and jockeys and trainers," said Bill. "That was her way of looking after us." Impulsive and pleasure-loving, Bess did things her own way. Notably, after becoming a widow in 1936 — several years after Dorothy's departure from the household — she sold the fine house on Sixty-second West Terrace, sold the other real estate she and her husband had owned, and turned the farm where young Bill met the billygoat into a roadhouse called the Cotton Club, after the famous nightclub in Harlem. The nightclub flourished, and Bess enjoyed the stir. Later, as a partner in a racing stable, Bess began traveling the racing circuits from Saratoga to Havana, in the company of a young horse trainer.

G.W. with his racer, 1930

It was through this restless and adventurous aunt that Dorothy came in contact with the lively side of Kansas City. The commercial property owned by Bess and George Coffey included the Mecca Hotel at Thirteenth and Wyandotte, in the center of the entertainment district that made Kansas City notorious. One block away stood the Gayety Burlesque, whose vaudevillians were frequent long-staying guests at the Mecca. In surrounding blocks were jazz clubs, speakeasies, cabarets, gambling dens, bawdy houses, and private clubs where businessmen and conventioneers could watch strippers while they ate a meal.

Bess relished this atmosphere. She kept a suite of rooms at the Mecca, and she enjoyed meeting the show people booked at the Gayety. Dorothy's brother recalled that Joan Crawford stayed at the Mecca

The Mecca Hotel, Kansas City (Joan Crawford slept here)

on one of her appearances in Kansas City, and that she and Bess became acquainted. Crawford had got her start in show business in Kansas City as a vaudeville chorine and always claimed it as her home town. In 1932, fifteen thousand fans turned out to applaud as Will Rogers welcomed her and Wallace Beery home for the premiere of the movie *Grand Hotel*. Beery had made his name as a comic actor in short films impersonating "Sweedie," a Swedish maid, so Rogers introduced him as "the girl you've all been waiting for," a joke twice over, since the real star of the movie was Greta Garbo.

The month *Grand Hotel* opened, the Kansas City *Star* ran a serialized biography of Joan Crawford revealing the tidbit that she had grown up in Oklahoma, where she was called Billie, a common nickname for Lucille, her given name (and Dorothy's middle name). "Billie Cassin still lives in Joan Crawford," said the *Star*. "It is because Billie Cassin is still alive that Joan Crawford still can look at life with the same breathless eagerness of the little girl who watched the hoofers in the wings." It is tempting to imagine that Dorothy's adolescent contacts with show business through Aunt Bess included an introduction to somebody as glamorous and successful as this swan from Oklahoma. She could easily have learned that a girl named Lucille might be called Billie, and that a guy could become famous in show business by cross-dressing.

Enrolled in Kansas City's elite college preparatory school, Southwest High, from age fourteen, Dorothy had orchestra classes every year, along with a course of academic subjects. During her first year she added lessons on the alto saxophone to her lessons on the piano. She played saxophone in the thirty-four-piece orchestra as a freshman and stayed with it all three years at Southwest, playing bland pieces such as "Moonglade," "Valse Melodic," and "Harvest Tide." If she had been a boy, she would have been able to join the band; if she had been black and a boy, she would have had even better opportunities for mastering those instruments at Kansas City's black high school, Lincoln, where the bandmaster N. Clark Smith trained a slew of jazzmen. In the absence of opportunity to play in the school band, she might have organized a band of her own. Some of the sheet music in her collection suggests that she was feeling her way toward a jazz musician's persona during those years of training, calling herself Tippy Tipton.

Band member or not, Dorothy was in the right city for picking up on jazz. During Prohibition, the nightspots were under the protection of the Kansas City police, with the business of pleasure open twenty-four hours. Bennie Moten's orchestra, one of the best jazz bands in the whole Midwest during the years 1926 to 1935, was wildly popular. Coincidentally, Bill Basie left the Oklahoma City Blue Devils to play stride piano, Fats Waller style, in Moten's band at just about the time Dorothy Tipton left Oklahoma City to learn classical piano at Miss Concannon's.

Maybe more to the point, Kansas City was then the home base of some strong female piano players. Mary Lou Williams, like Basie, had moved on from Oklahoma City to find work in Kansas City. Just four years older than Dorothy, Williams was pianist, writer, and arranger for Andy Kirk's band, Clouds of Joy. She often told a story about being inspired by a piano player named Lovie Austin at a theater in Pittsburgh one night while she was a teenager: "I remember seeing this great woman sitting in the pit and conducting a group of five or six men, her legs crossed, a cigarette in her mouth, playing the show with her left hand and writing music for the next act with her right. Wow! My entire concept was based on the few times I saw Lovie Austin." Another well-known jazzwoman in Kansas City was Julia Lee, who played in a band second only to Moten's, led by her brother George, and also soloed in various clubs, such as the Yellow Front Saloon. Lee was famous for her barrelhouse and boogie piano style and for the sly lyrics of the songs she liked to perform. According to a contemporary of Dorothy's, Southwest High School kids regularly went down to her place on Troost Avenue, "because Julia Lee was so great on the piano and sang crazy songs of her own making — 'King-Size Papa' and 'Two Old Maids in a Folding Bed.' She recorded those — I have the record stuck away."

Both Mary Lou Williams and Julia Lee were black, but as this recollection indicates, the bands they worked for regularly played for white audiences. ("Kansas City, Missouri, wasn't too prejudiced, for a Midwestern town," Mary Lou Williams commented in a memoir.) Particularly popular were the big air-conditioned dance halls such as PlaMore, the newly opened "million-dollar ballroom" with a springboard dance floor that could accommodate three thousand dancers, and the El Torreon ballroom, where Bennie Moten played jazz and held well-advertised "battles of the bands." This popular spectator sport of the time put competing bands at opposite ends of a big ballroom, where they took turns to see which could get the most dancers onto the floor, voting with their feet.

Even if Bess didn't take Dorothy to such places, dance music and jazz were inescapable in Kansas City. Dorothy and her high school friends could absorb a lot of it even in the middle of the day, without bothering anybody's sense of propriety. They could visit record shops where photos of local jazz artists hung on the walls and where patrons sat in booths spinning new releases. Bennie Moten was a bestseller on the Victor label, with titles such as "Boot It," "South," and "New Vine Street Blues."

Dorothy would have heard live music on the streets, too. On her way to the Mecca Hotel after running errands for her aunt and uncle, she could have detoured onto Twelfth Street — the street celebrated in the rag G.W. and Reggie had played, making the piano "get up and walk." Kansas City's version of Bourbon Street or Harlem, Twelfth Street was lined with little clubs where musicians went to jam after hours in sessions that could last well into the next day. Mary Lou Williams called Kansas City "a heavenly city — music everywhere in the Negro section of town," and recalled that there were "fifty or more cabarets rocking on Twelfth and Eighteenth Streets" alone. She also told about dropping by a club called the Sunset after her own work was over for the night, to hear the pianist. "Pete [Johnson] might be playing something like 'Sweet Georgia Brown' or 'Indiana' when we got there. I'd go home to bathe and change, and when I got back, ten to one Pete would still be jamming the same tune . . . Of course, we didn't have any closing hours in these spots. We could play all morning and half through the day if we wished to, and in fact we often did."

If Dorothy and her friends wanted to hear a dance orchestra, at lunchtime any weekday they could drop by the fancy Hotel Meuhlebach, where Bernie Cummins's Orchestra broadcast over station WDAF. They might have dropped in on the sensational dance marathon that ran for 117 days at the El Torreon during the winter and spring of Dorothy's junior year at Southwest, providing a showcase for all kinds of local bands.

But Dorothy's most continuous and influential exposure to music was the radio she kept in the big bedroom where she practiced her saxophone, on the second floor of Aunt Bess's house. Late at night, listening to any of the numerous stations that broadcast remote, "Tippy" could slip into nightclubs in New York and receive impromptu lessons from the biggest names in jazz. On local stations she could hear Kansas City's own notables: sax wizards such as Tommy Douglas, Harlan Leonard, Buster Smith, Ben Webster, and Lester Young, or pianists such as Count Basie and Jay McShann. The hours Dorothy spent listening were as important as the hours she spent preparing her lessons for Miss Concannon. The radio dial could break all the rules that separated children from grownups, black from white, the serious jazzmen from everybody else. If she was to make a career in jazz, Dorothy would have to ignore the boys-only rules, take lessons anywhere she could, and practice, practice, practice. And women *did* play jazz. As Mary Lou Williams said about her own apprenticeship, "They don't think of you as a woman if you can really play . . . If [women] have talent, the men will be glad to help them along. [And] working with men, you get to think like a man when you play. You automatically become strong, though that doesn't mean you're not feminine."

Dorothy also took part in the Masqueraders, a drama club at Southwest High School. During her junior year she held the office of secretary. But according to the classmate who was president of the club that year, "Clubs like the Masqueraders didn't draw us together. We had sororities and fraternities at Southwest and were maybe standoffish, snobbish. To give you an example, at Christmas we had the kind of parties where the men wore tails — my brother even had an opera hat! Dorothy wasn't a member of a sorority, and I don't think she had any close friends." This woman recalled Dorothy as someone who was impossible to get to know, "distant and bashful," a girl who brought her lunch in a brown bag from home and ate it every day by herself, who refused offers to join the gang, who never fit in.

Possibly Dorothy was still plump and awkward, not socially acceptable to the sorority girls. Or maybe she chose her friends from a different set. Her brother recalled that from time to time she entertained her high school pals at Aunt Bess's, and he distinctly remembered her coming in late one night in a car driven by a boyfriend, which caused some kind of ruckus. Did Dorothy ever have a real boyfriend? And what kind of entertainment did she seek out with her high school buddies? Did she and the other Masqueraders ever watch the female impersonators at the Gayety Burlesque? Did *she* ever go to the Yellow Front Saloon to hear Julia Lee play "Two Old Maids in a Folding Bed"?

As soon as school let out every year, Dorothy and Bill climbed several rungs down the social ladder for a three-month stay with their mother and Charlie Herr. Reggie's new husband was kind to the little boy. "Charlie had no children of his own from his first marriage, and I was real small when they married," Bill said. Charlie's projects as an engineer for the Oklahoma State Highway Department carried the family all over the state: east to Muskogee and on to Sallisaw in the hilly country bordering Arkansas, and then south to Tuskahoma, deep into the former territory of the Choctaw Nation. Electrification had not yet come to Tuskahoma during the summer the family boarded at the town's only hotel. The children bathed in a washtub and never had to practice the piano, despite Aunt Bess's instructions — "Mother babied us a lot," Bill conceded — and Charlie rented a pony for Bill to ride. Those summers were idyllic, at least for Bill. "Charlie loved me," he said. "And he always made sure I had jingles in my pocket."

It seems, however, that Dorothy didn't much like her mother's husband. Very likely she felt the loss of her real father, who now took little notice of her. Possibly she noticed a strain in the marriage. Having married in haste, Reggie was soon repenting at leisure. Charlie is remembered as tall, dark, and handsome, he is remembered as kind and hardworking, but he is not remembered as exciting, and that is what Reggie was used to in her marriage to G. W. Tipton. "Mother loved my dad until the day she died," Bill said, acknowledging that Charlie Herr was no match for her.

In 1931 the marriage went aground and Reggie fled Charlie, seeking refuge in her destitute sister Cora's one-room apartment in Muskogee. When she eventually sued Charlie for divorce, Reggie had a long list of grievances. Charlie, she claimed, had cursed, threatened, and abused, struck, and bruised her without cause or provocation. (Charles Herr waived his right to answer.) She also claimed that he was guilty of gross neglect of duty, failing to support her for the past year or to provide suitable lodging. It had become necessary for her to earn her own living. But how was she to do so? She had been a housewife since the age of . . . , well, sixteen, actually, but fourteen was what she usually claimed.

In the summer of 1932, estranged from Charlie and out of money, Reggie decided to go after G. W. Tipton once again. She returned to Oklahoma City and took him to court, requesting custody of the children and payment of some long-overdue child support. G.W. had recently been gaining renown as a builder of racing planes, and Reggie no doubt saw his picture on the front page of the *Daily Oklahoman* when one of his designs was entered in the transcontinental Cirrus race of 1930. Optimistically, she must have concluded that G.W.'s fame was bringing him fortune. She wanted the money he owed her: about $100 to date, and mounting.

Reggie also wanted custody of Dorothy and Bill. "The children have not been properly disciplined, maintained and educated commensurate with their talent," her brief alleged. "Dorothy Tipton is now seventeen years of age and has each year expressed a sincere desire to change her surroundings and course of education and is, at this time, with her mother in Oklahoma City and has expressed her dislike to leave her mother and return to Kansas City for further control and discipline of said Mrs. Bess Coffey." Oh, it was an ill wind filling the

sails of Reggie's argument that she, as mother, was "the proper person
to further direct the course of education and discipline, companionship and association of the said Dorothy Tipton, her daughter." The
same went for her son, now ten years old.

The hearing was held in early September 1932, the week that
Dorothy and Bill were supposed to return to Aunt Bess in Kansas City.
Reggie won her motion to modify the divorce decree and was granted
custody of both children, but G.W.'s pleas of hardship resulted in a
halving of the monthly child support payments. On paper, each won a
round. But Reggie did not in fact keep both children with her. By now
she was homeless. Nor did G.W. ever pay her what he owed her. By late
1932, there just wasn't enough money left in anybody's pockets.

Foiled in her effort to achieve financial security by reclaiming her
children, Reggie became desperate and selfish. "The Depression was in
full swing, but the way they had lived, so well, she didn't know how to
economize," Madeline recalled. "Suddenly she was destitute too, and
there she was, wanting to live in our little one-room apartment in
Muskogee, where we were having such a terrible time. She was constantly contacting our uncle [G.W.] for more money. Finally he sent
her two dollars. Instead of putting that on groceries, she went down
and spent it on face cream. That's when she told my mother, 'My face is
my fortune.'" Eilene too remembers Reggie as callous in those days,
indifferent to anybody's struggle but her own, and what she got she
hung on to. "Aunt Reggie had lots of clothes, and we thought if she
only gave Mother one of her dresses, things would have been a lot
better. But she gave Mother nothing."

"She didn't really want the children with her," Madeline said. "I
believe she felt they aged her, especially Dorothy — a teenage daughter was a liability, made her appear older." Bill held a more generous
view of the way Reggie abandoned him once again, and of her marriage
to Charlie Herr, seeing her as the victim of circumstance. "Marriage
was her only lookout," he said. "Mother would have loved to come and
take me, but she couldn't do it. Wrote to me occasionally, and of course
I always went to stay with her in summer — that didn't change."

And what about Dorothy? "Dorothy was very independent," said Bill.
"She didn't care for strictures. Aunt Bess was quite strict, wouldn't let
her do things she wanted to do, and had ambitions for her to be a
concert pianist." If Aunt Bess had her way, Dorothy was going to finish
high school and be dispatched abroad to put the finishing touches on

her musical training. Then, if Dorothy failed to marry, she would have the opportunity to pursue a career as a concert pianist, or, in the worst case, she would be able to support herself by teaching music, like the Miss Concannons of the world. Bess, it seems, was determined that Dorothy wouldn't turn out like spoiled, helpless, dependent Reggie.

By urging Reggie to regain custody and remove her from Bess's influence, Dorothy resisted those enlightened plans. She was immensely attached to Reggie and, it appears, troubled by Reggie's vulnerability. It may be that Dorothy, feeling grownup, had resolved to renounce her affluent life in Kansas City in order to provide moral support for Reggie during the divorce from Charlie Herr.

In September 1932, while Reggie battled G.W. in the courts, Dorothy moved in with her mother and started her senior year of high school in Muskogee. She stayed for one semester and then transferred to the Connors State College High School in Warner, a private boarding school associated with the college. Her tuition was paid, her brother recalls, by their father. Meanwhile, Reggie went back to Oklahoma City to improve the chances of collecting arrears from G.W., since his lawyer had noted that her residence lay outside the jurisdiction of the Oklahoma City courts. She got a job working at Kerr's Dry Goods, one of Oklahoma City's best department stores, and waited for G.W. to pay the $245 he owed her. When her divorce from Charlie Herr was final, she regained the name Tipton.

Dorothy completed her senior year at Connors State, where she studied music for a semester, receiving a grade of 95 (out of 100) — far and away her best performance in four years of academic work. She did only middling well in physics, English, and U.S. history. But that year, for the first time, she was allowed to play in the high school band. Farewell, Miss Concannon, Liszt, Chopin, and Rachmaninoff! She was ready to play stride piano and to make headway on the saxophone.

Dorothy finished all of her courses at Connors State, but the records suggest that she did not apply for graduation in 1933. Why not? A high school diploma was a fairly important credential in those days. But maybe Dorothy, a new girl twice over in her senior year, didn't have much invested in the rituals of leaving high school. Maybe she didn't have the money to spend on parties. Maybe she couldn't wait to get out on her own. In any case, she now prepared to follow Reggie back to Oklahoma City.

Her close relationship with her little brother was a casualty of these decisions. "When Dorothy moved down with Mother, she *stayed*," said Bill. "She just refused ever to come back! 'Course I missed her tremendously. To Dorothy, I would always be Little Brother. But we were separated from that time on." And how did their relationship change? "I became the go-between in the family," he remarked as we turned the pages of sheet music from his mother's piano bench in the dining room of his home. Aunt Bess's Spode china stood on display alongside Aunt Dove's ruby cut-glass goblets; painted wall hangings from Dove's home had been unrolled and spread out on the carpet to help his memory. "I was friends with everybody and could go to anybody's house. The other ones couldn't." Reggie couldn't, he meant, and later Dorothy couldn't. "Aunt Bess kind of hated Mother. I remember Aunt Bess talking about what Mother was trying to get out of Dad in the divorce, and of course she took his side."

But for Dorothy, at eighteen, the angry old family question "Whose side are you on?" had already turned into a fascinating new question: "Who, really, are *you*?"

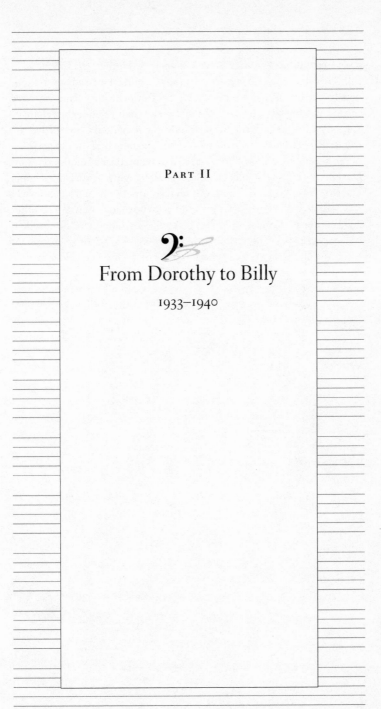

PART II

From Dorothy to Billy

1933–1940

· 4 ·

The "In" Sex

═══════════

1933–1934

STRAIGHT MAN: How many sexes are there?
BILLY TIPTON: Three. The male sex, the female sex,
and the insects.
— "Gee Quiz," circa 1955

WHEN DOROTHY TIPTON stepped off the train in the summer
of 1933, returning to her birthplace, she entered a city undergoing a
transformation. In 1928 the oil boom had finally arrived in Oklahoma
City, and by 1933 many of the old landmarks had been engulfed or
reconstructed. The historic Santa Fe station itself had been replaced
by a modern stucco building that looked like a movie set, while on
every side oil derricks raised a carnival architecture, zigzagging from
the outskirts right through the center of town and onto the lawns of
the state capitol. Enormous lights hung on the rigging, turning the
nights as bright as day. The smell was sickening, and the filth, a blend
of crude oil and the Dust Bowl grit that came billowing off the plains,
was inescapable. Everybody had a story about the gusher "Wild Mary
Sudick," which had blown out the drilling tools and spewed for eleven
days, uncapped, in 1930. High winds had spread a mist of oil so thick
that for almost two weeks Oklahoma City residents were not able strike
a match to light a smoke or cook a meal.

This torn-up world was to be the site of Dorothy's transformation
into Billy. During 1933 she undertook one of the twentieth century's
most sustained acts of female defiance. Wild Billy Tipton! Why on
earth did she do it? Too bad for us that, unlike some of the male
impersonators we know about, Billy did not write a memoir or leave a
letter marked with the instruction "To be opened after my death." We

will have to substitute imagination for the absent documentation. Perhaps what happened went something like this.

It was a hot day in the summer of 1933 when Dorothy stepped off the train in Oklahoma City, wearing a cotton dress limp from many washings and left over from the humid summers of her Kansas City girlhood. Her luggage carried the real trophies of her old life. A velvet-lined case held her alto saxophone, and folded into a leather suitcase lay the coats and skirts and dresses purchased in the days when Aunt Bess had been grooming her for the concert stage. These were the last gifts she expected to receive from Aunt Bess, who was angry at her for leaving Kansas City to live with Reggie. The good clothes would have to last until the saxophone got her a job.

Reggie met her train and they rode the streetcar to the grandly named Cadillac Hotel, where Reggie paid five dollars a week for their dingy room. It was a catchment area for the heat of an Oklahoma City scorcher but located in a respectable neighborhood, and that's what mattered to Reggie. Dorothy and Reggie would share the bed and the dresser; they shared the bathroom with everybody else on their floor.

The hotel had no dining room, so Reggie had been eating at a boardinghouse just across the alley from the hotel, a big old house that looked very like the place where Dorothy had lived as a little girl. Depression foreclosures had turned family homes into dwellings for transients, and many widows made a living by renting out rooms and converting their dining rooms into economical family-style restaurants. Dorothy arranged to work in the kitchen several hours a day in exchange for meals for herself and Reggie. The boardinghouse also had a piano where she could practice. Playing music, she quickly became acquainted with the roomers and began enjoying herself.

For Reggie, however, there was no comfort in these arrangements. Reggie was downright phobic about dirt — fastidious housekeeping was perhaps the one legacy of her upbringing by the nuns, who had been preparing her for life as a domestic servant. In her own home, relatives remember, Reggie washed dishes in water too hot for most people's hands, then rinsed them with boiling water. A spot of grease on the floor of the garage would send her into a paroxysm of scrubbing. She wouldn't put anything dirty in her washing machine, so she washed everything first by hand. Now she was eating with greasy cutlery off chipped dishes, sleeping on a stained mattress — something like the princess in the fairy tale, Reggie could *feel* the stains on a mattress — and bathing in a tub used by men who didn't know enough to clean the scummy ring left by the water they fouled.

The boardinghouse served filling meals, a lot of biscuits and gravy and cabbage and the bologna they called "dog." Poverty could make you fat. Reggie hated the food and tried to keep trim by eating little and smoking a lot. She could have worn to perfection the bias-cut satin gowns that clung alluringly to the hipbones of movie queens, but she was finding it hard just to keep herself presentable for work as a clerk at Kerr's Dry Goods. She was calling herself Reginald Tipton again, and took to her work the attitude of the affluent customer she had been in her old life. As she often said, she would rather do without than look cheap. That was one of the lessons she drummed into her children: "If you're going to buy something, buy the best." She liked being surrounded by well-dressed people and fine goods. People might have noticed a resemblance between Reggie and the gold-digging salesgirl played by Clara Bow in the 1927 movie *It*.

Reggie craved attention, and made Dorothy her emotional ally. To Dorothy, she could pour out her sadness and fear. She worried constantly about money. Saleswomen were relatively well paid, but they were easily replaced by part-timers. Her job was so insecure! And she never seemed to feel very well anymore; her feet hurt, her back hurt, she was sensitive to the heat, the stench of oil nauseated her. And she fussed about her looks. She could rarely treat herself to those little luxuries that made so much difference to a woman her age — a manicure, a permanent wave. If she lost her looks, she could lose her job. And how was she going to meet any men?

Living in tight quarters with her needy, obsessive, fretful, flirtatious mother, Dorothy began to develop a strategy she would later use with the other women in her life: she soothed. Reggie needed to be cheered up, so Dorothy started collecting jokes and trying them out on Reggie and the other boarders. Dorothy could make a good story last and last. She was also an artful mimic, like her father. Reggie needed to be distracted, so Dorothy, who was already running with a girl she had met at the boardinghouse, took her out to a local bar to hear the friend sing. Maybe most important, Reggie constantly needed money, so Dorothy provided it. Right away she had been able to relieve Reggie of the cost of meals, and she was optimistic about finding a job in a band. Despite the hardships the Depression imposed on the rest of Oklahoma, in the capital musicians were enjoying the benefits not only of the oil boom but of the new liquor laws. After the repeal of national Prohibition, the sale of alcohol became legal in most states, but Oklahomans continued to stagger to the polls and vote dry, as Will Rogers joked. Prohibition was not lifted in Oklahoma until 1959, but lawmakers struck a minor compromise in 1933. They declared that beer with an alcohol content of 3.2 percent — "near beer" — was not intoxicating and permitted its open sale in licensed bars. In oil-rich Oklahoma City there were customers, and the honky-tonk came into its own, making plenty of work for piano players. As one musician put it, "Why, anybody that had an empty building in Oklahoma City had a dance floor back in 1933." Musicians were also needed by radio stations to provide advertising spots and sound effects, and some of the big moviehouses hired musicians to play brief stage shows during the intervals between features. The very best-paid jobs were with the large orchestras or "society bands" that played dance music in hotels and supper clubs.

Dorothy appears to have been optimistic about finding work in this lively town. Sometime during 1934 she spent some money on eight-by-ten-inch studio portraits, maybe thinking she would need them for professional purposes. In one she poses in a stylish cloche with a soft brim; in the other she wears a beret and a silk ascot. Both portraits have been lightly hand-colored, as if by a makeup artist who has tinted Dorothy's lips, penciled her eyebrows, and lengthened her eyelashes with mascara. In each portrait, Dorothy's short hair waves back from her temples in feminine curls. She gave copies to Reggie, who preserved them in an album: this is Reggie's dainty daughter, age nineteen.

But if Dorothy was aiming for a job with a society band, she quickly learned some rude lessons. Oklahoma City was not only full of farmers who wanted to pass as oil workers and widows renting their family homes piecemeal as furnished rooms and unskilled women down on their luck trying to keep respectable jobs as department store clerks, it was full of young people trying to be musicians. The ones who eventually made it did so through luck as much as talent. For example, Clarence Cagle, who later played in the first band Billy led, recalled the subterfuge by which he landed his first gig.

Dorothy in a cloche and in a beret, 1934

I was about thirteen or fourteen years old, and heard there was a band that needed a fiddle player. I went out there and told them I'd like to play. They said, "Sorry, we just hired a fiddle player, what we need is a piano player." I said, "Well, don't hire nobody. I'll be back tomorrow night." Guy said, "Why can't you start now?" I said, "Well, you can see I'm pretty young to be out here — I've got to go home and tell my mother where I'm going to be at." "Okay."

So I went along home and got Mama up, and said, "Mama, I need some help. I promised to play piano with that band out there, and I don't know anything." She said, "You just learn. You go pick the chords offa the guitar there, and I'll play the piano and show you chord for chord what chord." So Mama helped me. By late the next afternoon I had discovered I wasn't going to become a piano player overnight — there was more there than met the eye! I hadn't ever played the piano — my sisters all played the piano, they got the training, but we were in the Depression when I came along and I didn't get any training.

Now, several weeks before that I had fractured my wrist cranking a car, so I put the wrist bandage back on my wrist and went out to the man and said, "You see, I've had some trouble" — I didn't lie, you see, held up my hand so they could see — "but I think I could maybe play accompaniment." And I did, I had learned enough that I could play accompaniment on the piano just from watching Mama. I can very well to this day tell you the first tune that I played chords on the piano for, "The Waltz You Saved for Me." So that's the way I slipped into playing the piano.

Another good-luck story was told by Jerry Seaton, who later knew Billy in Joplin, Missouri. At about Dorothy's age he was invited to try out for a local band, the Missourians.

Now, the Missourians were a country-type band that had a radio program out of Joplin. Happened that a fella named Slim Wilson knew me and my mother. My mother told him where I was, working in a filling station out on College Street, and he drove up in their big Buick limousine to the filling station, said the Missourians were looking for a piano player. 'Course I was all excited about getting to play on the radio. And the other things too, just playing with a band!

So he drove me over to the house — it was only a block away — and I played a song for them on the piano. He said, "Good enough, let's go." So I packed a few things in a little suitcase and left my mother crying, and we headed for Joplin.

Walked into the studio just as they were going on the air. I had never seen these guys. They said, "Our theme song is 'Sunbonnet Sue' in the key of E." Well, I couldn't play in the key of E and never heard of "Sunbonnet Sue," but I played it anyway. Went on the road, played every night in a different town, plus two radio broadcasts in Joplin every day except Saturday and Sunday. Pay was two dollars a night. That was the start of it.

Such stories describe the lucky breaks that came the way of the male musicians Dorothy was competing with for jobs. What was it like for her? A musician named Paul Jensen remembered meeting her in 1934 in Oklahoma City in the middle of California Street, across from the Goody Goody Lunch, a bar and grill where he was playing in a band. (He recalled the meeting, he said, because he was reluctant to stand chatting in the middle of the street. Childhood polio had left him with a withered leg, and he walked with a cane, never very far.) Dorothy, dressed in women's clothes, was introduced by "an older lady who was running around with her. I didn't know her ladyfriend at the time, but she knew us because of the band — everybody knows you if you're in a band. She wanted to introduce Dorothy. Probably she thought she could get Dorothy a job at the Goody Goody. Didn't work out, because we already had a piano player." Dorothy, he recalled, was occasionally sitting in on the piano in a dive called the Green Lantern, across the street from the Goody Goody. "But she didn't last long, because the males didn't like female musicians. And management wouldn't hire her, because they didn't want a girl playing in a place like that."

Dorothy may not have felt as squeamish about the Green Lantern as Paul Jensen did, and she certainly needed a job. The music scene in Oklahoma City was beginning to look like Southwest High in Kansas City. Were only boys going to get to play in the band, even in the honky-tonks of Oklahoma City, where piano players were hard to come by? Why couldn't *she* get a job, if she was willing to play in a dive like the Green Lantern? Well, she couldn't, and soon she couldn't afford the rent, and Reggie couldn't afford to keep her.

Dorothy returned in defeat to Muskogee, to sleep on the floor at Aunt Cora's. The cousins recall that they were "in dire straits," living in a one-room apartment. Their father had taken up with another woman, leaving Cora with two teenage daughters and a new baby to support. "But Mother wouldn't have turned her away for anything," said Eilene. "To Mother she was just another child that needed help. And Dorothy really tried to find work. She went looking for a job and just couldn't find one."

She couldn't find one, but the cousins were there the day Dorothy finally figured out what to do about that. "Some way or another Dorothy heard about a band that needed a saxophone player," Eilene recalled. "Back in those days you know they didn't have girls traveling with bands — it was just frowned on. Anyway, she wasn't helpless and appealing-looking like you'd expect a woman to be. So she said, 'Well, if I can't go as a woman, maybe they'll take me as a young man!' She took a piece of old worn-out sheet and wrapped it around her chest and pinned it real tight. I never will forget the big safety pin we used in it! Some way she had picked up some clothes. Dressed as a boy, she got this job and left with the band." Madeline added, "That's what I admired and loved about Dorothy — she was so innovative! She didn't cry or go around asking for help, she took responsibility for herself, and here she was, just a kid. She chose it out of absolute necessity. What

The graduation portrait, 1935

were the alternatives? A girl in her position might have ended up as a prostitute!"

Despite the dearth of options, it does not seem likely that Dorothy would have ended up as a prostitute, in the sense that Madeline's exclamation conveys. A great difference separated Dorothy from her cousins, a difference in background and character that made it possible for her even to think of dressing as a man. Call it the sense of entitlement bestowed by talent and by the affluence of her early life. Her cousins, who lived in perpetual fear of poverty and degradation, sought the security of marriage to decent men. But Dorothy apparently gained from the brutal economic pressure of the early 1930s an enabling insight, namely, that playing saxophone was not just playing an instrument, it was playing a role, for which trousers were required. (Everybody was in drag! Why else would the photography shop add lipstick and mascara to the image of Dorothy in her stylish little hat?) Hence her elegant solution to the problem of finding work with a band. If saxophone players are supposed to be men, play a man while you play the music.

Dorothy commemorated this decision in an inscription on yet another photograph she submitted for inclusion in Reggie's album. Datable to 1935, this is the earliest known photograph of Dorothy wearing a man's slicked-back hairstyle and a man's clothes: a tie; white shirt, pants, and shoes; dark double-breasted blazer with a boutonnière. On the back of the snapshot, in Billy's handwriting, is penciled the note "Your Child/Graduation." Perhaps labeling her cross-dressing as the equivalent of a high school commencement was intended as a joke that would give the family a way to accept it. The family did not accept it. "Aunt Bess and Aunt Dove thought it was just absolutely terrible," Dorothy's brother recalled. "Bess went to Oklahoma City to try to straighten Dorothy out, but it was no use. Dad was furious, and completely disowned her. When Dad was riled, he was riled! Mother didn't like it either, but she had to go along with it because they had to make a living." Reggie evoked those hard times in a letter written two decades later: "My darling . . . I remember the years back. Lay there at night and everything comes back to me. 1933–1934 and every year since. I can't help it. I'm sure you think of them too. But I hope you don't cry over them."

It is unlikely that Dorothy cried over them, for the blowup following her decision completed her separation from her father and her aunts. No longer answerable to the older generation, she was obliged to develop her talents as she could, to support herself. She embarked on developing the character of Billy.

The person that Dorothy became is most understandable when viewed as driven by the motivations of an actor, an artist whose subjectivity is both submerged and expressed in a role. "True acting," wrote the director Peter Hall, "is a revelation of parts of the self, not an imitation of somebody else." Born and raised female, Dorothy had been socialized into feminine roles. The studio portraits show her enacting "the feminine." Watching Reggie struggle to keep up appearances would have reinforced the message that femininity required maintenance. But femininity did not a musician make. That Dorothy also found in herself the components of a masculinity and studied the art of performing it is one message of the "graduation" image, with its celebratory boutonnière.

The expression of that masculinity, in Billy's case, began with clothing, the clearest set of cues by which others judge our social status. It was clever of Billy to figure out that wearing men's clothes would make her actual sex invisible, despite the disadvantage of being only five feet five inches tall. But within a few years of this first stint of cross-dressing, Billy achieved a style of self-presentation that few onlookers ever questioned. Wearing a coat and tie and well-pressed trousers, holding his body in a relaxed but notably erect posture, Billy left the impression of a man compensating for his short stature. At some point in his career he also began wearing obvious lifts in his shoes, a prop that strengthened this impression.

Billy also wore a pants-filler that he "dressed left," as the tailors say. A jockstrap filled with a rolled stocking would have served the purpose, though later on, when Billy started passing with women, he apparently adopted more complicated gear. The women who thought Billy had a penis always mentioned the jockstrap that Billy hung on the bathroom doorknob and that routinely appeared in the laundry basket. Such props not only affected the hang of his trousers but may have permitted him to use a strap-on dildo when making love in the dark (Billy never removed all of his clothing when making love). The women would have been used to feeling straps on his body.

Having established the look of conventional masculinity in his clothes, Billy followed through with a repertory of other cues. His walk, his speech, his attitude, all conveyed the socialization of a male. He never crossed his legs or fumbled with his hair. Careful barbering and oiling took care of the hair. He expressed aggression through humor or in stony silence. If a fight broke out, Billy held the coats, but since he was a piano player, nobody seems to have expected him to risk his hands by making fists. When he began assuming leadership positions in bands, he defused conflict with a grin or a joke — a mean, coarse, sexist, homophobic joke if need be.

These were the outer signs of masculinity among the musicians Billy worked with, but the inner Billy had resources to tap as well, for risk-taking played a prominent role in the character she enacted.

This was an aspect of identity that she had absorbed from her father. Though Billy was not an exhibitionistic risk-taker, as was G.W., she put herself in considerable physical danger throughout her life by cross-dressing. Since she aimed to be an entertainer, the thrill of successfully negotiating the tricky bits surely provided her with a trust fund of self-confidence upon which to draw in her work. The vigilance and discipline required to sustain the masculine role gave a profound theatricality, gratifying in itself, to the banal routine of Billy's everyday life.

Moreover, the style of heterosexual masculinity that Billy eventually developed — the persona of an upbeat, sharp-dressing, warmhearted, good-humored big brother — addressed a number of emotionally significant problems she carried over from the breakup of her family. Though she had been disowned by her father and her aunts, Billy mastered skills that they respected, becoming an entertainer in a family that admired entertainers, a musician in a family where the important adults prided themselves on playing piano. Her way of life not only expressed their values, it compensated for their failings. The men in Dorothy's family were always walking out on the women. Billy became a protector, the kind of man who solved the problems created for her mother's kind of woman by her father's kind of man. Throughout life, Billy surrounded herself with creatures that needed protection: small dogs, young men, vulnerable women, and eventually children.

Possibly Billy was able to undertake this masculine role-playing with such self-confidence because she had entrusted the hidden female identity to her mother's keeping. For Reggie, Dorothy was first, last, and always a daughter. When writing to her, Reggie never addressed her by name; she was simply "my darling." But Reggie gave a fullness of meaning to this endearment that Dorothy/Billy could receive from no other source, and that was enough to sustain in her an emotional core of confidence. As long as Reggie lived, she and her child never let go of this love.

There were other female identifications in the role of Billy as well. Billy's musicianship was in part an expression of the influence of the piano-playing Reggie ("*your* child"). The movies of the day were also full of prompts to female liberation. The year before Billy started cross-dressing, MGM released *Queen Christina,* in which Greta Garbo wears male attire to express her authority as sovereign and "to be free," as she explains to the Spanish ambassador she has duped. The film's romantic, heterosexual plot is undercut by Garbo's evident relish for the role. Studiously unfeminine, she strides rather than walks, flirts attentively with a lady of the court, reads in bed (and makes reading in bed seem manly), dresses without shame in front of her male valet, slouches in a chair while the French ambassador tries unsuccessfully to address her with appropriate courtesy, and finally sails off to an unknown destiny. Think of Billy watching Garbo act out the solution to the problem of *being female in a role reserved for males,* before her very eyes!

Once she had created the persona of Billy, however, gender categories apparently ceased to have much importance to her personal sense of identity. The evidence for this judgment is that she hung on to attachments formed in both the feminine and the masculine identity throughout her life. About a year before she died, Billy explicitly told one of her cousins that she considered herself a "normal person" — specifically, not a hermaphrodite, and by implication not a lesbian; certainly not a man. "How many sexes are there?" asks the straight man in Billy's nightclub routine. "Three" was Billy's answer: male, female, and a third position, disquieting, indeterminate, in-between, a surprise erupting from the obvious and causing a startled laugh, the meaning concealed in the homologue "insects," the word concealed in a homonym, "in" sex.

By age nineteen, she had won the necessary freedom to pursue this new identity. Her most provocative act of defiance was the name she traded for Dorothy: Billy, with a *y.* Today the name is redolent of jazz; Billy Eckstine (1914–1993) and Billie Holiday (1915–1959) and Billy Strayhorn (1915–1967) were contemporaries of Dorothy Tipton. But in 1934 she could not have known of the others. They were black, she was white, and all of them were just getting started in the music business.

No, the name was a pure theft from the males in the family — from her little brother, who was too young to oppose her, and from her father, whose renown as an aviator still resounded in Oklahoma City. She was something like a girl in a myth being changed by a god, except that most girls in such stories become trees or fountains or birds, escaping the wiles of men, whereas Dorothy bestowed on herself the privileges of men. No myth or legend I know about ever endowed a girl with the satisfaction that I imagine swept over Billy the first time she was called by that name in Oklahoma City, as she picked up a saxophone: "A *one,* a *two,* y'all *know* what to *do* . . ." Take that, G.W.! Disown her, would he? Mistreat her mother, would he? She would raid his title and take his place. Just like the original Billie Tipton, she would break rules — she would break *his* rules. She would make her own rules, and make others complicit in keeping them. And unlike the *women* in the family, she would never need a man.

· 5 ·

Graduation

1934–1935

BILLY TIPTON: Hey, Pelvis, do you know the difference
between a mosquito and a fly?
STRAIGHT MAN: No, Melvis, what is the difference
between a mosquito and a fly?
BILLY TIPTON: You can't sew a zipper on a mosquito.
— "Hound Dog," circa 1956

IN 1934, when Billy first started cross-dressing, "graduation" was still
a year away. She returned to Oklahoma City wearing men's clothing
and began auditioning for jobs. As the saying goes, if they didn't ask,
Billy didn't tell. A rare early glimpse of this strategy survived in the
memory of the musician Clarence Cagle, who was thirteen years old
when he first laid eyes on Billy.

> My dad had a string band in Oklahoma City, called it Uncle Charlie
> and His Boys. Well, we went to this place to play, and this real well-
> dressed person came up and said, "Uncle Charlie, I sure would like to
> play in your band." Dad said, "Well, that's all right. Get your instru-
> ment." So Billy went out and came back with a saxophone, sat in for
> an hour or so. We didn't have no crowd anyhow that night.
>
> When it was over, Billy packed up the saxophone and went out the
> door. My dad, you know, didn't know a whole lot about nothing, just
> looked after Billy at the end of it all and said, "Why, I believe that
> saxophone player was a lady!"

Cagle added that Uncle Charlie and His Boys wasn't a "real" band
anyway, just himself and his father and the paper boy, all wearing
overalls and playing string instruments they carried around in old flour

sacks. Billy, dressed in a gray three-piece suit and carrying her horn in a leather case, had her hair cut short and neat as a boy's. She would sit in anywhere, anytime, just to keep her music going and to practice getting comfortable under the gaze of an audience.

Dorothy's new look, however, made her an unacceptable roommate for Reggie, too weird to be introduced as either a daughter or a son. To complete the metamorphosis into Billy, she had to seek an environment where she could shed habits and expectations formed while being raised as a girl and where she could test a repertory of masculine gestures and postures and attitudes on a range of audiences. Meanwhile, she needed protection from natural enemies. By sheer good luck, Billy found herself a room in a boardinghouse run by Helen Teagarden, the matriarch of a brood of up-and-coming jazz musicians. Though the distance between Reggie's hotel room and Billy's new residence was only a couple of city blocks, with this change of address Billy left the world of her mother, in which marriage was "the only lookout," and alighted in a demimonde of show people, where she quickly came to feel completely at home.

The name Teagarden was already famous in 1934, when Billy Tipton moved into the boardinghouse. Jack and Charlie Teagarden were pulling down good salaries in New York, playing in Paul Whiteman's orchestra. Jack played trombone, Charlie trumpet, and they had made dozens of records with other jazz artists, some featuring Jack as a vocalist. Their visits to Oklahoma City drew local musicians from all directions for impromptu jam sessions. Chances are that Billy was on hand for some of these visits, sat in with Jack, and later commemorated this brush with greatness in the boast that he had traveled with the Teagarden band. (Billy Tipton never played with a Teagarden band.)

According to Jack's biographer, Jack's visits were the stuff of local legend.

After greeting her son warmly, Helen Teagarden introduced seven brawny oil workers as her boarders. In a matter of hours the local musicians heard of Jack's arrival and came around bearing gifts — all bottled. A spirit of celebration descended upon Mrs. Teagarden's household and when Jack and the musicians left for a survey of the town's night haunts, the oil-men fell to quarreling . . . They became violent and began overturning the furniture. A stern knocking on the door interrupted them. It was the police summoned by aroused neighbors.

Desperately Mrs. Teagarden begged her boarders to subside. She reminded them of the favors they had enjoyed while lodging on her premises, the savory meals she provided. This took effect. The oil-men paused, their expressions suddenly contrite. But the police could be delayed no longer. Helen opened the door and gave them the familiar Teagarden smile. The officers looked beyond to see seven disordered giants and a woman, all innocent of mien and surrounded by scattered pieces of furniture. The law departed, understandably puzzled, and the oil-men righted the chairs. Tranquillity was restored only to be shattered by the return of Jack with a noisy contingent of the local musicians' union.

Jack and Charlie, known as Big T and Little T, were the most cele-brated members of the family, but their siblings were professional mu-sicians too. Clois ("Cub") Teagarden was a drummer and a singer, barnstorming around the Texas oilfields. Norma was the pianist in a dance band based in New Mexico, a "territory band" that traveled great distances to play in regional dance halls.

Their mother has her own brief entry in the *Grove Dictionary of Jazz*, as a pianist, and at the Monterey Jazz Festival in 1963 she performed the high-speed version of "Tickled to Death" that she had learned as a girl of nine. But mainly she is credited as the person responsible for the musical education of these talented children. Despite the poverty that followed early widowhood and deepened during the Depression, Helen Teagarden made music the center of their lives from the time the children were very small. Norma told an interviewer, "We never had music lessons from anyone but Mama. About the time we learned to read and print ABC, we learned where middle C was on the piano." The lessons were incessant and informal. Helen set the children to practic-ing while she worked around the house. Ironing in the next room, she'd keep her ear on them. "She'd holler to us, 'No, it's B-flat!' Mother just loved to spend time with us," Norma said. "She could never do any-thing financially for us. In fact, it was always the other way. But she sure did love us." The family remained close, even as adults. Norma and Clois and Clois's wife, Irene, lived with Helen Teagarden through-out the Depression.

Billy Tipton became a paying guest in this musical household shortly after she began cross-dressing. Helen's niece recalls that Helen and Billy became friendly because "Billy was very outgoing" and liked talking about music. "Helen was always feeding musicians," the niece remarked, and Billy, it seems, needed someone to mother her. Like Reggie, Helen played ragtime piano, which she kept up despite the hard work of running her boardinghouse, and like Reggie, she encouraged her children's musical abilities. But where Reggie got her children started, Helen kept her children going. Jack had been a prodigy on the cornet and piano at five and on the trombone at eight; at sixteen he joined Peck Kelley's band and started earning his own living. Norma began taking jobs while she was still in grammar school. Helen provided a stable home base to which the itinerant children could always return, even though hard times had pushed them early from the nest.

Norma returned from New Mexico in 1934, shortly after Billy moved in, and they became acquainted. Norma remembered that to escape the summer heat, the roomers would often spend most of the night in a nearby park. Norma would join them after work, bringing a wind-up Victrola and a stack of records. "I met Billy, oh, of course," Norma recalled. "She was like a little puppy, very friendly," always on the lookout to join up with Norma when musicians were around.

Right away Norma found a job with a big band from California, the Les Jenkins orchestra, playing dance music at a fancy nightclub. "Nobody was doing *well* in Oklahoma in those years," she said, "but I had steady work, and was working with the better musicians in town." And Billy? "She was working around town, just getting started. I never played with her, though, and I never heard her play." Was Billy dressed as a man at the time? "Oh yes, but she never pretended to be a man, you know. She just always wore men's clothes. I mean, slacks and things, coats, and had a boy's haircut. But I could understand that. Playing in a front line, she wanted to be in uniform the same as the rest of the musicians."

Billy's desire for acceptance by other musicians was obvious and touching, Norma recalled. "Billy seemed very young. She would work a job once in a while, but it wouldn't have paid much. She wanted to be a musician so bad! She just followed us around." She wanted, specifically, to be a musician like Norma, a jazz instrumentalist. Norma specialized in stride, a propulsive style of piano playing that developed out of ragtime in which the percussive left hand keeps strict time, alternating chords with pedal notes in a strongly marked rhythm — a basic style amenable to a range of improvisations. Later, when Billy had acquired a masculine identity, he played stride piano sometimes and told people that Norma Teagarden had taught him. Though Norma said she never played with Billy and never heard him play, Billy must have been studying Norma's presentation, even if Norma didn't know that she was teaching.

Norma Teagarden's professional life presents a kind of counterpoint to Billy's, as she was one of the few white women of her generation who successfully made a career in jazz. She had boyish looks herself, with a trim, wiry figure and shoulder-length hair styled in a pageboy. When asked whether she, like Billy, wanted to be in uniform on the bandstand, she explained, "I wore a suit, very near what the men wore. Never wore men's clothing. I had uniforms made of the same material as theirs, only mine had skirts." Was it unusual for women to wear men's clothing and a man's haircut? "I don't know whether it was unusual — I didn't know many women musicians." During World War II, however, Norma played in a girls' band in Long Beach, California, where there was a well-defined dress code that allowed no mixed signals (though the trumpet player had to wipe off her lipstick and the drummer had to remove her high heels before they could play). The women all wore "beautiful long evening gowns," she recalled. "'Course, they would last you two or three years, but you'd have to have maybe three or four of them." Norma remembered exactly what she paid for a good evening gown in 1942 — "Sixteen seventy-five, nineteen seventy-five — nothing over twenty-five dollars" — and this would be merely for the fabric, since her mother sewed the gowns. "In fact, the only time I ever forced the union to give me two weeks' notice, I had bought a lot of evening clothes. I wanted them to use me for two weeks because I'd spent so much money on my clothes."

In printed interviews, Norma in her understated way called attention to conditions in the music business that worked against a woman who wanted to be a musician as strongly as she wanted it and as Billy wanted it. Very few female instrumentalists made it onto a bandstand; even during wartime, when many musicians had been drafted, few women found work as anything but vocalists in bands. The jazz historian Nat Hentoff tells a story about the time "my high school buddies and I, giggling and slapping our thighs, went to see the Woody Herman band and its freak show when it came to Boston," the freak show being the female trumpet player, Billie Rogers. (Woody Herman also hired at various times the vibraphonists Margie Hyams and Jerry Ney, the latter of whom doubled as a vocalist. Herman was unusual in this respect, though he did tend to hire women with unisex names and even occasionally endowed them with masculine stage names.) As for Norma, "I did things . . . and put up with jobs that my brothers never would have done," she told one interviewer. "It was much harder for a woman to get work when I started. They'd use anybody before they'd use a woman."

This was Billy's situation too, but it appears that the Teagarden connection did not pave the way to opportunities for her. Her lucky break was to come from another quarter entirely. As Norma acknowledged with Oklahoma-style reticence, Billy acquired a companion while she was living at Helen Teagarden's: "Billy lived, roomed, with a woman who dressed like a man, except she wore a skirt. She wore dark tailored clothes, man's shirt and tie, and she had a man's haircut, and she was a lot older than Billy was. I remember her hair had some gray in it. We didn't know anything, Mama and I. No one I knew . . . Hadn't been around any homosexuals. Mama just couldn't understand why a woman dressed like a man." This was the "older lady" remembered by Paul Jensen, who had tried the preceding year to get Dorothy a job playing piano at the Goody Goody Club. Her name was Non Earl Harrell.

Non Earl! In this story there are plenty of women whose names might have been the names of men or boys — Mattie, Reggie, Billie — and men with names or spellings of names usually assigned to girls — Bonnie, Billie. Now along comes a person whose name sounds like a joke on the difficulty of keeping the sexes opposite.

Non Earl was outrageous. Born and raised in rural Oklahoma, buckle of the Bible Belt, she was a maverick who liked to dance and drink and smoke. One of her distant cousins remembered that she was held up by the Baptist relatives as "the example of a bad girl. The saying went, 'If you go to dances, you'll end up just like Non Earl!'" But a niece defended her: "Non Earl just followed her inclinations. I don't mean that she got into trouble, but she didn't put down roots like the rest of us. Oh, but she liked to tease and joke — she'd do anything for a joke.

Like her father. Her mother was a disapproving type, used to like to sit in her car on market day and pass judgment on the town. But her father was a good ol' boy himself, and would go along with anything Non Earl wanted."

Non Earl wed a local farmer at age sixteen and divorced him after their twin boys were stillborn, before divorce was very common in rural areas. Next she married a man named Earl Ezra Harrell. Earl and Non Earl — like the vaudeville routine Pete and Repeat, except that Non Earl's husband was not an entertainer; he was a quiet, somewhat melancholy man, not much of a match for his lively bride. For several years they ran a bakery in the farming town of Stroud. Then, in 1930, they moved to Oklahoma City, where Earl found a job with a baking company and Non Earl became a secretary for the local Metro-Goldwyn-Mayer distributor. When she lost her office job and the Harrells couldn't make their rent payments, their marriage began to fail. Non Earl decided to take up marathon dancing. In 1931 she entered a walkathon and became a "horse" — a pro on the circuit, making a living with her feet.

The walkathon was an endurance contest that had evolved out of the twenties fad for dance marathons. Contestants had to keep on the move twenty-four hours a day, in couples, for forty-five minutes of each hour, with fifteen-minute breaks. They participated in frequent special events such as relay races to break the tedium. During the Depression, entering these contests provided a way of life for entertainers, who were hired on seasonal contracts. The jazz singer Anita O'Day got her start in walkathons at age fourteen, as did the actress June Havoc, sister of Gypsy Rose Lee. "We were starved into dance marathons," wrote Havoc, who was a runaway when she entered her first walkathon. Her memoirs tell some of the tricks of the trade. "I knew how to sleep upright, hands in pockets, chin pointed straight ahead. To keep my mouth shut, never fight, listen to no one but the management." She developed three-inch calluses and had to learn to walk on them, as if wearing platform shoes, and to apply olive oil to prevent them from cracking and splitting. As long as the contestants stayed in the competition, they had regular meals and a roof over their heads. Locals were paid nothing except the coins tossed by admirers, but promoters paid professionals as much as $75 or $100 a week, depending on their ability to pull in customers.

The film *They Shoot Horses, Don't They?* captures this life with documentary realism. The master of ceremonies, played by Gig Young, attempts to tease drama out of the essentially dull spectacle by weaving the contestants into the plot of a soap opera. The pros would take part in fake romantic rivalries, fake fights, even fake marriage ceremonies. Contestants would have postcards of themselves printed for sale to fans.

Non Earl's scrapbooks contain a number of such souvenirs of her life as a walkathon horse. A postcard of "Non Earl and Buster" is inscribed, "He & I had gone 1442 hrs when this was made (My second partner)." The sloe-eyed Non Earl, in full makeup, wears a flowered gown and high heels, Buster a three-piece suit and tie. One of "Joe and Nonearl" shows her from the rear, looking like a farm woman in a baggy dress and drooping socks, draped over her partner as if sound asleep. The back of a third postcard, showing "Nonearl" posed against a walkathon banner, reads "Regards, Non Earl Harrell, 1287 hrs."

In 1932, Non Earl had the thrill of playing a leading role in a melodrama that pitched walkathon finalists against the local Baptist ministers, who were pressuring the city government to close it down. A thousand-dollar prize was at stake. Non Earl's partner took out a court order to attach the promoters' property, claiming that if the contest were terminated prematurely, he and Non Earl stood to lose the benefit not only of the prize money but of "the right to be declared and advertised as a champion of that particular kind of public entertainment." The Baptists won and closed the show down after 1972 hours (eighty-two days); the four surviving contestants shared the prize. Non Earl received $250 — about three dollars for each day of the spectacle.

One woman had reason to remember her parents' stories about this contest. "My folks would keep the radio tuned to the station where they broadcast the walkathons. When Non Earl Harrell was about to pass out, they would hear about it on the radio, and they would get in the car and drive down to urge her on. 'Wake up, Non Earl, you've got to win that prize!' When I was born, in 1934, and my parents were trying to think of a name for me, my mother said, 'What about Non Earl?' And my father said, 'That's it!'" Many years later, Non Earl Harrell met her young namesake and told her that the main thing she had to show for winning walkathons was big wide feet, spread to a size E.

It was Dorothy who met Non Earl, in 1933, but it was Billy who lived

Non Earl Harrell as a marathon horse, 1932–1933

with her, beginning in 1934 at Helen Teagarden's boardinghouse. Billy was going on twenty, Non Earl was thirty-four. To Norma Teagarden and Paul Jensen, who were in their early twenties, Non Earl seemed an "older lady," but photographs show a woman in her prime, short and strong, with black curly hair, a big sexy mouth, and a bit of a squint. At the time they met, Non Earl was the proprietor of a little hole-in-the-wall restaurant near the Goody Goody and owned a Model T Ford — great resources, both, for somebody in Billy's position. As a walkathon contestant, Non Earl had worked and bunked for months at a time in close quarters with roustabouts of all ages, and as a consequence, she was worldly-wise. She brought the whole weight of her worldliness to bear on the shaping of Billy. Non Earl "looked after Billy," people recalled — helped her find work, gave Billy someone to come home to. Maybe more important, she encouraged Billy's boldness, helped her discover the advantages of eccentricity and impropriety, and prompted her to channel energy into becoming an entertainer.

Non Earl in trousers, 1932

It may even have been Non Earl who first put the thought of cross-dressing into Dorothy's head. One of Non Earl's nieces, raised to believe that a woman must wear a skirt, recalled that once Non Earl got to Oklahoma City, she took to wearing trousers (or sometimes overalls), long before anybody back home on the farm had ever heard of such a thing. It was a sign of her independence. (Right through the 1930s, even farm women wore skirts. When Greta Garbo was spotted "striding swiftly along Hollywood Boulevard dressed in men's clothes," it was cause for headlines: GARBO IN PANTS! The less reticent Marlene Dietrich devoted a whole interview to the subject, "Miss Dietrich Defends Use of Pants," in the *World Telegram* of 17 January 1932.) Non Earl had adopted a mannish look for one of the souvenir postcards sold at a marathon in which she was competing back in 1932, wearing an open jacket and fly-front trousers, hands thrust into pants pockets, a faintly belligerent expression on her unsmiling face. Non Earl projected the image of what people in the know might have called a "he-she." Was it directed to members of her audience who were in the know?

Probably. Like other cities where the entertainment business brought women together outside the boundaries of feminine propriety, boomtown Oklahoma City had its zones of specialized sexual geography, including what we would call today a homosexual subculture — one so carefully undercover that it might well have remained invisible even to Helen and Norma Teagarden. Not that Oklahoma City could vie with Greenwich Village or Paris, yet if a woman was seeking a female companion, she could find places to look. The black women were very bold, according to a musician nicknamed Doebelly, who knew the club scene on both sides of the color line. He lived on Deep Deuce and made a living as a restroom porter at a whites-only nightclub called Jake's Cow Shed. "Colored women who was bull dykes, they didn't care who knew," he said. "And they would fight over the women — they'd say, 'I don't need no man. I got me a woman.'" In white Oklahoma City — at Jake's, for example — "they were there, but it was kept quiet and you never knew which ones they were."

That was the way it worked, even in the provinces. Nightclubs flouted Prohibition, lifted inhibitions, and enabled people who would never meet anywhere else to mingle freely. A white woman might go to the Blue Moon Cafe (later the Ten-Penn Barbecue) up in the north end of town, near the city waterworks on Tenth and Pennsylvania. Lesbians also mixed with other Prohibition scofflaws in the nightspots along the strip on Reno Street, just outside the city limits. For a valuable consideration to the current sheriff, illicit behavior was tolerated outside of town, and the law took an interest in prostitution, gambling, and bootlegging only from time to time. Chief Jim's, out on West Third, open all night for dancing and chicken dinners, was among the liveliest clubs. It had a big dance floor and was known for its "liberal interpretation of the Prohibition laws." A woman who used to go dancing in those days remembered a couple of other wide-open places in the Lime Creek district "that reputedly had gays. At least, that was the talk — I never went to those places myself. It was all very hush-hush." These were not gay bars, strictly speaking, just places with a known tolerance for the presence of women unaccompanied by men. (As Paul Jensen put it, "We always thought that there were a lot of homosexuals there, but we never could pin it down.")

But to speak of gay bars and a homosexual subculture, even of lesbians, is to impose a contemporary frame of reference on the Oklahoma City of the 1930s. While there is ample evidence that in real life, like-minded women were able to find one another, they were not yet subject to official classification. As one researcher commented in 1914, "That such a relation as Lesbian love exists is unknown to the majority of even the most intelligent people," and that remained the case until after World War II, when the Kinsey Reports moved a medicalized vocabulary about sex into common parlance. In the 1930s in Oklahoma City, "he-she" was the polite name for a mannish woman who openly sought the social and romantic companionship of other women. "Homo" was the rude word, and "bulldagger" was the "colored" term. Norma Teagarden's stumbling explanation — "We didn't know anything, Mama and I. No one I knew . . . Hadn't been around any homosexuals" — suggests that invisibility was promoted by the very absence of such categories. An individual could therefore be regarded merely as eccentric, rather than as a member of a social minority or, worse, as pathological.

That brings us back to Norma Teagarden's memory of Billy's roommate and her elision of clothing with sexual orientation. Commenting on 1934 from the perspective of 1994, Norma assumed that Non Earl and Billy were lesbians. But trousers alone do not make a lesbian, and as historians point out, working-class women were less constrained by feminine dress codes than middle-class women and donned men's garb for a variety of reasons. Entertainers, a class of their own, were also permitted liberties in their dress. So it is conceivable that Non Earl was not what we would call lesbian or bisexual and that Billy was not sexually involved with her. Non Earl had a lot in common with Billy's mother — age (Reggie was born in 1896, Non Earl in 1900), outlook, disposition, even a slight physical resemblance. Perhaps Billy found in Non Earl a companion with whom an overtly sexual liaison was psychologically out of the question. Moreover, Billy had been raised with great expectations. Possibly she still held herself above the low-life surroundings in which she had to look for work, and if so, she might have held herself aloof from the stigmatized homosexual identification as well. Dorothy's brother Bill, for one, does not believe that Dorothy and Non Earl were lovers. "Non Earl was her first girl," he acknowledged, "but I don't think it was an out-and-out marriage situation. I would say they were more like roommates." It is possible that these skeptics are right. For her own unknowable reasons, Non Earl may have cooperated in Billy's disguise because, as her cousin put it, she followed her inclinations, loved to tease and joke, didn't put down roots like the rest of us. Non Earl may just have decided to provide Billy with protective coloration, "like roommates," for as long as the arrangement suited her.

It is conceivable, but it is unlikely. Billy's attraction to her own sex goes back as early as anyone's memory takes us into her life as an independent woman. She is remembered as having a romantic friendship with another woman during her earliest days in Mrs. Teagarden's boardinghouse, when she was "running with a girl who sang at a local bar." If we ask the musicians who knew them whether Billy and Non Earl were romantically involved, the answer is, "Well, I would think so," or, "Oh, everybody knew that, they just didn't discuss it," or, "Yup." Billy and Non Earl represented themselves as a married couple in Oklahoma City from 1934 on, while Billy was establishing herself in the music business (and legally this made Non Earl an adulteress, a crime punishable under Oklahoma State law). They registered as man and wife when they rented rooms together and when, moving up in the world, they rented a house together. *Somebody* served as Billy's sexual initiator. *Somebody* provided safety while Billy acquired the sexual techniques that later proved so convincing. *Somebody* gave Billy the confidence to take big risks in the pursuit of worldly women. Non Earl is the obvious, if circumstantial, candidate for the role of Billy's first important love. Later, when Billy was an established entertainer, he wrote a joke into one of his floorshows that can be read as an homage to this era in his life, the era of meeting Non Earl and discovering what Billy was going to like:

STRAIGHT MAN: When did you first begin to like girls?
BILLY TIPTON: When I found out they weren't boys.

Moreover, that photograph in Reggie's album that Billy inscribed "Your Child/Graduation" was accompanied by several other snapshots taken

Non Earl's husband with his wife, 1935

on the same occasion. One shows Non Earl and Billy embracing, with Billy's arms under Non Earl's chalk-stripe blazer. This photograph suggests that whatever Billy meant by "graduation," Non Earl was part of it.

While her role in the evolution of Billy's sexuality may be open to debate, Non Earl was unquestionably a crucial figure in developing Billy's gifts as an entertainer. Marathons were mere sidelines in show business, but Non Earl was an enthusiast of the trouper's life and participated in any way she could, including vicariously. She was by temperament the perfect person to draw out character traits we find attributed to Dorothy from girlhood on: her delight in play-acting, her impulses as a cut-up and prankster, her tomboy daring. Living

with Non Earl showed Billy the costs and benefits of the entertainer's life. Billy emerged from that critical year, 1935, with the begin-
nings of an adult character firmly in place, founded on the pride of the
illusionist, the comic, the improviser. This pride, I think, is the key to
the joke in Billy's nightclub routine about the difference between a
mosquito and a fly ("You can't sew a zipper on a mosquito"). Maintaining "difference" is what civilians do in the straight world, but in the
world Billy shared with Non Earl, there were other possibilities. You
can sew a zipper on a mosquito: it's called "fantasy," the stuff of dreams
and jokes and sex.

· 6 ·

The Playboy

================

1935–1938

BILLY TIPTON: I used to teach drums at the YWCA.
STRAIGHT MAN: How did you get into the YWCA.
BILLY TIPTON: I lied about my age.
— "Wall Street Broker," circa 1960

SATURDAY NIGHT at the Locust Grove in Enid, Oklahoma: a good-looking boy steps to the front of the bandstand and takes a chorus of "Maiden's Prayer" on alto saxophone. This is a new Bob Wills tune, a slow dance with a two-four beat, the only thing anybody wants to hear tonight. When the next request for it comes around, the same boy picks up a megaphone and this time performs the vocal in a high tenor that causes a flurry in a cluster of girls on the sidelines. One of them brings a folded note to the bandstand. Would that cute little singer join her and her friends at a private party out on Highway 54 after the dance?

Something like this was always happening at one dance hall or another across the state of Oklahoma in 1935, the year Billy Tipton, postgraduate, landed her first real job, going on the road with an eight-piece territory band named the Banner Playboys. On the bandstand, Billy played saxophone most of the time, piano some of the time, and a boy all of the time. The impersonation was so successful that Billy, like a character in a farce, occasionally had to fend off the advances of smitten women, especially when performing as a vocalist. The publicity photograph she had taken that year, at the aptly named Pose-Ur-Self Studio, shows why. Billy looks delectable groomed as a boy.

Appearances alone sufficed for the bandstand, but defending herself from inquisitors offstage required cunning. By 1935, Billy had in place

Delectable, groomed as a boy, 1935

the rudiments of a strategy that she would deploy for the rest of her life. Primary in the strategy was an explanatory lie. In 1935, the lie was about age, because Billy was not passing full-time as a man, she was dressing for work as a man. A lot of people in Oklahoma City knew that Billy was female, but she didn't want them to think about it when she was working. She avoided curiosity by acting the part of a young kid just getting started — maybe fifteen years old was the speculation, not worth bothering about. (Billy would in fact be twenty-one at the end of that year.) "Kid" is a word unmarked by gender, and until a person is "of age," gender is not particularly socially significant, an insight Billy wrote into the YWCA joke for one of his floorshows many years later. For a guy, looking like a kid comes darn close to looking like a girl (little boys, we know, are permitted to use the women's bathroom). If Billy's sex should be detected, she might still by a stretch of the imagination be accepted as a tomboy, a female who hadn't yet settled down into feminine roles.

Just as important to Billy's lifelong strategy was the presence of a female partner who played a role "opposite" to Billy's. Non Earl was the perfect complement to Billy's act during the early years. Looking old enough to be Billy's mother, she did not conform to most young men's idea of a girlfriend, yet she was exhibitionistic and sexy, a vivid "show-type person," as one musician described her, and she seemed to be romantically involved with Billy. A decade or two later, "butch" and "femme" would be the social labels applied to their kind of female couple, but at the time they attracted no such generalizing categorization. They were just show people, a good enough explanation for those who knew that Billy was female. In the eyes of those who didn't observe that Billy was cross-dressing, Non Earl, being so emphatically female, both confirmed Billy's heterosexual masculinity and kept him off-limits to other girls: Billy was already spoken for. Among the band members, Non Earl's presence also reduced the tension that Billy's good looks and nice clothes might have caused, taking Billy out of competition for women with the young men in the band.

The final picket in Billy's fence, always, was the complicity of a man in a position of authority. In 1935 the man was D. L. Hickman, manager of the Banner Playboys. In his late fifties, Hickman had developed lung trouble while running the Banner Laundry in Oklahoma City, so he sold the laundry and opened a booking agency, reserving his old business name for whatever group of musicians he could put together to fill a gig. Billy was a regular in the Banner Playboys, and as part of the pay, Billy and Non Earl roomed in the Hickmans' home that year. The Hickmans knew that Billy was female, but they applied Oklahoma-style discretion to the situation, and most of the musicians Billy played with ad hoc did not know. Non Earl's partnership, Billy's musicianship, and Hickman's sponsorship were sufficiently prominent features to forestall inquiries.

The Banner Playboys worked a circuit of one-nighters. They might drive as far as 150 miles out of Oklahoma City, a trip that took as much as five hours in the 1930s, but they would return to sleep in their own beds, since motor courts were beyond their means. On the road, the musicians often had to double as mechanics. Mary Lou Williams's lively memoir of that era noted "the miles of dirt and turtle-back roads" over which a band had to travel in those days. On her first trip to Oklahoma, "these excuses for highways were studded with sharp stones . . . every forty to fifty miles we stopped to change tires or clean out the carburetor. To top it all, it was August and hot as a young girl's doojie." They could tell when they were getting close to Oklahoma City by the smell of oil in the air.

All of the boys in the band were kids. Hickman, who had the reputation of his booking agency to protect, struggled to keep them in line, as somebody was always hearing a rumor about work in some other band and dropping out, or showing poor judgment in romantic matters, or getting too drunk. One night the Banner Playboys had a job in the town of Shawnee, and they arrived so short-handed that it looked as though the band would break up then and there. But Hickman knew of a local musician named Son Wallin who played on the Shawnee radio station, and went to see whether he could scrounge a few band members for an evening. He learned that Wallin wanted to expand his own band, the Cavaliers, so the two bandleaders ended up negotiating a permanent merger. With a handshake, an eleven-piece band was formed: the Banner Cavaliers.

This handshake was to change Billy's fortunes, for Son Wallin was not only a bandleader, he was a man with a plan. He wanted to put the Banner Cavaliers on the radio.

Wallin's model in this marketing strategy was the Tulsa-based radio star Bob Wills, the most popular musician in Oklahoma. After making his living for several years playing fiddle at country dances, Wills had evolved an eclectic style of music he labeled "western swing." Adding horns and drums to string bands, he introduced the swing tempo and sporadic improvisation into traditional country music, expanded his band's repertoire to include the blues, and modeled his patter on the call-and-response of gospel congregations. The jazz inflection was daring, as horns were associated with "race music." Wills dressed his band like cowboys, but he named them "Playboys" to suggest jazz-age sophistication and to attract university audiences. This cross-fertilization of country music with jazz proved to have great commercial appeal. By 1935, the Texas Playboys were reaching huge audiences via the most powerful radio transmitter in the region, Tulsa's megawatt station KVOO ("The Voice of Oklahoma"). The Wills band could be heard by listeners as far away as Oakland, California, and though it was broadcast at intervals throughout the day, the noontime live broadcast grew to be one of the most popular radio shows in the Midwest. Farmers would haul their big battery-powered radios into the fields so they wouldn't miss the midday show, bars and cafés would turn up the volume, lower-case playboys and their girlfriends would wake up and tune in, schoolkids coming home for lunch would be greeted by sounds of the Texas Playboys. One man recalled that as a teenager he could walk three blocks to a store in Houston on a noon errand for his mother "and never miss a word to a song. In the summer every window was open, and every radio station was tuned" to Bob Wills. At night the Texas Playboys broadcast live again, from Cain's Dancing Academy in Tulsa or from any of the twenty-one remote locations where KVOO had a wire.

D. L. Hickman, who was savvy about marketing, had added the Wills brand-name "Playboys" to the name of his laundry in forming the Banner Playboys. Son Wallin wanted the Banner Cavaliers to sound like the Texas Playboys, if they could, and then capitalize on the craze for western swing. Billy's saxophone was a necessary ingredient in the sound Wallin was aiming for; in fact, among the Banner Cavaliers, only Billy and the drummer, Bob Green, made what would otherwise have been a string band into a western swing band. Wallin proposed that the Banner Cavaliers follow the same circuit as Bob Wills, advertising themselves on the tiny stations that also carried the Texas Playboys. Small-town radio would be the key to their success, for radio provided the only entertainment regularly available in farm country. Bob Wills's band dominated the airwaves with KVOO, but the many local stations that had sprung up also wanted to carry live music. Wallin knew from experience that local businesses would be inclined to attach their names as sponsors to the Wills imitators if the Banner Cavaliers could come up to the mark.

This strategy soon began paying off in steady work. Hickman would see to it that the band arrived in town early enough to drop by a radio station and play a few tunes. The announcer would mention the band's upcoming appearance at a local dance hall. Radio play enabled the band to negotiate a higher fee elsewhere. In a really good week they might play six radio spots and six dances, rehearse new numbers on a

The Banner Cavaliers, 1935

couple of afternoons, and maybe even be hired for a funeral or a wedding. Playing dances from 9 P.M. until 1 A.M., they were making about two dollars an hour apiece. (For comparison, Norma Teagarden recalled that in beer bars — the lowest-paying jobs — band members received two dollars each for a five-hour night, with no intermissions.) Hickman and Wallin received the money, paid the bills, and saw to it that the boys ate regularly, but doled out cash in driblets. "Those were hard times," Wallin said. "You needed to make sure the money would last."

While Wallin was going forward with his ambitious plans for the Banner Cavaliers, he wasn't paying much attention to the individual members of the band, including Billy. But when the weather heated up, he decided to put them all in T-shirts and had a run-in with Billy. "Billy just wouldn't put on a T-shirt," he recalled, "and the fellas really got mad. That's when Hickman told us that Billy was a girl. We were all really surprised — my gosh, those dirty jokes we told! Up to that time she had been behaving like one of the boys. Well, she never would put on a T-shirt, but we continued treating her like a boy. Didn't matter to us, 'cause she got along real good with everybody. Just thought she was a kid who played good saxophone."

A photograph taken in 1935 confirms this observation. Son Wallin, on the far left, is identifiable by his helmet of dark hair; Hickman, next to him, has lost his. Above the musicians' heads is the luggage rack on their homemade band bus, a seven-passenger Buick with the engine removed, towed by another car when they were on the road. Billy squats in the front row, smiling. At this point she must have been making little effort, among the musicians, to disguise the contours of her body. All in white, she wears a man's haircut and fly-front slacks, but a belt encircles a female waistline, and the tucked-in shirt pulls across her bust. She seems to be wearing a wedding ring on her left hand. Plainly visible is Billy's right hand, clasping the hand of a guitarist from the former Banner Playboys, who is grinning.

Morale was high among the Banner Cavaliers in late 1935. They had become a tight group, well rehearsed, but they were still mainly in the business to enjoy themselves. Their manager, Hickman, was over fifty, but most of the musicians were in their teens and early twenties and fond of horseplay. Guitar and banjo players would jam a burning cigarette onto the dangling end of an instrument string and shove it surreptitiously into another musician's arm while they were all playing, a jab of heat to test his cool. The piano player, whose back was turned, often became the brunt of such jokes, since it was easy to slip a lighted cigarette under his rump as he bounced on the piano bench. Son Wallin recalled that Billy, who mainly played sax with this band, seemed to love tormenting the piano player and was a ringleader in pulling such pranks.

Most of the musicians in the Banner Cavaliers were talented but untrained, and were not permitted to join the union, which was reserved for those who could read music. Wallin, for one, could not read music; he said he "just picked it up by ear" after he bought a bass fiddle somebody left in a beer joint in Oklahoma City. The band's success was based on disciplined rehearsal and a level of professionalism intolerant of casual participation. After six months or so, its name began to get around, and Wallin became even more ambitious. Why not try for a slot on a megawatt station that would broadcast the Banner Cavaliers throughout the whole territory in which they played one-nighters?

The breakthrough came in late 1935 with an invitation to audition for WKY, an NBC affiliate and the premier radio station in Oklahoma City. Every radio station was looking for the next Bob Wills, and WKY offered the Banner Cavaliers a one-month contract, renewable, at the precious noon hour, playing "old-time Western songs" for fifteen minutes, testing the market. Their theme song was a lively version of "Alabama Jubilee."

WKY paid each performer thirty dollars for the month's work, and the money was guaranteed. A dollar a day for fifteen minutes of music was very attractive to the boys, and Billy, they discovered, had a flair for radio performance. The Kansas City burlesque house in Billy's background began showing up in the "silly business" she worked up for WKY, singing falsetto and wisecracking like a vaudeville comedian. Again the model was Bob Wills, who bantered with the Texas Playboys on the air and punctuated the band's songs with his audio signature, an elated, long-drawn-out "aah-haaa." Listeners had come to expect a bit of improvised frivolity from radio performers, and the Banner Cavaliers counted on Billy's gift of gab to provide it.

They were pleasing the radio audiences so much that they were shocked when WKY didn't renew the contract at the end of their thirty-day trial period. Possibly the Banner Cavaliers failed to conform to the standards of sophistication being introduced by the station's ambitious management. According to a historian of Oklahoma radio, WKY's chief executive "considered the new studios to be fully as advanced as anything NBC might have in New York and Los Angeles, and he ran the operation with the same kind of discipline he thought David Sarnoff might employ." The manager was trying to purge the station of its country sound, including any trace of an Oklahoma drawl in the voice of an announcer. He himself monitored the requirement that male employees wear coat and tie at all hours, whereas the Cavaliers "were all kinda relaxed about dress," Wallin admitted. (All but Billy, that is, for Billy rarely appeared in public without a vest and tie, except in the hottest weather.)

But for the Banner Cavaliers in general and Billy in particular, being let go by WKY turned out to be a lucky break, because the band's option was immediately picked up by Buck Thomason, the programmer at KFXR, a small local station that showcased local talent. Buck Thomason *loved* cornball country music, *exaggerated* an Oklahoma drawl, and appreciated everything about the Banner Cavaliers, including their silly business, including their cross-dresser. Buck was a cross-dresser herself.

How Buck Thomason became part of Billy's story is a story of its own. She started working at KFXR in 1935, just out of high school, when her father bought the radio station. Her high school classmates remember her as a tall, shy girl named Mary Louise who lettered in team sports. "Not a bit pretty," she had an awkward manner and wore "thick bottle glasses." Once she started announcing on KFXR, calling herself Buck, Mary Louise Thomason underwent a personality change: she cut her hair, put on weight ("got so she looked like Orson Welles"), and began wearing a man's suit in a distinctive and memorable shade of brown. Recalling a first encounter with Buck's new persona, a friend said, "One night while I was working as a carhop at the Triple X, a convertible rolled in, with a woman and a man in the front seat. The man looked familiar, but I couldn't place him. Had a real pretty blonde with him, lying on the front seat with her head in his lap. I said to a friend, 'That man looks familiar,' and she said, 'That man is Mary Louise Thomason!'"

Buck developed an outlandish style of announcing that appealed especially to younger audiences of KFXR. Particularly notable was her habit of tunelessly singing along with the recorded music she played. As one listener remembered, Buck "couldn't sing *at all,* but she was always singin', throughout the broadcast. I remember her theme song — 'Just Because You Think You're So Pretty.' Oh, I've thought of this woman many, many times in my life, and find myself singing that song." With live musicians in the studio, Son Wallin recalled, "She'd say just about anything she wanted to say" to get them going. "She was very crude, with a rough-sounding voice," another listener remembered. "I don't mean naughty, just not precise and down the middle of the road the way they are now. The insight on it is, she was funny — a jovial character."

Buck also inaugurated a policy of inviting live audiences to her evening show. The broadcasting studio was still a novelty in those days, and Buck was ready to share the fun of being a radio personality. Some

listeners would drop by the station just to check her out. "People said
Buck was a hermaphrodite," recalled a person struck by her distinctive,
gravelly voice. Another woman remembered, "The only time I saw
Buck, I noticed that he had breasts. Looked like he needed a bra, not
just prominent pecs. 'Hermaphrodite' was a word I heard applied to
Buck." A woman who had known Buck as Mary Louise said, "'He-she'
was the way we referred to her when she started calling herself Buck. I
think they had an expression like 'hermaphrodite' for her, yes. Well, we
were so naive! Things like that weren't discussed in polite company."
Yet another woman, who had spent a little time on a bandstand herself,
sympathized with Buck's gender ploy. "Back in the days when I played
music, the boys used to bother us so much! They were always high on
dope and booze. So no wonder those women wore men's clothes."

From the time Buck and Billy met, Buck gave the Banner Cavaliers
regular airtime on KFXR, including the precious noon spot, which
attracted audiences on their lunch breaks. The tiny studio, furnished
with bulky Buck and an upright piano, held only three band members
at a time, but Billy was always one of them. Son Wallin recalled, "It
wasn't so much the music Buck liked, but the mischief," of which Billy
was ringleader. The band's regular appearances on KFXR put its name
in circulation and snagged the Banner Cavaliers one of the best jobs in
town, at Swing Time, a dance club in South Town. Wallin recalled that
the club had an address that already sounded like a radio jingle, 2929
Twenty-ninth. Non Earl got a job as a waitress at a club called Happy
Time, in the same part of town. Since Hickman's services as booking
agent were no longer needed, Billy and Non Earl moved out of his
place and into rooms in a hotel in downtown Oklahoma City.

Only a few months later, however, in mid-1936, Son Wallin developed lung trouble and was abruptly sent to a sanitarium. Wallin's bad
luck was Billy's good luck, for when the Banner Cavaliers disbanded,
Billy salvaged a couple of the best musicians — Lloyd Payne and Fred
Loveland — and found a new piano player, Clarence Cagle. With
Buck's influence, Billy hung on to the job at Swing Time, becoming for
about a year the leader of a band of her own.

Buck's influence — what improbable good luck, that Billy should
meet up with a cross-dresser whose father owned a radio station! Yes,
Buck was a curiosity, but her father's position made for tolerance, and
Buck was high-spirited and knew everybody Billy wanted to know in

the music business. And she liked Billy Tipton's style of humor and kept her on the air for the next couple of years.

Buck's patronage gave Billy's career its first real momentum. For Billy, a typical day would begin with the noon show at KFXR. The band would play for fifteen minutes and return every two hours throughout the afternoon, at two, four, and six. Billy would sometimes sing, sometimes play the piano; saxophone was for the bandstand only. At the end of each performance, Buck would announce the dance that night at Swing Time and read the ads Billy had scouted from local businesses, bartering airtime for life support in the form of gasoline, haircuts, laundered clothes, and food. Clarence Cagle remembered that a favorite sponsor was a café called Bill's No. 2, where they could cash in a fifteen-cent chit for a meal of toast, jelly, eggs, coffee, and a small steak.

Billy and Non Earl looked after Clarence, whom they often had over for a supper of cornbread and beans before driving out to the Swing Time. "My folks was gone, so for two years I was in limbo there, a single teenager," he remembered. Thinking about the hard times they lived through together during the Depression, he paused. "You're not going to get me to say anything bad about either one of them! I wouldn't even think about it, you know, because they were nice people." And he and Billy were also struggling *young* people — that was the crux of the matter for Clarence, who avoided applying a pronoun to Billy. "I never thought of Billy as nothing but kind of like me, a teenager like me who was just trying to get by."

Billy and Non Earl profited together from the opportunities that came Billy's way through the work on the radio, for as bandleader, Billy was able to attach Non Earl to the group as a "kitty girl" who would pass the hat for tips and requests. Non Earl came over to the Swing Time after finishing work as a waitress at the Happy Time. "Twenty-ninth was way out in the country then," Clarence remembered. "Billy and Non Earl drove fancy cars, when they could. That was *her* money." Clarence, who was avid about cars but too young to drive, recalled that in 1937, Non Earl still had her old Ford, "because I very well remember this Ford coupe that was a 1932 model, first year of the V-8 engine."

The boys would arrive at the club around eight-thirty. Dancing began at nine and continued until 2 A.M. — three on the weekend —

without intermission. As bandleader, Billy announced the numbers with a line of patter and let Cagle do all the piano playing. The other members of the band were Freddie Loveland, on electric guitar; Lefty Payne, on fiddle; Oral Hulsey, on bass; and Skeeter Prendergast, on banjo and drums. It was "a pretty good working band," Cagle said, but it was tough being the piano player, which is maybe why Billy played sax. "The piano player got no breaks," Cagle explained. "The other players were one man at a time, but that piano was constant. If you had to go outside, you just stepped outside and came right back, but that was it."

The Swing Time was a small club, maybe sixty by forty feet, and is remembered as "a *wild* place, rowdy — a place where they wouldn't shoot anybody but people were always getting in fistfights." The wooden tables and cane chairs shoved to the side of the dance floor were easily breakable and served as the only kind of insurance carried by the Swing Time, since management didn't want any fatalities when fights broke out. Non Earl would arrive late in the evening and stake out a table where she could sip a nickel Coke that held a splash of bootleg gin. Like everybody else, she carried a brown bag to the club. (Billy didn't share the bottle, preferring never to drink on the bandstand.) When things got lively on the dance floor, Non Earl would go around with her hat, teasing for tips, and when things were slow, she would go from table to table, joshing with the regular customers and collecting requests. In 1936, Cagle recalled, everybody wanted to hear "Steel Guitar Rag," Bob Wills's big hit. The boys worked out a deal with Non Earl: "Steel Guitar Rag" could be requested only once in twenty songs. So Non Earl would hector the customers, asking, Who'll place the next nineteen requests so we can dance to "Steel Guitar Rag" again? "She worked the kitty and got all the money, but she paid us two dollars a man per night," Cagle explained. "She was a pretty good hustler of that money. Well dressed at all times, always looked dressed up. There were five of us, so after the first ten dollars come in and we got our two bucks each, the rest of it was hers. She was probably hustling out about twenty-five dollars a night." Each of the other boys would take home four dollars, two dollars from the club manager and two dollars from Non Earl. Billy would take home Non Earl.

On weekends, Buck usually showed up with her girlfriend after the last show on KFXR. After Billy and the boys finished the last set, Buck helped them load up their instruments and the whole gang headed for an after-hours place. The Goody Goody was popular, as was a place called the Cave, on Deep Deuce. This was Billy's time to unwind and have a drink or two. Son Wallin remembered that after hours, "Buck and Billy would often get to acting silly and Buck would start driving like a wild thing, going all over the road. She'd just scare the waddin' out of us."

A few of the musicians might stay into the early morning hours, jamming. Non Earl and Billy were usually among the last to leave. Billy didn't seem to need much sleep. Back home after a fifteen-hour work-day and several hours at a jam session, she might put on a record — maybe "I Ain't Lazy, I'm Just Dreamin'," recorded before Benny Good-man's band became famous, with Teddy Wilson on piano and a vocal and trombone solo by Jack Teagarden, all favorites of Billy's — and play it several times while Non Earl fried potatoes and scrambled some eggs. Billy liked a big breakfast before turning in. They would sleep until nearly noon, when the routine set in all over again.

It was during this tenure at Swing Time that Billy applied for a social security number. Something prompted her to take a very bold step and apply *as a man*. Did she have to join the union, and did she have to be a man to qualify for union membership? Or was she laying the ground-work for the masculine identity she later assumed? Clarence Cagle doubted that Billy needed a union card to play at the Swing Time: "Horn men in the north part of town playing country club dances would have been union, but not country musicians," he said. Of course he, like the other musicians Billy worked with at Swing Time, knew that she was female. Nonetheless, the application was submitted un-der the name of Billie Lee Tipton (a spelling corrected in Billy's official signature), a white male, age twenty-two, born December 29, 1914. What Billy did lie about (her sex) and what she didn't lie about (her age) formed the first riffs in a long improvisation, set the first strands in a web that became increasingly tangled as the years went on, and brushed the first strokes by which Billy began painting herself into a corner.

Billy and Non Earl had been enjoying the unprecedented prosperity of their joint income at Swing Time for about a year when they were toppled like dominoes from what had always been a precarious secu-

The Swing Billies, 1938; Clarence Cagle is on the far right

rity. In 1938, Buck's father was forced to sell KFXR. Buck was forced to step down as announcer and programmer and could no longer provide Billy with the visibility of daily air play. Not long afterward, Billy's job at Swing Time became a casualty of a love affair that heated up between Freddie Loveland and a vocalist named Louvenie Perkins, the lead singer of a popular hillbilly band called the Arkansawyers. Their romance caused the Arkansawyers to disband. Celebrities in Oklahoma City, the Arkansawyers had been able to walk into a nightclub and bump any other musicians out of their jobs, so when several of the band's former members approached the manager of the Swing Time looking for work, that was the end of Billy's band. As Clarence Cagle recalled, "Just overnight! We'd been there about two years and they took our job!" As it happened, the ex-Arkansawyers didn't bring a piano player with them. The owner of the club pointed to Cagle. "'Here, this boy will play piano with you!' Well, rather than be totally out of work like the rest of them," Cagle admitted sheepishly, "I switched over." They called themselves the Swing Billies.

Meanwhile, Louvenie Perkins formed another band, christening the new group the *Western* Swingbillies and hiring Billy to play the piano. Louvenie, a radio personality, had no difficulty getting them a job as house band at a popular beer bar named Brown's Tavern and a daily show on radio station KTOK. Billy was glad of the steady job, but this was still a demotion. A promotional postcard ordered by Louvenie to advertise the band's appearances on KTOK shows us a scaled-down version of Billy, very much in the background, arms limp, eyes covered by rimless spectacles. The men are dressed alike, in white clothing that provides a frame for the dark-clad, heavyset figure of Louvenie and the big guitar she holds forward in hands with polished fingernails. Of the two extant photographs taken at this session, Louvenie of course chose to publish the one more flattering to herself, a version that crops her thick ankles and darkens the background in a way that conceals her bulk without diminishing the heft of her presence. She's the leader, all right.

Meanwhile, Buck and Billy went their separate ways. Buck, out of work in 1939, forged her father's name on a ten-dollar check she passed at a haberdashery and was sentenced to serve time in the state penitentiary. During the war, calling herself Mary, she became a mechanic at Douglas Aircraft, and in the 1950s, briefly calling herself Marion, she

Louvenie's Western Swingbillies, 1938

worked as a machinist and ran an elevator in the Oklahoma Club. In the 1960s she listed her name as M.L. and her occupation as artist. While she was Billy's friend and champion, though, Buck helped advance Billy's standing in the music business, and it is reasonable to wonder what the citizens of Oklahoma City thought about this Laurel and Hardy pair of cross-dressers who spent so much time together in public, both often with girlfriends on their arms. Didn't they leave a trail of anecdotes?

No. Oklahoma musicians who played with Billy in those days swear they didn't think much about the cross-dressers in their midst and are somewhat mystified by probing questions about them now. "It was common knowledge," said Wayne Benson, a bass player with the Arkansawyers who appeared regularly on KFXR, and who also worked with Billy off and on between 1936 and 1938. "Buck was real nice. I keep referring to Buck as *her* rather than *him,* even though he called himself Buck. But she was always very nice to all of us, she'd laugh and kid with us. We really didn't have a problem with it at all."

And Billy? "Well, there again, it was common knowledge, you know, with the band and the guys and everything, that she was a female. She was, to me, always very nice — she'd kid around. To me, there was nothing wrong with her. I really didn't see anything unusual. I'm trying to think back. Normal person who dressed like a man, but we knew she was a woman — but very nice." Didn't that seem remarkable? "Not to me, it wasn't. It was just one of those things. She dressed as a man and she played good piano. Really, no one thought anything about it around here, that I know of. I have nothing in the world to say against her, and I don't think you'll find anyone who will, either."

When reminded that people made a lot of Billy's subterfuge after her death, Benson said, "Evidently. When I read that newspaper article — well, I had a friend that played guitar, played in another band, never played with Billy, but he and I lived next door to each other out West. He knew Billy. When I read this article I called him. I said, 'Jim, do you remember Billy Tipton?' He said, 'Sure — everyone down here knew she was a woman.' I said, 'That's what I've been trying to tell everyone!' But no one thought anything about it, no one cared, the people I knew — no one cared at all! So what!"

While Buck may in some ways have been a model for Billy, people who knew them both do not remember them as at all similar. For one thing, "Buck and her girlfriend were pushy — Buck's front teeth were knocked out in a fight during those years! Billy wasn't pushy. She kept herself in the background. And Non Earl wasn't pushy either," as one acquaintance recalled. Then there was Billy's style of dress. Everyone who talks about Billy has something to say about the way her clothing set her apart. As Clarence Cagle put it, thinking about the band that played at the Swing Time, "The rest of us was country musicians and knew we were. Wore overalls and what have you. Billy wasn't really a country musician, and Billy was always well dressed. Immaculate, I'll put it that way. Just a teenager, but real well dressed at all times, and well spoken. She could talk to you about anything." It was part of Billy's legerdemain to make her cross-dressing appear as costuming rather than deviance. Billy did not look dressed *as a man*; Billy looked dressed *for the bandstand*. She directed the beholder's gaze elsewhere, toward her purposefulness as a musician. Not perceived as wild or odd, she is remembered as dedicated, singleminded, "a teenager like me who was just trying to get by." Paradoxically, it was her clothing that made it possible to get by. Many of the musicians Billy knew dropped out from lack of ambition or were forced out by economic hardship, but Billy — with Non Earl's substantial help — worked steadily at just one thing, and that was playing music while looking just like everybody else, only a little better.

· 7 ·

Reggie's Daughter

≡

1937–1940

> I'm like a nurse, a fireman, or a cop on the beat — they
> all wear their uniforms to work, and I'm no different.
> — Drag queen RuPaul, *Lettin' It All Hang Out*

DURING BILLY'S YEARS in the Oklahoma City music scene, she
was actually serving two apprenticeships, one in music and one in
cross-dressing. By 1937 she was so practiced in moving and talking and
looking like a man that the performance of masculinity came as naturally as the motion of her fingers on the keys of her instruments. We
have seen how ungrudgingly the musicians closest to Billy accepted
her as a leader even though they knew she was female and referred to
Billy as "she."

Acceptance by members of her family was more difficult, but once
Billy had established her independence, she began attempting to over-
come their resistance. Her mother's second remarriage provided an
opening. In 1935 Reggie quit her job at Kerr's Dry Goods to wed Lynn
Fullenwider, a recent widower. Lynn's first wife and their only child
had been killed when a train hit the car they were riding in, and Lynn
was still grieving for his little boy. At the time he married Reggie, he was
working as a mechanic for Oklahoma Gas and Electric, a secure and
steady job. Security had become very important to Reggie. She was
overjoyed when Lynn was promoted and transferred to Enid, a couple
of hours' drive north of the urban squalor of her recent life in Oklahoma City. They bought a spacious house and planted a garden, which
Reggie tended with the same zealous attention to detail that she lav-
ished on their home and their car and their garage.

Settled safely on her perch as a middle-class housewife again, Reggie began to see more of her children. Billy became a frequent guest,

Non Earl, Reggie, and Reggie's son Bill in Enid, 1938

often accompanied by Non Earl. These visits must have required a certain amount of accommodation by Reggie's new husband. Lynn Fullenwider is remembered as a "Kentucky gentleman," a conservative, reserved, soft-spoken person who was considerate of ladies and very old-fashioned about the proprieties. Moreover, he had known both Reggie and G.W. since their high school days back in Chandler, and he had worked in a garage managed by G.W. during the 1920s and watched Dorothy grow from a toddler into a little girl. Perhaps this memory was the source of the diminutive Dot, with which he always addressed her in letters — and a way of minimizing the impact on him or her changed appearance.

Reggie and her children, Enid, 1938

Billy and Non Earl were apparently accepted comfortably in Reggie and Lynn's home, however the reunion had been accomplished. Photos taken on the front porch of the house in Enid show Reggie and Non Earl posed as chums, with Non Earl's hand resting companionably on Reggie's knee in one. Group photographs place Billy and Non Earl with Reggie and Lynn. How did Reggie and Lynn explain Billy to each other in private? No doubt with some version of the explanation offered by family members years later: Billy's work in the music business required trousers and a man's haircut and a name that either sex might wear. Photographs taken in Enid show Billy looking like a woman wearing pants more than like a man, her stance making the female body under the clothing faintly visible. Dorothy was now in uniform, so to speak, her clothing entirely practical. This explanation, which may have been promoted among family members by Billy herself, made it possible for the errant daughter to bring together the parts of her life that had been split apart when she went off to live in Helen Teagarden's boarding-house. Contact with Billy's world may even have seemed exciting and interesting to Reggie and Lynn, for Billy and Non Earl were visitors from the parallel universe of show people, which respectable working folk like the Fullenwiders knew only by hearsay and through the movies. Dorothy's sexuality would never have been acknowledged as an element in her friendship with Non Earl. It would not have been acknowledged even if Dorothy (or Billy) had had boyfriends. Among family members, sex was unmentionable.

Whether or not Reggie approved of her daughter's cross-dressing, she had now accepted it as Billy's choice and was able to take pride in Billy's achievements. The cousins remember that Reggie's letters and phone calls always carried news of Billy's whereabouts and doings. Conceivably, Reggie recognized the creativity in what other family members, including Reggie's sister Cora, viewed as outrageous. Dorothy began appearing in her mother's photo album in her own "pants role" the same summer that Katharine Hepburn was appearing in local movie theaters in the pants role of *Sylvia Scarlett,* a film credited now "for its undermining of socially constructed norms of femininity and masculinity." (At the time, it was said merely that Hepburn was "better looking as a boy than as a woman.") Possibly Reggie saw Dorothy as participating in a life more urbane and glamorous than her own and took vicarious pleasure in Dorothy's rebelliousness. Her daughter was well on the way to making a living in show business, playing music and playing Billy. Did Reggie remember the sharp red fingernails that had attracted so much attention in her high school days, and wonder whether the keyboard of a jazz piano might have taken the place of three marriages in her own life?

Reggie also collaborated in Billy's need for discretion. In the letters Billy saved, sent to business addresses, Reggie's phrasing is extremely circumspect, referring in code to the secret. And what delicacy she showed in replacing "my daughter" with "my darling," preserving the hidden initial of the name Dorothy, which she was no longer permitted to use.

Billy tried to make up with her father during those years as well. By 1937 G.W. had returned from Kansas City, where he had been living in his sister Dove's apartment building. Having divorced his second wife, a French girl named Marie, he had married a woman named Irene and started another family. Settled once more in Oklahoma City, he set up a repair shop where he rebuilt and resold airplanes. Billy may have felt that the time was propitious for a reconciliation, but G.W. was unappeasable. Family members recalled hearing G.W. say that he didn't want to have anything to do with his daughter, that she ought to change, that what she was doing was wrong. "But I never did get into a discussion with him about it," Dorothy's brother, Bill, said. "It wasn't my position." Dorothy never did meet the half-brother born to G.W. and his third wife.

Dorothy's brother, now in his mid-teens, was also a regular visitor in Enid. By 1937, he too had been bitten by the jazz bug and had taken up the trumpet. He enjoyed reunions with his lively, jazz-playing sister and her antic girlfriend. In Reggie's photo album, he mugs with Non Earl and poses with Billy, looking for all the world like a twin brother. One summer he spent a few days hanging out with his sister in Oklahoma City. "Dorothy was living in a nice house subdivided into small apartments, with a screened-in porch around it," Bill recalled. "Of course she was dressed as a boy. I know I had my trumpet with me on that visit. She said, 'Oh, you are playing that thing wrong! You're going *rucky-tuck, rucky-tuck, rucky-tuck.*' She wanted to show me how to make it swing!" Bill even sat in with Billy's band on one occasion. "Some way or other the string bass man didn't show up or wasn't there, and I stood there and beat on that string bass while they played the dance." He also remembered driving down from Kansas City and meeting his sister at the nightclub where she was working. "It wasn't the best place in the world — wild and woolly, a lot of drinking going on. After the dance a fistfight broke out on the gravel parking lot, over a girl. Dorothy wasn't involved, nor was I. Turned out to be pretty bloody."

Bill's visits to his sister's turf were apparently limited to these few occasions. As he explained, "If I had gone where she was playing, she'd have had to introduce me as her brother, Billy Tipton — upset her apple cart something terrible. It's human nature for people to take something that's a little out of line and twist it around." Bill believed that his sister was wearing men's clothing, even at home, because she had no choice. "She was deathly afraid of being discovered, and any change would have brought that out. She'd have lost her job." While he was young, he accepted this as his sister's business. Did she talk to him about it, justify herself? "She wouldn't have thought she needed to! I was uncomfortable about it, but that's what she wanted to do, and that's that." As a grown man, however, he firmly distanced himself from Billy's masquerade. "I didn't condone it and still don't," he said. "I kind of admire her for what she pulled off, but at the same time I hate that she did it. It's not the normal run of life to do something like that. I believe she could have done better, broken it off at a later time and straightened up."

For Dorothy, the reunion with Bill mended a broken connection and established continuity between her childhood and her adult life. Bill's wife remarked that at their rare meetings, Dorothy continued to call Bill "Little Brother." She had converted her old role of tomboy, fighting his battles, into the role of big brother, and extended the range of her dominance, flexing her muscles in the field of music, which they shared. Bill pointed out, apparently without rancor, that she had eliminated the possibility that they would actually both work in this field by using his name and getting there first. A Jacob to his Esau, she had managed to steal the birthright and receive (though not from her father) the blessing and the entitlements of the elder son.

In the circle of her family, as in the circle of her peers, Billy accomplished her complex negotiations by deploying a winsome, unthreatening boyishness. But by 1937 or 1938, her professional ambitions began outreaching this persona. During the mid-1930s, music was undergoing one of those revolutions that happen when technology and talent combine to redefine a field of art. Recordings, radio, and to some degree film were making big-band jazz wildly popular. The popularization of swing — the commercial name for this music, which obscured its origins as "race music" — is usually credited to the Benny Goodman band's Saturday night music show, *Let's Dance,* broadcast over NBC beginning in 1935. Arrangements for the Goodman orchestra cleverly retained the sound of jazz improvisation within tightly structured ensemble playing by brass, reeds, and rhythm sections. The nationwide audience that danced to Goodman's music across the sweep of time zones reached by NBC responded with hysterical enthusiasm to live performances. Swing titles dominated the Hit Parade, and bandleaders became celebrities.

Billy listened to this kind of jazz on records and over the radio, and she both listened to jazz and played jazz at after-hour jam sessions. Players from traveling big bands often went to local clubs after-hours to jam, since the big-band framework restricted their solo time and the clubs gave them scope. Records were also a source of inspiration. In his autobiography, Teddy Wilson describes how he acquired the piano style of Fats Waller and Earl Hines as a teenager, using the speed regulator on a gramophone to slow a record to the speed he wanted. "You could hear exactly what a player was doing in a particularly intricate passage and match it to your own piano pitch," he wrote. Wilson, who could read and write music, said he "copied the solos from records note by note and memorized them," capturing both in his annotations and in his memory "the intricacies of jazz rhythm, the little shades" that make jazz magical. By the mid-1930s, Billy Tipton was doing the same thing with Teddy Wilson's solos on recordings by the Benny Goodman Trio and the Benny Goodman Quartet.

That was how Billy wanted to make a living — by playing in a swing band, making records, living the life of a jazzman. She was a good enough musician to do so, according to her piano player at Swing Time, Clarence Cagle. "It was very obvious that Billy was a better musician than any of us. Billy was a fair sax man too, played very well for a woman, but Billy had the piano *boiled and ready!* Really and truly, I can't figure out why she left the piano to me. I kind of felt terrible playing piano, knowing that Billy sitting there could outplay me by a whole handful." He and Billy had similar views of Teddy Wilson, Cagle recalled. "Billy asked me, 'What kind of piano do you want to play?' and I told her, I said, 'Like Teddy Wilson.' She said, 'Well, you really picked a good one!'" Knowing this, we can catch glimpses of Wilson's musical ideas in the few existing recordings of Billy Tipton at the piano — the mellifluous, striding left hand, the airily melodic feel both pianists had for uptempo numbers as well as ballads like "Moonglow" and "Exactly Like You."

But Billy was making her living in what were basically modified string bands that got paid to play popular dance music, "current songs of the day done in the country manner," as Clarence Cagle put it. Musicians experienced a kind of professional schizophrenia, fulfilling umpteen requests for "Steel Guitar Rag" on the bandstand, then at jam sessions trying out new ideas pulled from the latest records and radio

Non Earl and her little brother Wayne, circa 1939

broadcasts. Not that the western swing they played wasn't jazzy. As a former member of the Wills band put it, "Western swing was not really country as Nashville is country. The guys in Wills's band were uninhibited about what they played, so they developed a jazz style from within. Jazz is a freedom you can form within any kind of group." But the Bob Wills style of jazz was completely different from the sounds that came over the radio from New York and Chicago and Los Angeles. Paul Jensen, who played in a five-piece band at the Goody Goody, remembered that when he made enough money in 1936 to buy a new Chevrolet, he paid extra for a radio in it, "so we could get up at intermission and go out in the alley back behind the Goody Goody and listen to the *Camel Caravan* direct from KFI in Los Angeles. It was hard to get us back in to play, 'cause who was on it? Benny Goodman!"

Another influence on Billy's ambitions in the late 1930s may have been the friendship she developed with Non Earl's youngest brother, Wayne, who joined them in Oklahoma City in 1936. Nicknamed Tiny because he was over six feet tall and weighed three hundred pounds, he carried his bulk on light feet. One of his women friends described him as "kind of a chunk, but a real nice-looking guy," with a handsome, expressive face. Non Earl adored this "little" brother. Younger by twelve years, he was her twin in disposition: talkative, gregarious, extroverted, warmhearted. He was also the best piano player in the family. Non Earl was good, according to her cousins, but Tiny was *really* good. "When Tiny was around home, he *had* to be on the piano. He played entirely by ear. Somebody hummed a tune, he could play it right off."

Just out of college in 1936, Tiny wanted to become an entertainer, maybe a bandleader, maybe even get into the movies. He went to Oklahoma City hoping to be discovered by Gene Autry, Oklahoma's most illustrious cowboy star. Autry was a loyal native son and returned to Oklahoma City now and then to make personal appearances with his horse, Champion, on the *Cain Coffee Program* over station WKY. One of Tiny and Non Earl's brothers knew him from the days when Autry had worked on the railroad. The brother offered to introduce Tiny and bankroll his efforts to get a start in show business. The whole family was sure Tiny had it in him.

But when Tiny arrived in Oklahoma City, all he had going for him was talent and optimism. For a while he may have depended on Billy and Non Earl for meals and a floor to sleep on, since by late 1936, Non Earl was working two jobs and had plenty of cash as well as connections to the music business from her days as a marathon horse. Hearsay suggests that Tiny was homosexual ("little bit funny, not normal"), and anecdotes indicate that he was the entrepreneurial type, someone who could walk up to a bandstand and get himself invited to sing a number or two. As one bandleader explained, "You know, when someone weighs five hundred pounds, they can pretty well do what they want." One of the musicians who hung around with Tiny recalled an occasion when Count Basie came to town. All the musicians wanted to hear him, but most of them lacked the money for a ticket. "Tiny said to me, 'You got your union card, I got my union card, and we're not going to pay to get in here.' He asked the guy on the door if he'd take a note to Basie for him. Guy came back and told us, 'Basie says come on in!'"

Despite the Depression-era climate of caution and pessimism, Tiny was convinced he was going to be a star. In 1937 he persuaded his home town's chamber of commerce to pay his way to an audition in New York for Major Bowes's radio show, *The Original Amateur Hour*. Singing "Red Sails in the Sunset," he won a position on the program's "all star unit," which led to work in New York nightclubs. A talent scout sent him to Hollywood, and in 1939 he bagged a seven-year movie contract with Paramount Pictures. In his first movie, *Some Like It Hot,* starring Bob Hope and Shirley Ross, he played a bandleader.

Between jobs and auditions and movies, Tiny would return to Oklahoma City to visit his sister. He was ebullient, fun, a spendthrift, and brought out the best in Non Earl. Were these visits important to Billy's sense of purpose in 1938? Working with the Western Swingbillies as Louvenie's piano player was providing Billy with enviable job security, but it was not advancing her aim of playing jazz or getting into show business. Nor did it improve the financial situation, for Non Earl's job as kitty girl had been an adjunct of Billy's role as bandleader at Swing Time. Some of the musicians Billy knew just gave up the music business for jobs less dependent on scarce disposable income. Billy hung on with Louvenie until sometime in 1939, when Louvenie was offered a job in Amarillo, Texas.

Billy didn't go with her. That year saw the nadir of Billy's early career. The name and address of William L. Tipton, musician, vanished from the directories of the cities he had worked in, and apparently Dorothy retreated to Enid, put on a skirt, and tried to find work playing the piano in local clubs. The source of this information is a musician who later played in a band with Billy. In 1939 he was still a schoolboy in Enid.

> I used to walk by the house where Dorothy's mother lived on my way to Longfellow High School with a friend. We knew that Dorothy Tipton lived there and that she was a fine jazz pianist. In Enid, everybody called her Dorothy, I can remember. Billy didn't dress as a man in Enid — they'd have run her out of town. Enid was a little Bible Belt town of the sort where nobody took a drink, even in their own home. If they wanted a drink, they left town to do it.

I cannot truthfully say I even remember talking to her. Most of my associations are from a distance, idolizing someone who played jazz piano. I thought of Dorothy as an older person. At that time, six months older would have seemed old!

Dorothy left Enid before I started in high school, in 1940. At that time a woman couldn't find work — I'd say there were maybe five or six women musicians active in the whole business. The next time I saw Billy he was wearing a man's clothes and a man's haircut.

This memory illuminates the second turning point in Billy's story. In 1939 the Depression was ending in the buildup to war, but Billy's career was stalled. What could she do? What were her alternatives? Well, a woman in her position might become a piano teacher — that's what Aunt Bess would have recommended. She might try out for a girls' band, as Norma Teagarden did around this time. Perhaps she did. Dorothy's cousins think that she formed a girls' band that year, though the people in Oklahoma City who would surely have heard about it don't remember it.

Luckily for Billy, Lynn Fullenwider was willing to support her, yet the months in Enid must have seemed to her like a regression. The situation was a mirror image of the one her worried cousins had witnessed in 1934, when she was sleeping on the floor of Aunt Cora's one-room apartment in Muskogee. Five years later Billy was out of work again, sponging off respectable, goodhearted relatives again. Back in 1934 she had wanted a job in a band — any job, any band — and "maybe they'll take me dressed as a young man," she had said. The persona she had developed for the purpose had been good enough to get Billy jobs in beer bars and roadhouses, but now she wanted a job with a big band, playing swing. For the past six years, performing in male attire, Billy had been building up an actor's capital, a diversified portfolio of roles. She would cash it in. Playing swing was a job for a man, so she would have to trade the persona of "kid" for the impersonation of a grown man.

By the end of 1940, Billy had retired the role of skirt-wearing Dorothy once and for all and was on the road again. Reggie's daughter no more, Billy mailed her a Christmas Eve postcard signed with careful formality, signaling a new era in their lives: "Dear Mom: Well, we're in Martin, South Dakota. Made it fine. We play a dance here tonite then go to

Nyder, Neb. Sure getting a kick out of traveling. Tell everyone hello —
Merry Xmas — Love — B. Tipton."

Social security records show that Billy had joined a big band with
good bookings in major venues in the mountain states. New Year's Eve
found him in Casper, Wyoming, at the grand old Gladstone Hotel, a
city landmark dating from Casper's days as a ranchers' town and an oil
capital. The Gladstone was where Wyoming elite gathered to banquet,
to dance, and to gamble, and Billy's saxophone greeted the new year
bathed in prismatic light from an enormous revolving mirror ball that
had been drawing crowds since the Roaring Twenties. In January the
band moved on to the exclusive Broadmoor Country Club, in the Edge-
water district of Denver, Colorado.

But by spring 1941 Billy and Non Earl had returned to the Midwest
and settled in Joplin, Missouri, a town in the Ozarks about 240 miles
from Oklahoma City. Very likely they had followed Tiny, who was then
operating a nightclub at Shadow Lake, a popular resort in an area of
the Ozarks full of caves, which had an outlaw history as bootleggers'
hideouts. When Paramount Pictures shot scenes of the movie *Jesse
James* in this area in 1938, Tiny got a bit part, and he went on to parlay
his celebrity into a successful business venture. During the summer,
Shadow Lake attracted trainloads of vacationers from as far away as
Kansas City, and these people wanted a bit of sophisticated nightlife to
enliven their holiday. Tiny — who was a good cook, according to one of
his cousins — oversaw both the dining room and the dance floor, serving as manager, bandleader, emcee, vocalist, and comedian. His example may well have influenced Billy's resolve to aim high in these pur-
suits too, for Billy seems to have shared Tiny's irrepressible sense of
entitlement and may have taken heart from his success. And though
Joplin was only a six-hour jump, as the musicians would say, from
Billy's home town, it was far enough for Billy to set up a new life. He
and Non Earl rented an apartment as man and wife in central Joplin,
listing "Mrs. Tipton" as Nona, and he found a job in a swing band at a
roadhouse called the Cotton Club.

It was at this moment in Joplin that Billy began passing as a man
full-time. Though since February 1937 he had held a social security
card designating him as male, it was not until Billy left Oklahoma City
that he left off cross-dressing and adopted a masculine identity in
all relationships. The distinction is important. Billy dressed in men's

clothing was, you might say, a critic — a de facto critic, one whose adoption of male attire was itself an eloquent comment on the sex segregation that prevailed in the world of musicians. Billy in a male persona was an artist, improvising with attitude, voice, and gesture. A self-made man, from now on, in both professional and personal life, Billy Tipton was "he."

Part III

The Impersonator

1940–1948

· 8 ·

Self-Made Man

1940–1943

BILLY TIPTON: Look at me! I'm a self-made man!
STRAIGHT MAN: That's the trouble with this cheap labor.

— Comedy routine, circa 1954

TWO GOOD HIGHWAYS swept directly into Joplin, Missouri, from the west, Route 44 from Oklahoma and Route 66 from Kansas, funneling thirsty folk from these two dry states across the border to buy a legal drink of hard liquor. The first stop would often be the local Cotton Club, just east of the state line on Route 66, with a parking lot that covered half a city block. A tall red neon sign flashed OPEN every night, including Sunday. The Cotton Club was strictly a bar and dance hall, with no gambling tables and not much to eat. A pair of bandstands stood back to back in the cavernous space, separated by folding doors. On weeknights the doors were pulled closed, creating intimate surroundings where a combo played to a small crowd of dancers. With the doors unfolded the club could accommodate four hundred, and one whole end of the building might be open to the night air.

On Friday the Fourth of July in 1941, customers were testing the truth of a claim running in the Cotton Club's ad for an all-night dance: *It's always cool on the open-air dance floor.* The short blond saxophone player set down his horn and stepped to the microphone. A flashbulb seized the moment: Billy Tipton is poised in midsong, perhaps performing his imitation of Lionel Hampton's vocal on "Exactly Like You," a dance tune popularized by the Benny Goodman Quartet. George Mayer, the tall, dark bandleader, is grinning, his eyebrow cocked, looking ready to lift his clarinet and perform his rendition of Benny Goodman's solo on the same recording.

Billy Tipton the vocalist, George Mayer the leader, Joplin, 1941

In that photograph, Billy Tipton and George Mayer present themselves as a duo. The other band members play in shirtsleeves, but Billy
and George are fastidiously uniformed in light-colored coats and pants
and look-alike two-tone shoes. The initials G M are emblazoned on the
music stands. George Mayer, by force of personality, had become the
leader of Paul Jensen's band, since Jensen, who migrated to Joplin from
Oklahoma City, did not serve as front man because his polio-withered
leg gave unsteady support on the bandstand. The eight-piece band he
managed was now called George Mayer and His Music So Rare, a
name copped from Jimmy Dorsey's hit "So Rare." (The running joke
had it that Mayer's music was rare because it "wasn't well done.")
Everybody in the business was imitating the tastemakers.

Billy Tipton's job at the Cotton Club, playing swing, gave him momentum for the first time as a musician. The sophisticated harmonic
progressions, rhythmic surge, and melodic openness of swing suited
Billy's disposition and permitted a full display of his talents. Among the
popular tunes in the Mayer band's repertory were titles recorded in the
1930s and 1940s by Teddy Wilson: "After You've Gone," "How High the
Moon," "Whispering," "I'm Confessin'," "Body and Soul," "Talk of the
Town," "Sweet Georgia Brown," "I Want to Be Happy." This music has

saturated American culture; we recognize the melodies, we can hear how the notes are carrying words even when we don't know what the words are. But often we *do* know — phrases flow through our mouths as if they had been dissolved in the music. As played by Teddy Wilson, the music is both familiar and ingenious, phrase by phrase. To a musician, Wilson's artful command of each sequence of notes, his interpretation of each instant, and his improvisations are apparent. No wonder Billy wanted to sound like Teddy Wilson.

Or to sound like Lionel Hampton singing "Exactly Like You." Billy had a tenor voice very similar to Hampton's. As one of the musicians who worked with him later put it, "Billy's voice was not high-pitched like a soprano, but in the men's tenor range, his was high. Yet I never thought of it as a female voice — here was sound coming from this man, it's a man's voice! Yes, it's a high-pitched voice, but it's a man." Its sound is preserved on a couple of recordings of radio broadcasts on which Billy sings harmony on several pieces and solo on "The Best Things in Life Are Free," "Love Me or Leave Me," and "If I Knew Then." He swings, to his own piano accompaniment, making an engaging and convincing presentation.

Billy Tipton had probably been playing music with George Mayer off and on for two years by the time they arrived at the front of this band. None of the people on the bandstand, including Mayer, knew that Billy was female. Mayer's ignorance was Billy's passport across the last frontier into full-time male impersonation. "Exactly like you, George," was the message. Mayer's unquestioning acceptance would promote that assumption among their changing cast of coworkers on the road and in the nightclubs, protecting Billy from curiosity in his professional life, just as Non Earl's presence continued to protect him from overtures by other women.

George Mayer was in every way an ideal partner for Billy at this moment in his career. Mayer had grown up in a nest of vaudevillians and had been in show business ever since his parents stood him on a Coke box to play the xylophone in a nightclub act when he was still too young for school. His mother and his aunt had been members of a family of self-styled "Spanish troubadours" that traveled vaudeville circuits all over the world. In old age they claimed they had shared the stage with the likes of Jack Benny, Bob Hope, and Arthur Godfrey. The family settled in the Midwest, and George's mother took her talented son to Oklahoma City to work in vaudeville when he was about ten years old. By then George could not only sing and dance but play clarinet and drums.

Mayer was in his early twenties when he met Billy Tipton. They may have worked together in a Major Bowes road show one season, possibly in 1939, and Mayer probably toured in the same band that took Billy to the Dakotas and Wyoming and Colorado during the winter of 1940. Like Billy, Mayer was ambitious as both a musician and a showman. He had taught himself to play the clarinet in the style of Benny Goodman, but he modeled his stage personality on Cab Calloway, "the cat who started scat." Calloway was an immensely popular entertainer at the time, heading the house band at the original Cotton Club in Harlem and broadcasting a radio show three nights a week. It was claimed that Calloway's band introduced New York City–style jazz to the Midwest. Young George Mayer might have been among the crowds at live performances during Calloway's tours through Texas and Oklahoma, and by the late 1930s he could have watched Calloway's manic, loose-limbed showmanship at the movies. Feature-length films such as *The Big Broadcast,* with George Burns (1932), and *The Singing Kid,* with Al Jolson (1936), along with a host of shorts, displayed the full range of Calloway's talents, including his rapid-fire jive and his sartorial stylishness. He liked to jump onto the stage as "cool as an ice cube in a white tuxedo with a white baton," as he put it. Then, from the first downbeat to the last note of a number, "he was all motion," said a fan from the Cotton Club days. "He waved his arms, he ran back and forth from orchestra to microphone, he danced in a frenzy to the music. His hair flew one way, his coattails another." Mayer, who bore a physical resemblance to Calloway, including a great big flexible mouth, adopted the Calloway style of bandleading, the Calloway strut in the Calloway zoot suit, and Calloway's signature tune, "Minnie the Moocher."

"George Mayer" was apparently a stage name. Nobody recalled whether he ever used his family name — the couple known as his parents were Philip and Lita de Castro — or why he chose a Jewish-sounding surname. One of his wives said that after several years of marriage she caught George speaking perfect Spanish, to her astonishment, and wormed out of him that he had been baptized Jorge Soto-Mayor and that his father had been Basque. But she didn't know whether to believe this explanation, since George often seemed to be

George Mayer as Minnie the Moocher

entertaining himself at her expense. His skin was dark enough to raise the question whether he was black, like the light-skinned Cab Calloway. Paul Jensen thought that "George Mayer was dark-complected, but he was not black, he was Hispanic-looking. He was part Indian, too." Jensen said that George told him his father was an Indian chief named Waywayotten, a medicine man who traveled around Oklahoma and the Southwest selling elixirs. George said he traveled with his father, playing a homemade horn made out of an old megaphone. Jensen loaned him the money to send to Paris for the Selmer clarinet that he is holding in the photograph. "Waywayotten" sounds like one of George's vaudeville jokes, but Jensen bought the story and was convinced that George had come directly from the medicine-show circuit when he joined Jensen's band. Another source recalled George saying he was from a gypsy family. A musician who played with him in Joplin had an entirely different recollection: "George was Castilian, I believe — lots of people of Hispanic descent were down there in Texas." George's aunt, however, said that the family ancestry was mainly Italian and included a world-famous violinist and a diva. Possibly Mayer produced this abundance of explanations to make a single point: he was not a black man.

By the time Billy and George played the dance captured in the photograph, they were an act. Their floorshows punctuated a night of dance music with intervals of what Billy called "monkey business." Each of them had specialties. George, impersonating Cab Calloway, would get the crowd clapping and singing the call-and-response refrain "Hi-de-hi-de-hi-de-ho." Later he would show off an act he said he had performed for Major Bowes, "tap-dancing" with lips, teeth, and tongue to "Bye Bye Blues," or improvise scat numbers and tongue-twisting song lyrics such as "Bob Hoppin Wot Hoppin No Stoppin Bob Hoppin Blues." George "was a nut, a child!" one of the musicians recalled. "Even at seventeen I could see that."

Billy was a different kind of nut, with a set of routines in which he performed female roles such as Little Nell and the Farmer's Wife, wearing a sunbonnet, or impersonated the radio personality Wee Bonnie Baker, who sang novelty songs on *Your Hit Parade*. Billy's signature number, "My Wubba Dolly," required little-girl gestures, a lisp, and a falsetto. "He'd sing this thing and the people would go crazy," this musician remembered. "'Billy, do "Wubba Dolly," Billy, *do* "Wubba Dolly," do "Wubba Dolly," Billy!' 'Awww, wish I'd never heard of that thing,' he'd say."

> My mommy told me
> If I'd be goody
> That she would buy me
> A wubba dolly
> Now don't you tell her
> I've got a feller
> Or she won't buy me
> No wubba dolly

Here is one of the moments when Billy's artistic risk-taking breaks the frame of his time to wave at ours: a male impersonator impersonating a female! Right through the 1930s, drag had been a staple of night-club floorshows, as it had been of vaudeville, and was regarded as wholesome entertainment, "particularly suitable for women and children." By the mid-1940s, though, female impersonation was gaining its present disrepute as "queer." As one scholar put it, "No one but a 'queer' would want to perform as a woman." Billy kept these female impersonations viable as entertainment by infantilizing the characters, playing the naive little girl or the gullible rube. Customers at the Cotton Club relished these acts, which made vulnerability and helplessness laughable, and both Billy and George had big personal stakes in carrying them off. "Silly business" endowed them with the privileges of entertainers — comedians can say anything. George playing Cab Calloway made theatrical use of his dark skin. Billy's acts drew on her own childhood, keeping alive the little girl inside, and also expressed her complex relationship to the conventions of femininity. It was okay for a man to *act* effeminate onstage, as long as it was just a shtick. Once the floorshow ended, Billy went back to playing the heterosexual man who sang those romantic love songs, with nobody else the wiser about the degree to which this role too was an act.

The choice of George Mayer as a sidekick illuminates an aspect of Billy's character that was increasingly important to his ongoing success in passing. Billy was a shrewd observer of the psychology of other people. He looked for common ground — with Mayer, a shared passion for Benny Goodman's music, which later became the mainstay of their small ensemble work — but he also subtly took charge of the personal dynamics, positioning himself in complementary roles that kept the relationship in balance and himself quietly in control. George was taller but Billy was older, so Billy indulged George's immaturity in the manner of a big brother. George was volatile, Billy was steady. George was a natural musician, but untrained and generally uneducated and embarrassed about it. One of his wives recalled that he would panic if asked to sign his name in front of another person. Billy's tactfully asserted expertise in such things as composing their arrangements concealed George's limitations. George, though married and the father of two children, was an impulsive skirt-chaser, while Billy lived a predictable, settled domestic life with Non Earl and was good at soothing hurt feelings on mornings after. George was a clown and Billy was too, but Billy was also a good listener. Attuned to the restless motion of

George's whims and fancies, Billy knew when to join in and when to fall back and applaud. George was full of himself; Billy mirrored back to him the attitude that George was very, very special. George was sensitive about his dark complexion; partnership with fair-haired Billy diminished the ambiguity. Maybe most important to Billy's security was George's lack of curiosity about other people. By keeping an eye on George's comfort level, Billy remained safe from his careful appraisal.

Billy couldn't keep an eye on everybody, though. Acquaintances from his old life in Oklahoma City and Enid were always turning up in Joplin, looking for work or passing through on their way to another job. In the summer of 1941, Clarence Cagle drove through Joplin on his way to Coffeyville, Kansas: "It was the middle of the night, and lo and behold, somebody hollered and flashed their lights. We pulled over, jumped out of the car — it was Billy and Non Earl! I hadn't seen them since I left Oklahoma City, 1939. We had the bass tied on top of the car, and they recognized us. They were working out there at that nice club west of town, nicest club in Joplin."

Cagle wasn't the only person who crossed the state line and bumped into the Tiptons, carrying baggage from Billy's past. Another musician recalls an incident that mystified him at the time. The band was playing at the Cotton Club one night when a ruckus erupted. "Somebody started calling to Billy, 'You used to be a girl name of Lucille back in Oklahoma City!' Now, there was a fellow that Billy allowed to sit in with the band. He really liked Billy, kind of was Billy's champion. He wasn't a toughie, but he knew how to handle himself. Three soldiers got into it with this fellow, and he dispatched them pretty quickly, but I remember hearing that — 'You used to be a girl . . .'"

Why wasn't Billy's secret exposed, once it *was* a secret? Was it because the world didn't provide ready-made labels for Billy as a social type? Maybe. And Billy was able to offer a socially acceptable explanation for the rumor. He told George Mayer and others that his mother had dressed him as a girl when he was a little child. Putting a very young boy into skirts and letting his hair grow out in curls was not a particularly uncommon practice among middle-class families, and Billy might have given his father's cousin, the bandleader Bonnie Spencer, as another example. Oklahoma City musicians would have recognized that name, since Spencer's society band was fairly well known. Billy told some people that that's what those strangers were remembering: as a kid he'd been dressed as a girl.

Retrospectively, some of Billy's acquaintances had different explanations for Billy's ability to pass as a man among the men he worked with. Billy was being protected out of respect, Clarence Cagle said. "Musicians I worked with in those days certainly wouldn't have said anything or done anything. They just would have said, 'That's Billy Tipton, that man playing the piano right up there.'" Another musician who knew Billy's real sex thought the secret was safe because it was a secret among Oklahomans: "Now, when you're born and raised in Oklahoma, you don't question your elders and you don't divulge secrets." A musician who was not in on the secret said it was just simple decency not to ask: "I'll tell you why. Back then there were not nearly the number of mean people we have today. This country is on a binge of ignorance and revels in it. Pickup-truck mentality. The attitude then, with us and with everybody you talked to, probably would have been 'What the hell difference does it make? He was a nice person, played well — what the hell difference does it make?'"

This kind of tolerance seems to have prevailed in Billy's world, but not everyone in that world was motivated by respect. Paul Jensen recalled that one of Billy's habits did excite curiosity among the other guys in the band. "We noticed that when we took intermission, most of us had been drinking a little beer, we'd have to go to the restroom. But not Billy. As soon as everybody else got on the bandstand, he'd say, 'I gotta go.'" One of the boys volunteered to spy on him but could only report that Billy never used a urinal but always went into a stall.

Billy's act grew even more dangerous after December 1941, when the United States entered the war in Europe. An undrafted man was subject to constant interrogation. One musician recalled that "if you were stopped, you had to have a draft card on you. That was a federal requirement. I carried mine for years." During the war, tens of thousands of soldiers were stationed near Joplin, at Camp Crowder, so Billy was continually surrounded by men in uniform. Billy's female cousins remember her worrying about having to show evidence of ineligibility. Thinking about her possible vulnerability, Paul Jensen recalls that Billy "got a doctor to give a statement that would exempt her from having to go, put her in 4-F." How did he know about that? "Well, Billy told us. We asked, are you going to have to go in the army? We wanted to know if we were going to lose a piano player."

George Mayer was classified 4-F because of a heart condition, but

Jensen had a lot of trouble keeping that classification, even with his withered leg.

> I was put in 4-F in Oklahoma City, but when I was playing in Little Rock, Arkansas, they put me up into 1-A because they had to meet a quota! I said I'd be glad to be in special service. They said, "No, you have to be inducted just like everybody else." I came back to Joplin, and they notified me here that a bus would be here for me at a certain time and I had to be on it. And I went, December twenty-eighth. They put me in Barracks 14, Company G, Fort Leonard Wood, which was a long way to the mess hall, I'll tell you. I had to crawl on my hands and knees — I didn't have a walker at the time, I just had a cane. I thought, Can't the fools see that I can't walk? I wasn't reclassified until after they inducted me.

Nor did classification end the discussion of the matter, as another musician remembered.

> I was playing with a band at the Monticello Hotel, near the Navy installation in Norfolk, Virginia, and it was made so miserable on us that we just stayed in the hotel all the time, ate in the coffee shop and slunk back and forth to work, which was just a couple of blocks. You got this "Hey, you 4-F sonofabitch!" You got that all the time. I was coming back from Las Vegas one time, and there were a bunch of guys going back to Fitzsimmons General in Denver, and one of them said to me, "Don't let it throw you, kid. They're just mad because you're out and they're in."

During this period Billy used the cover story that he continued to deploy for the rest of his life in every situation that required explanations about his physical condition. He said that several of his ribs had been crushed in an accident. Now and then he said he had been kicked by a horse, but usually he claimed that the injury was caused by a head-on collision in a car. Sometimes he mentioned that his pelvic area had also been damaged and needed the support of gear he purchased from medical supply houses.

By late 1942, musicians were thin on the ground in Joplin, plucked away by the draft. Paul Jensen, as manager of the band, began reaching into a pool of young customers at the Cotton Club who played in high school bands. To the kids, the Cotton Club seemed as glamorous as a

nightclub in the movies. Its band had the best live music around —
"George Mayer, the music that gets in your hay-er," the kids called it.
The band's first high school recruit was a trumpet player named Bill
Pierson, seventeen years old and in the last months of his senior year in
the little town of Granby, twenty-six miles southeast of Joplin. Pierson
and his friends would go to the Cotton Club whenever they could
scrape together the $1.25 for round-trip bus fare to hear the pros play
swing. Pierson "was trying to play trumpet the way Benny Goodman
played clarinet, lots of notes," and he remembered the night he met
Billy Tipton because of that. "The band was playing a Meredith Will-
son tune called 'Two in Love,' with George Mayer and two or three
other reeds — it was written for all clarinet, four or five clarinets, real
pretty arrangement. At intermission, why, we went up to the bandstand. Paul Jensen recognized us. 'How are you guys?' I said, 'Oh, fine,
fine, Mr. Jensen. Where did you get that arrangement for "Two in
Love"?' And Paul said, 'Oh, Billy Tipton wrote that. You want to meet
him?' 'Yeah!' Billy came over and shook hands with all of us."

Jensen asked Pierson to join the band, and Pierson gave up sleeping
most nights, catching the bus to Joplin in time to be on the bandstand
from nine until the last customer left the floor, catching the bus home
to Granby at six-thirty in the morning, arriving just in time to change
for school. "For this I was paid two-fifty a night." He managed to
graduate from high school, then immediately moved to Joplin, took a
room at the YMCA, and began working full-time at the Cotton Club. "I
was happier than hell, you know! I was seventeen, had my own home,
even though it was a tiny one-room cell there at the YMCA. Could
come and go as I pleased, making my own money, and I was writing and
playing in a band!"

In March 1943 the Mayer band added a high school student who was
even younger than Pierson, and a girl at that. Roberta Ellis, a self-
taught drummer, was sixteen years old when she became the band's
percussionist, but she had been performing in shows since she was
five, singing and tap-dancing on a half-hour radio broadcast five days a
week as part of a sister act. When she was ten, Roberta began gaining
weight and "wasn't cute anymore," which interfered with her mother's
plans to put her three daughters in show business. Obesity was to be a
lifelong affliction, Roberta said, noting that she "always felt because of
my body I couldn't accomplish a lot of things." But she took up drum-

A wartime quartet, 1943: Billy (with a mustache) on piano; Bill Pierson on trumpet; Paul Jensen on sax; Roberta Ellis on drums

ming and found that her big body was acceptable in that role. "I was proud of being the only percussionist in the high school band," she said. She also joined a dance combo at age thirteen. "All the girls envied me. I was the one girl in the Ritzy Seven. Six lovely boys and me. But to the guys, I was just one of the guys."

As a condition of hiring an underage female, the management at the Cotton Club required Roberta to be chaperoned by a family member. Her mother was happy to spend her evenings at a nightclub, and family life was eased by the extra income. Her mother was a dance teacher, her father a car salesman. Roberta found that "at age sixteen I was making as much money as my dad was, selling cars, and that's the truth." She could even afford to pay her older sister to do her homework.

George Mayer gave her some lessons in drumming, teaching her rhumba and "a lot of other beats I didn't really know yet." George and Billy also took her into the floorshow. "There were two thirty-minute stage shows a night, variety type. Billy Tipton was featured, then Mayer would do his Cab Calloway act, 'Minnie the Moocher,' then I was an added attraction. I was quite graceful as a tap-dancer — people thought it was unusual for a large person to be able to tap." Roberta's mother helped her work out a song-and-dance routine to "I'm a Corn-fed Girl from Indiana." "Mother loved music and wanted to help me any way she could. She knew I had my obesity against me, so she found a way that I could use my size to its fullest, in comedy."

Billy looked after these youngsters much as he had looked after sixteen-year-old Clarence Cagle ten years earlier in Oklahoma City, treating him like a little brother. He would take Pierson along with him to the afternoon movies. "There was a moviehouse, the De Ray, down on Third and Main, that we called the Dead Rat," Pierson said. "Every once in a while they'd have a triple feature of ghost movies. Now, Billy freaked out on ghost movies. It would be, 'Hey, Pierson, we've got to go to the movie tomorrow, got to go to the movie!' I could take about two of those and then I'd say, 'Man, I have to go get ready for work.' He'd stay and see all three of those movies and then maybe start all over again. 'Ghost movies today, man, ghost movies today!'" With Roberta, Billy was protective. "He took a caring attitude toward my being young," she said. "He saw to it that all of them treated me with the respect of a daughter, wouldn't let them use profanity around me."

Girls were supposed to be kept ignorant of sexual matters, Roberta noted, but the surroundings of the Cotton Club presented certain challenges to this principle.

> I remember one time talking to Billy about a man who would come every evening to the Cotton Club with a little black bag and disappear into the men's room. I asked Billy, "Who is that person?" Billy said, "Now, Roberta, you really don't want to know and you're not old enough to know." Later I found out he was filling the condom machine.
>
> What I did know about life I learned on my own. My mother was the type not to tell any of us girls anything. Later, when I went on the road with another band, she gave me only one piece of advice: "Keep your underwear on and you'll be all right." I said, "Why is that?" And she said, "You will find out as you go along."

During 1942 and into the spring of 1943, the George Mayer band kept knitting itself back together, using high school kids like Bill Pierson and Roberta Ellis and soldiers from Camp Crowder. In the summer of 1943 it finally unraveled. Paul Jensen, who had a college degree in math and physics, took a job at a big mining and smelting company, relegating his clarinet to weekend service. George Mayer moved to Corpus Christi, Texas, where his family had opened a nightclub.

Billy seized the opportunity to form his first jazz ensemble, the Billy Tipton Quartet, and put his own stamp on it. Retaining Roberta Ellis on drums and Bill Pierson on trumpet, he added a bass man, Floyd Conness, and fitted them out with a new look. Pierson later remembered Billy's remark that a successful band would have a suit for every day of the week. "That stuck with me," said Pierson. "Never did make it." Neither did Billy's quartet, but their uniform was classy: royal blue tuxedo jackets, black trousers, white shirts, maroon bow ties. Roberta Ellis wore a black skirt, but aside from this concession she dressed like the men. And Billy began sporting a thin, elegant, Teddy Wilson–style mustache. (After Billy's death, one of the musicians' wives said she had noticed that Billy had helped along his mustache with hair dye and eyebrow pencil.)

Billy wrote new material for the quartet, including routines in which he played both piano and sax, and worked up a number of one-man impersonations. His version of Jimmy Durante's "Ink-a-Dink-Adoo" was popular. He also gave Ellis a number of new roles in the band, singing ballads and performing comedy acts. Roberta felt that he was encouraging her career, helping her make the best of her talents.

About a year after Billy formed the quartet, Bernie Cummins came through Joplin with his society orchestra, which was based in Kansas City. He knew Billy and dropped by the Cotton Club, where Billy introduced Roberta Ellis. Shortly afterward, possibly through a suggestion from Billy to Cummins, Ellis received an offer from an all-girl band in Kansas City that was looking for a drummer. She was tempted but loyal, and she told Billy she would stay in Joplin if he needed her. Billy strongly encouraged her to accept the offer. "He told me this might be the only chance I'd receive in a lifetime — after the war, nobody knew what would happen. He said, 'If you're ever going to succeed, this is the time.' I believe now that he must have been thinking about what it had been like. As a woman, Billy had encountered the same problems that I would encounter in this business."

Ellis also thought she understood why Billy had taken the route of hiding out in a male identity.

> Male bands were superior. In retrospect, after traveling for three years with the girl band I later belonged to, I can say that the musicians were very good but were more or less held down, especially in jazz. Very few women have gone into jazz; most went into commercial or philharmonic, that sort of thing. Jazz was a man's world. I was fortunate to be born and pursue the career I had when the war was going on, lucky to enter when women were in demand. I got to play music and travel. That was our time, the forties were our time to make it! I was a girl drummer. That's what we were pushing — female. But if I had been able to get into a male band, with musical expertise all around me, I probably would have become a better musician.

During Billy's transition from sideman to bandleader in 1942–1943, he and Non Earl were still living together, but under conditions that promoted Billy's new need for secrecy. Their old freewheeling way of life changed completely once they settled in Joplin. In Oklahoma City, Billy had been conducting what would now be labeled as a lesbian relationship with an older woman, one who brought to the partnership a number of financial and social assets. When they first became a couple, in 1934, Non Earl had the car, had the connections, worked the crowds, made most of the money, and was, presumably, more sexually experienced than Billy. In the world where they circulated as a female couple, they possessed a mild outlaw glamour, but mainly they were known as show people, who lived on the fringe of respectable society no matter how they lived. The move to Joplin, where Billy started passing as a heterosexual man, reconfigured the relationship to the social disadvantage of Non Earl. By default, she was demoted to the position of the older wife of a young man (in 1942, Non Earl was forty-two and Billy was twenty-seven). To make ends meet, she went to work as a clerk at the Montgomery Ward outlet in Joplin. Billy had the glamour, the spotlight, the show business to himself. When Roberta Ellis joined the band, for instance, she was amazed to learn that the friendly middle-aged woman who dropped by the Cotton Club to sit and chat with the older women almost every night was Billy's *wife*. Roberta had thought she was Billy's *mother*.

Roberta also noticed that after Non Earl went home, Billy would perk up. He even began flirting with Roberta's eighteen-year-old sister, Doris Dean, a pretty blond tap-dancer. He would ask her to dance during intermissions and hold her tight in the foxtrot. Billy's attentions caused a flutter of speculation between the sisters, Roberta recalled: "Billy was such a good-looking man! His hair was beautiful, wavy; and he had a smooth face. But we also said to each other, 'He certainly has a big butt for a man!' Most women are built this way, not men. Yet we never, never had any inkling Billy was a she. Billy had a crush on Doris Dean, and you could tell it. Whenever Doris Dean came into the room, Billy's eyes would light up. We thought he was married, though, so she just treated him very friendly."

Meanwhile, Non Earl was getting bored. Maybe it occurred to her that if she was going to be regarded as married, it might as well be to Earl Harrell, the husband she had never gotten around to divorcing. During Non Earl's absence, Earl had been managing a nightclub and residing with a woman named Winnie, whom he listed in the city directory as his wife. In 1943, Non Earl returned to Oklahoma City and took Earl away from Winnie. Non Earl and Earl invested in real estate, and as a hobby, Non Earl began raising parakeets. She became a land-lady, renting one of her rooms to a bootlegger, a lingering connection to the bar culture where she had spent her thirties. In her late forties she decided to become a nurse and went to work for several years at the

Oklahoma City Bone and Joint Hospital. She became a devoted daughter and a regular at family reunions again, reentering the family photograph albums wearing eyeglasses and house dresses. The cousin who recalled having Non Earl held up by the Baptist relatives as the example of a bad girl commented on how surprised she was when she finally met Non Earl at a family reunion. "Nonie was just an older married woman, perfectly respectable. I'd look at her and think, 'Who *was* this girl who used to dance?'"

With Non Earl out of the way, Billy began leading a bachelor's life in swinging Joplin. One of the musicians he worked with recalled that he was not above bragging about his conquest of a pretty young woman who frequented the Cotton Club: "Billy talked about laying with her, and he mentioned that she was a virgin. He said that you could tell that, you know." By the autumn of 1943, however, Billy had found a glamorous new companion, who was to become the next Mrs. Tipton.

· 9 ·

Swinging

≡≡≡≡≡

1943–1946

Bill Tipton is just 5 feet, 4½ inches tall, but every fraction
of an inch is packed with talent . . . His wife is a talented
vocalist.

— *The Dial*, March 1944

SATURDAY AFTERNOON in the late autumn of 1943: a dressed-up
young couple walks purposefully down Main Street in Joplin, Missouri. She is diminutive, small-boned as a bird; he holds her lightly by
the elbow, possessive. He's wearing a fedora and a double-breasted
suit, somewhat threadbare but fastidiously brushed and pressed. She
has hung an unbuttoned polo coat over her shoulders like a cape,
partially revealing a knee-length dress with a gored skirt. On her feet
are platform shoes, and she has applied pancake makeup to her
shapely legs; fashion, contributing to the war effort, dictates raised
hemlines, to save fabric, though hosiery is hard to get. The street is
crowded with buses depositing load after load of soldiers and a few
women in WAC uniforms, up from Camp Crowder for the weekend.
The couple's civvies stand out amid the khaki. Is that why they stare
straight ahead, meeting no one's eyes? They are headed for afternoon
drinks and people-watching at the Rendezvous Lounge in the grand
old Connor Hotel, where a jazz ensemble plays in the afternoon. Then
they will go on to drinks at a lounge in the Keystone Hotel called the
Glass Hat, where the customers sit as if arranged on display behind the
plate-glass windows.

This is Billy Tipton and his new wife, June, who had married each
other, they said, in October. June was eye-catching, "oh so hip and so
cool!" according to a musician who was just seventeen when he first

laid eyes on her. Women recall that she had clean-cut, small features set off by a short pageboy hairstyle and that she was "tiny," "very slight," "petite," well proportioned. Men say that she had great legs and, despite her small size, a buxom figure. And a good voice. Though June was not really a professional singer and had no regular job with a band, she was sometimes billed as a torch singer, as in "carrying a torch," as in "tortured." Her style evoked comparisons with some of the best jazz vocalists, such as Anita O'Day and Ella Fitzgerald. One musician who backed her occasionally during the late 1940s recalled, "June could sing up a storm. She did a lot of the jazz things, not quite as bluesy as Billie Holiday or Sarah Vaughan, but certainly capable. Very, very talented, and very nice. I was just young, a kid, and not married. If it hadn't been for her being older than I was — which I don't think was much of a roadblock to me at that age — and if she hadn't been attached to Billy, I think I would have chased her."

Within the limitations of the wartime economy, June was also a clotheshorse. One of her friends remembered an occasion when she and June dressed up to go to the club where Billy was playing that night. June appeared in "a gorgeous, beautiful evening dress, kind of a pale peach color, and she said that Billy told her that she looked like a gumdrop in it." As for Billy, clothes made the man, and what gave the finishing touch to his manhood was this beautiful doll draped over his shoulder, a doll that other fellows wanted to steal.

June was a local girl, maybe ten years younger than Billy. She lived on the outskirts of Joplin with her mother and her older sister, Virginia Stanfield, who supported the family. A nightclub waitress, Virginia had earned the name Jitterbug because of the way she would "just skip across the floors and dance around the tables with a big load of dishes up and down her arm." Virginia's boyfriend was Clark Stewart, the son of the nightclub owner Gladys Stewart, and he was dating Jitterbug on the sly, against Gladys's wishes. "Mother must have told me a hundred times, *do not date the waitresses*," he said, but he found Virginia unusually attractive. Back in 1938, when a film company had invaded the Ozarks to film the outdoor scenes for *Jesse James*, the crew had driven up to Joplin for a little urban entertainment, and the stars — Tyrone Power, Randolph Scott, and Henry Fonda — had often showed up in Gladys Stewart's nightclub. One of the crew took a shine to Jitterbug and began squiring her around in his big cream-colored Oldsmobile.

That was the sort of man she could charm, so Clark Stewart thought he could justifiably make her an exception to his mother's rule.

No wonder the likes of Henry Fonda and Tyrone Power found their way to Gladys Stewart's nightclub. Joplin's distinctive character as an entertainment center dated back to the mid-nineteenth century, its earliest days as a mining town. Banks would be open Saturday night from seven to eight to pay the miners, and everything else was open all night, every night, to take their money. The mining industry cycled between surge and recession, but the entertainment business it fostered never left. One long-time resident recalled that before World War II, Joplin "had a red-light district second to none. People used to say that Joplin had more whores per capita than any town in the United States. They had a whore town, with girls sitting in the windows and knocking on the glass. These were mostly residential homes. It was all taken care of — the city physician checked them out all the time." In the center of town, bars were clustered six or seven to a city block, in two-story buildings where gambling flourished in the rooms upstairs. "For years, gambling was a pretty accepted part of the downtown business scene, drew a lot of people into town," this resident commented.

Widowed young and left with two children to support, Gladys Stewart was still strikingly good-looking when Billy worked at her club. She kept a poster board in the corner of the bar that showed her pouring a bottle of Walter's Premium Beer, a memento of her days as a beautiful girl, when a photographer had used her as a model. She prospered by turning a series of supper clubs into entertainment extravaganzas. Her establishments had the usual amenities: a well-stocked bar, a restaurant, and dance music, from a quartet at the best of times, sometimes just from a piano. She also had a nickelodeon loaded with records by the Andrews Sisters, which customers could use to drown out a combo they didn't like, and she installed pinball machines and a miniature bowling alley that had the same effect (or so the musicians remember). Upstairs at the Champagne Buffet, she had a number of rooms for gambling "when gambling was more or less legal" during the late 1930s. Her son recalled that they "had all kinds of games, such as twenty-one tables and slot machines — everything but roulette." Others remember that they also had prostitutes. As one person put it — a person who thought very well of Gladys — hers "was not a rough crowd, but if she had to have whores, she had whores."

In most details, Gladys's was like several other supper clubs in town

— Minnie's Dine & Dance, Dana's Bo Peep, the Golden Door, the Swingaroo, the Holiday Inn, the Roof Garden of the Connor Hotel. To compete for the attention of the free-spending soldiers during the 1940s, Gladys began having Atlantic lobster and oysters and sea turtles flown in several times a week for her restaurant. One of her former customers remembered that she "would go out in the middle of the night to meet deliveries at the airport," to be sure that the order met her standards. "You could call her up and ask, 'How fresh are the lobsters?' She would say, 'Maybe you want to come next week.' She was that kind of businesswoman." Patrons of her Champagne Buffet and later her Heidelberg Inn would enter the club through a canopied archway, to be greeted by a display of live turtles, some of them four feet across, and lobsters on seaweed-covered ice, framed by mounds of oyster shells. You could choose your dinner on the way to your table. *That* was the floorshow people went to see at Gladys's.

Billy began doing gigs at Gladys's during his earliest years in Joplin, at both the Champagne Buffet and the Heidelberg Inn. During the war Gladys moved her business out of downtown Joplin to a place that had previously been called the Cottage Inn, because it was both a nightclub and a tourist court with a dozen or so one-room shotgun cabins out back. She liked having show people around and made a few of the cabins available to entertainers who were short of money. Billy rented a cabin from Gladys after Non Earl left Joplin, and he and June shared it after they married. He became quite friendly with Gladys, as he had with Helen Teagarden back in his Oklahoma City days. Both of these landladies were active, independent widows who had seen a lot of life, women who provided a refuge for entertainers.

They also provided a refuge for entertainers' pets. It was while living with June that Billy began adding pets to his life. As children in Kansas City, Dorothy and her brother had lived with dogs and cats and horses, so a lapdog must have seemed like a convenient sort of pet to accommodate in Billy's itinerant worklife. But June and Billy unwisely adopted a nervous little red Pekingese that they soon named Troubles. June had a monkey too, more trouble yet. Billy told one of his friends about the time they left the monkey in their car while playing a gig. When they came back to the car, "it looked like there'd been a snowstorm in there. The monkey had torn up the upholstery and scattered the stuffing all over!"

But Billy and June and Gladys got along fine. A shrewd manager,

June and Gladys with friends at the Champagne Buffet, Joplin, circa 1944

Gladys was on the job at all hours. One customer recalled that "sometimes she'd be doing her sewing right there in the front of the place, and when someone came in she'd get up and serve beer." Her daughter said that until Gladys broke her hip, at age eighty-six, she was cooking shrimp and lobsters and waiting tables at the Heidelberg, her arms laden with heavy platters. When she died, at ninety-three, readers of her obituary joked that a newspaper wouldn't dare to print some of the things Gladys knew.

Joplin's history as the place "to go out for a little action" fostered tolerance of a different kind from that in Oklahoma City. According to a former fire chief, Harry Guinn, wartime Joplin was a haven for lesbians and gay men. He observed that "a lot of Gladys's clientele might have been that way — she was kind of known for that." Guinn had opportunity to observe this firsthand, since his fire station was directly across the road from the Heidelberg Inn. But, he added, the Heidelberg was not their only hangout. "There were a lot of places. Seems like [lesbians] were around quite a bit during the war," some wearing men's clothes. In the 1940s, when Gladys Stewart was Billy Tipton's landlady, her nightclub "was a beehive," said one of her friends, a gathering place for every sort of customer. "Gladys had a lot of friends. I guess you could say she was a liberal. If entertainers came through town and they were broke, she put them up there, and the kind of people that went there were kind of an oddball bunch. Don't know about Gladys, but she was probably the sort that did everything once. I don't mean that in a bad way. I liked Gladys. Liked her kids. She raised some good kids."

Gladys's son indicated that growing up around his mother's clubs made him savvy about a lot of things other people might not notice. Consequently, he was able to see through Billy's disguise as Billy went around with June on his arm. "Billy dressed like a man but had little boys' shoes on," he said. "There were some of us kids that were street-wise that knew she was a lesbian, but nobody ever made any mention of it. Billy never caused any trouble with anyone, and I guess it's obvious that he wasn't a fighter. He didn't talk like a woman, not like they do now. He looked a little funny, but I guess people just figured they were show people and didn't pay much attention to them."

Guessing Billy's secret, Clark Stewart observed that Billy and June were very discreet in public, "never did smooch or anything, never held hands. I remember they'd come down the street walking with their heads up, just looking straight ahead, arms hooked, like you were escorting someone into a dance." Stewart's sister, who had not guessed their secret, remembered rather wistfully that Billy was very much in love with June and "spoiled her to death. He was that kind of person, sympathetic and understanding. If he loved you, he spoiled you." Nor did Billy's musician friends observe anything at all unusual about this couple. A comment by Jerry Seaton, one of Billy's cronies, is typical: "Why, we all played our different jobs around the clubs, then we'd all meet downtown at the Horseshoe Cafe, just off Fourth and Main. We'd eat, sit around and unwind, just talk. Didn't stay very long, some-times an hour, then all go our different directions. And June would almost always accompany Billy. She was singing, or sometimes she'd just go with him. I don't know that I ever knew much about where she came from."

Most of the musicians the Tiptons worked with shared Seaton's view of them as an ordinary married couple trying to get by in the music business. Wartime rationing was making life difficult for everybody, but especially people who had to travel for a living. Automobile tires and inner tubes were among the first items to be rationed, the speed limit was reduced to 40 mph and then to 35 mph, and the gasoline ration was cut to four gallons per week per motorist, all in order to avoid wear on tires. High production in the Midwest oilfields meant that black market gas was readily available, or so former cabdrivers recall, but rationing discouraged customers from driving out to nightclubs. They stayed home and danced to music on the radio.

Possibly it was the combination of rationing and the draft that diminished and then terminated Billy's job at the Cotton Club early in the new year, 1944, abetted by the climate of suspicion the war produced in Joplin. The town of thirty-seven thousand was the nearest weekend playground for the forty thousand troops quartered at Camp Crowder during each training cycle. Billy might well have felt he would be safer from exposure in another community less full of shoulders with chips on them. By March 1944 he had found a job in Springfield, Missouri, sixty miles east of Joplin on Route 66, working as replacement pianist on the staff of radio station KWTO ("Keep Watching the Ozarks") for a salary in the range of twenty-five or thirty dollars a week. He is remembered as "real polite and courteous," a fine piano man, able to read and play whatever was set in front of him. Yet his competence was compromised by the sheer fact of his availability. Why wasn't he in the war? A brief profile published in the station's promotional magazine indicates how incessant and inescapable was the requirement that a young man explain himself in those days.

Bill is the new staff pianist whose playing has done much for KWTO programs during recent weeks, since Paul Mitchell went in the Navy . . . When Bill was twelve years old, he was badly injured when kicked by a horse while visiting on an uncle's farm . . . and he has tried without luck to enlist in various branches of the services, as a result of that old injury. Bill wanted badly to go into the United States Army Cavalry at the time his brother enlisted. His brother is now a First Lieutenant in the Cavalry . . . and is serving over-seas. However, we all know that good music helps morale, so we console Bill by telling him that his musical ability is at least doing some good on the home-front, and that his programs before soldier audiences are more than appreciated.

Bill's musical education fortifies his natural talent, for he studied classical music in the Horner Conservatory in Kansas City, and has had the best private instruction available in the middle west. However, when Bill "gets in the groove" on boogie-woogie, his specialty, he always says to himself, "If my teachers could only hear me now."

Bill is 24 years of age and has been married since October. His wife is a talented vocalist.

June accompanied Billy when the radio broadcast from remote locations, and she left a strong impression on one of KWTO's announcers, Virgil Phillips. June "backed him up in spirit, really showed her enthusiasm for the music," Phillips recalled. "I've seen her sitting there in the studio cracking fingers and twisting her arms around, making gestures with her hands and arms — she was one of those kinds of girls. What we used to call a live wire."

But if Billy hoped to remove himself from the public eye by working at the radio station, he miscalculated. The announcer George Wilson recalled that as many as fifty or sixty people would come in from the

"His wife is a talented vocalist": Billy at the piano, June waiting to sing with George Mayer and his orchestra, Corpus Christi, 1945

The pearl-gray La Salle

country to watch the live performers in the studio's glass booths. Billy's position at KWTO did not last very long, and hearsay suggests that rumors about his gender had followed them to Springfield. In mid-May 1944 the couple moved on once again, this time on the promise of a good job in Texas. Billy's old partner George Mayer was forming a band down in Corpus Christi, in a new nightclub called the Palmero. As George later recalled, Billy jumped at the offer but was broke. George had to loan him a hundred dollars to buy a used car. Billy went shopping and came up with a pearl-gray 1939 La Salle convertible that carried the couple to Texas in style.

But wartime Corpus Christi did not suit Billy at all, according to George. "Corpus Christi Texas was a Navy town. There were lots of free-for-all fights among the sailors who came to the Palmero where we played . . . When a fight broke out, beer bottles flew in all directions. Billy was ready to quit. The manager put up a screen of chicken wire to protect us from the flying bottles. That calmed Billy down until one night a shot rang out and a bullet whizzed by the bandstand. Billy said 'That does it!' and he quit the band on the spot."

One of Mayer's acquaintances pointed out that this story, told after Billy's death, bears a suspicious resemblance to a scene in the movie *The Blues Brothers*. In fact, Billy and June were in Corpus Christi for nearly two years and returned to Joplin only early in 1946. By then, a certain distance had opened between them. June continued to use June Tipton as a stage name but began seeking work outside Billy's band. Financial problems may have been pressuring them: social security records show that Billy drove a cab after returning to Joplin. Later that year he joined a band organized by a local musician named Williams and went on the road, traveling a big loop through Illinois, Indiana, and Kentucky. It was hard for musicians to make much money while traveling, and Williams quit the music business entirely a short while later and bought a Chevrolet distributorship — by them he knew a lot about cars.

By the end of 1946, Billy and June were no longer together. Billy had a double identity, and quite possibly June had fallen in love with only half of it. "Why not take all of me?" was such stuff as songs were made of, but marriages needed firmer ground, and Billy's desire to pass as a married man placed the relationship on a fault line. What June alone knew could always be used against him.

In any case, when Billy and June separated, their parting was called a divorce by the people who remember it, and Billy got custody of their dog, Troubles. One musician remembers something else, as well: "Now this woman named June that he married, she circulated a story after they broke up and supposedly got a divorce — I don't know that they ever really got married, but they claimed they did — but she later circulated the story that he was a *hermorphadite*, had both sexes. She'd wiggle her little finger up and down, you know, like Billy was the size of a pinkie."

This memory raises a number of questions about the years when Billy went from cross-dressing to passing. What did June know about Billy's body when she became his wife? She may have been using the term "hermaphrodite" as a euphemism. Sometimes rather poetically mispronounced "hermorphadite" (a woman morphed, as we might say), this was common parlance for "lesbian," as was evident in the way people phrased their recollections of Buck Thomason, the radio announcer. Was June a closeted lesbian, like Billy? Or was "hermaphrodite" Billy's term, an improvised explanation meant to allay the outrage June might have felt upon discovering that she had been deceived?

What actually was Billy's biological sex? As we have seen, certain aspects of Billy's body were commented on by people who knew him as a man. Paul Jensen observed, with reference to the strength of Billy's piano playing, that he "had arms big around as some people's waists almost. Real strong-looking arms." Another musician said that Billy's large buttocks earned him the nickname Pear Shape, after a male character in the comic strip *Dick Tracy*, though to female observers this feature looked female. Among the many reasons we can summon to explain Billy's choice to live as a man, was there a biological reason?

The social conventions by which we recognize only two sexes and call them "opposite" conceal a number of biological actualities. Sex difference is defined at several bodily sites. Outside lie the genitals and, after puberty, the secondary sex characteristics: breasts and hips on a woman, Adam's apple and facial and body hair on a man. Inside lie the gonads (ovaries in the female, testes in the male), which direct sexual development through the production of estradiol for female development, testosterone for male. Yet male and female bodies synthesize variable amounts of both sex hormones, and the complexity of the interactions of the hormones results in so much variation that sex difference is best understood as a spectrum or continuum. One contemporary biologist has claimed that there are actually five discernibly different and biologically coherent human sexes. Female and male are two of the five. The others are mixtures. "Herms," or true hermaphrodites, possess one testis and one ovary; female pseudohermaphrodites, or "ferms," have ovaries and some aspects of the male genitalia but lack testes; male pseudohermaphrodites, or "merms," have testes and some aspects of the female genitalia but lack ovaries. "Each of these categories is in itself complex," the biologist Anne Fausto-Sterling observes. "The percentage of male and female characteristics, for instance, can vary enormously among members of the same subgroup." In the medical literature, the hermaphroditic types are classed together as "intersexes." The condition is thought to occur in possibly 4 percent of newborns.

The external sex organs in human beings are visibly as different as a pair of gloves, one turned inside out: what is extended in one is concealed in the other. Yet in a newborn, the clitoris can be long, the penis abbreviated, the scrotum similar to labia. Such ambiguity is well known to pediatric endocrinologists, the usual referees when a baby's sex is not immediately obvious. Until very recently, medical treatment with hormones or surgery was often undertaken immediately, to insure that the external and internal sex organs matched up and gave one clear message at puberty. The treatment would be done early to help the child develop a secure psychological gender identity — the conviction, which is thought to form by age three, that one is a girl or a boy.

June's husband, circa 1946

Such medical intervention has grown controversial in the wake of recent reassessments of the notion that gender identity is an either-or proposition.

This brings us back to Billy. Evidence from the autopsy performed on Billy's corpse indicates that she was not a herm, for she possessed no testes. Was she a ferm? June's memorable finger-waggle suggests that she possessed an unusually large clitoris with some of the characteristics of a penis, but the autopsy report — a better source than hearsay — does not support this conjecture. "The body habitus is that of a normally developed, adult female (despite the name and past history of male identity)," the report says. "The genitalia are those of a normal adult female."

Yet as people remember and as photographs confirm, from time to time beginning in the 1940s, Billy sported a trim little mustache. At least two explanations are possible. The mustache could have been a cosmetically assisted feature of a normal woman's facial hair pattern, or it could have been the result of elevated levels of androgens. Billy's chromosomes were not examined during the autopsy to learn whether her cells carried the Y chromosome, which would make her male, or two X chromosomes, which would make her female. A Y chromosome might have caused an increased production of androgens if she had androgen insensitivity syndrome, a genetic disorder that prevents the full development of masculine traits in males. Another possibility is that Billy had a condition, not uncommon in females, called polycystic ovary syndrome, an enzymatic defect in the ovaries that causes them to produce too much testosterone, the steroid hormone that stimulates the production of male sex characteristics. Billy's chunky upper body, tendency to obesity, relatively undefined waistline, facial hair, and masculine walk could have been the developmental outcome of a flood of testosterone from polycystic ovary disease. Another result would have been a reduction in the number and strength of menstrual periods, a great convenience in Billy's way of life. Neither the presence of the Y chromosome in Billy's cells nor the effect of polycystic ovary disease would have made her any less than the biologically normal female described in the autopsy report. "Normal" is a very capacious category. Conceivably, though, Billy's fortitude got a little biochemical lift from testosterone.

As far as Billy's relationship with June and other women is concerned, we can assume that after she separated from June, being Billy full-time solved the psychological and social difficulties presented by Dorothy's strong masculine gender identification and her sexual desire for women, quite aside from solving the problem of achieving professional status in a man's world. Billy wanted to be happy, and for Billy it was easier to be happy as a man than as a lesbian. Confiding in sexual partners therefore became both unwise and unnecessary.

This decision inaugurated the final phase in the development of the persona of Billy Tipton, and it can be attached to a photograph of Billy with Reggie and Lynn Fullenwider at the Green Frog Café in Abilene, Texas. The nightclub's photographer captured them in their finery that night. Both men are in coats and ties, and Reggie wears a hat with a veil and a triple string of pearls. The spine of a matchbook on the table reads "Merry Christmas," so the occasion is quite possibly a celebra-

Lynn and Reggie Fullenwider with Billy Tipton at the Green Frog Café, 1944?

tion of Billy's birthday, 29 December. Possibly the year is 1944, when Billy was working in Corpus Christi. Billy turned thirty that year.

At least three prints of this photograph were made. One, nicely framed in ivory leather and covered with protective glass, was found among Billy's scrapbooks and memorabilia after his death. Another print was pasted into Reggie's photo album, probably by Reggie herself. This one has been trimmed of Billy, all except the hands, and has become a picture of Reggie and Lynn in a nightclub with some anonymous third party who is fiddling with a cigarette lighter. The third print, framed in silvery metal, always traveled with Billy. In this print, the figure of Lynn has been trimmed away, leaving Billy alone with his mother.

This keepsake in its three versions seems to be a record of the permanent transfer of Billy's secret into Reggie's keeping, for Reggie's album preserved portraits only of a daughter. From now on, Reggie alone held the part that once was her daughter's heart, the part now

fully masked for everybody else by the professional persona of Billy.
"Dorothy was my mother's daughter," Dorothy's brother often remarked, and Reggie's photo album seems to have served as the repository of that identity.

In Billy's show copy of the photograph, which he took on the road
with him, Reggie's personal history has been scissored away, probably
to improve her usefulness as a prop. Reggie's presence gives this birthday party its authenticity, so to speak. Mother and son are out on the
town, with a popping flashbulb confirming his celebrity and her pride
in it. This is the only image of Reggie that any of the other women in
Billy's life would ever see.

Billy's private copy of the full, uncensored print is the most interesting of all, for it shows that by age thirty, she had won acceptance not
only from Reggie but within the family life that Reggie formed with
Lynn Fullenwider. The same private filing cabinet that preserved the
photograph also contained a rather long letter from Lynn, dated 1961.
The letter thanks "Dot" for a Father's Day present and invites her for a
visit. "I hope you can make it to Okla this year. Both of us would love so
much to see you," Lynn wrote. "Thank you again Dear for the swell
Father's Day remembrances. With lots of love." This suggests that Billy
continued to put a good deal of effort into the preservation of her role
as a member of the family, and that this effort was successful in spite of
the potentially humiliating difficulties that her charade presented to
those who loved her and had to play along. In 1944, Lynn was there as
stepfather to celebrate the birthday of a successful entertainer whose
public persona was masculine, and he continued to affirm their relationship as Billy extended the disguise. For Billy did not choose to live
alone after he and June parted company in 1946. He had already met
the next woman he would call his wife.

· 10 ·

The Son-in-Law

1946–1949

I suppose if I'd been a little older and more worldly-wise,
maybe I'd have questioned this, but . . .
— Betty Cox, recalling her life with Billy Tipton

I N 1946, Betty Cox was eighteen years old and just off the farm, living "in a little bitty flea-bitten motel" in Joplin. Days she waited tables in the lunchroom of the Connor Hotel, and at night she served lobster dinners and drinks at the Heidelberg Inn. On her breaks, she danced. To Betty, the job at the Heidelberg felt like working on a movie set. "Growing up," she said, "I wanted to be like Ginger Rogers. I wanted to sing and dance with a band."

Betty was the middle daughter in a big, fatherless family and had moved to Joplin because her older sister Juanita lived there and because Joplin was a swinging town, full of music. Everybody in her family played music. Her mother, Lula Mae, always had a piano in the house, no matter how many necessities the family did without. Two older brothers played string instruments, and Betty and her two sisters learned keyboards. Betty joked that she started collecting sheet music when it became clear that she had no talent. She was known in the family as the one who "couldn't play 'Come to Jesus' in the key of G." During high school, working part-time at a bookstore, she culled free copies of popular songs from the damaged stock and the closeouts. By the time she moved to Joplin and went to work at Gladys's, she had "every kind of sheet music you could find in the world."

Betty was sexy. Her wide smile showed a chip in a front tooth, a little flaw that drew attention to her sumptuous mouth. She had a mane of dark wavy hair and a full-breasted, small-waisted body that she liked to

Betty Cox in high school, 1944

dress in form-fitting bodices and swishy skirts. Vain about her small feet, she wore strappy spike heels. "I feel," she said, "that when I sweep into a room, by God you'd better know I'm coming!"

Flirting with the musicians, scrounging their discards for her collection of sheet music, she became friends with Billy Tipton, whose quartet was house band at the Heidelberg Inn. During intermissions he would often sit with Betty in the kitchen, drinking coffee and chatting about music. He treated her like a kid sister. After the Heidelberg closed he would sometimes take her and her roommate cruising around in the little black '39 Chevy roadster with which he had replaced the La Salle, which he had wrecked in Texas when he was traveling with June. The roadster had a rumble seat, room for three.

"We'd go out and park on a country road and talk, the three of us. He was as comfortable being around my girlfriend as he was with me," Betty remembered. "Billy had a funny lopsided smile and always found the *humor* in something. He was a nice, nice person to talk to."

When Billy and Betty met, in 1946, June Tipton was still singing with Billy's group at the Heidelberg. They seemed like a solid married couple. Betty remembered that before June went onstage, she would say to Billy, "Kiss me, it makes my lips softer." But one day June vanished. Billy said that she had had a chance to go with a bigger band and had "just kissed him goodbye." Soon afterward, he started inviting Betty to come by his place and visit him and Troubles, the irritable little Pekinese. "And then I don't know how it happened. We were just sitting and talking one night, and it happened." Billy told Betty that George Mayer was forming a new band in San Angelo, Texas. He would be leaving in the fall. Would Betty come along? Betty was thrilled and amazed. Billy Tipton was in love with her! Of course she'd go with him.

Did she love him too?

Oh, I certainly did! It was . . . I don't know — fun, it was comfortable. He was neat, clean, and he didn't use foul language with me. He was a lovely human being, with twinkling blue eyes and such soft skin. I thought he was cute as a bug! Such a nice smile. If I had to list the five or six things that made us compatible, right at the top would be his sense of humor. Then, gentleness. Very seldom angry — well, not that he didn't lose his temper; he did. But he was considerate of other people. Very. Bend over backwards to do whatever he thought would make you happy.

And he wasn't . . . well, I don't know if you know musicians. Some musicians are standoffish — stand in the corner and don't give you the time of day. Well, he was gregarious, always talking to someone, always laughing. People took us to heart, we made some good friendships. I think that shows he was very outgoing. Women especially found him very attractive.

Betty and Billy decided that they would live together and that later they would marry. It was a bold step for Betty. To understate the matter, cohabitation "really wasn't approved of" in her world; in those days it was called "living in sin." To allay the concerns of her family, she and Billy claimed they had married, and Billy was welcomed as a son-in-

Betty's husband, 1947

law. Of course, Billy had been presenting himself as a married man with one woman or another ever since he had begun playing music. But his other women had been show people like himself. In Betty he was apparently seeking the comforts of a heterosexual marriage to a woman who would look up to him, who would let him make the rules, who would give him a sense of belonging to family again.

Billy chose well in Betty. She put her whole life at his disposal. She was used to working several jobs at a time, since she had started working at age twelve, when her father deserted the family. All the while she lived with Billy, wherever they stayed for more than a couple of weeks, she would find a day job, then join him at the club until the wee hours and go on with him to a jam session if anything turned up. Sometimes she would get a job at the nightclub as well. In San Angelo, she worked as a hat-check girl at the Melody Club, where Billy was playing. None of her jobs paid much, but they put food on the table and gave her a sense of partnership with Billy.

The food Betty put on the table was good food too, cooked by Betty herself — cheap, tasty dishes she had learned from her mother. Homemade noodles with slow-braised beef. Biscuits with fried eggs and ham and grits. Fresh berry pies baked in a dutch oven. Whenever they went on the road, they would carry pots and pans and a hot plate in the trunk so Betty could turn out a meal any night they didn't sleep in the car. A kitchen table became the center of the home Betty made for Billy in motels all over the Midwest and Texas, and later in Oregon and Washington, Idaho and Montana.

Billy fit right into Betty's family. "Among my folks," Betty commented, "everybody gets together when anybody comes through town." Home base was Nevada, Missouri, north of Joplin. Reunions were frequent, and usually took place at Lula Mae's home. She and her husband had acquired a tiny cottage during the Depression, shortly before he walked out. The cottage was just a tarpaper shack built on homestead land, but by working two jobs and getting help from her five children, Lula Mae was gradually able to replace the cardboard walls with clapboard siding, expand the single room to four, and add indoor plumbing. She hadn't yet acquired a toilet in the days that her new son-in-law sat at her kitchen table drinking coffee, though; the family still used an outhouse in the back garden. A bathtub had been the luxury Lula Mae chose when she could finally afford some hot running water.

Betty knew that Billy's own mother lived somewhere nearby, in Oklahoma, and that the divorce of Billy's parents had left the family in disarray. "I suppose if I'd been a little older and more worldly-wise, maybe I'd have questioned this, but Billy never wanted to dwell on any of the bad things," she said. "All I knew was that he had been raised basically by his aunt in Kansas City." Billy never suggested that Betty should meet this aunt, let alone his mother. It was odd, because when they were on the road, Billy called Reggie at least once a week, usually from a pay phone. No, the only mother they went out of their way to visit was Lula Mae. Whenever Billy was working in the area, they would drop by to see her, Betty recalled.

We'd roll into Mother's at four or five o'clock in the morning, and Mom would call my brother and sister and her husband. They'd all get out of bed and come over. Mother would fix breakfast — we're hearty eaters in my family — and we'd sit around and tell dirty jokes. My brother's a good storyteller. He and my brother-in-law Clyde, now deceased, were both truck drivers, and you know they hear a lot of stories. Well, he and Billy would get going with "Can you top this?" You sometimes had to prod Billy to get him started, but he could hold his own. God, we'd stay up all night talking when we were at home, if my brother was there. Billy was very much accepted into the family. My brothers didn't have an inkling about Billy. There just wasn't any question.

Lula Mae and Billy shared "a special understanding," Betty said. Billy loved to dance with Lula Mae and could always get her into swapping stories and home remedies. Billy did his own doctoring, and often took his complaints to his mother-in-law for advice. Lula Mae remembered Billy consulting her about the hemorrhoids he got from sitting so much. The worst thing about being a piano player, he said, was sitting on those hard benches. Lula Mae counseled him to carry a jar of Vicks with him in the car, as it was very soothing. Perhaps Billy complained about persistent hemorrhoids to explain the blood spots on his underwear, something a wife or mother-in-law would notice when she washed his clothes.

Billy and Betty never did get around to marrying. Betty said that they once "went to a little town to have the ceremony, but it was a justice of the peace, and we decided it wasn't worth it. Thought, Well, scratch this." Yet Betty was accepted as Billy's wife by everyone they knew. She used the name Tipton on her driver's license and other documents. At one point she even thought she was pregnant: "Now, you'll laugh at this, but do you know, I honest to God believed it! It was down in Texas. We'd gone to a show. It was pouring down rain. Running across the street, I ran into a cab — the car just slid around the corner and hit me — so of course I thought, Oh dear, now I've really made a mess of things. Shows you how ignorant I was. I was so sure I wanted a baby that when we went back to Joplin, I had tests done to see why I couldn't get pregnant."

Betty said that though she wasn't a virgin when she took up with Billy, she didn't know much about sex. "I think in those days you didn't discuss it. You certainly couldn't ask your mother. God, even when I got my period I thought I was dying, I really did, thought there was something terribly wrong. I had to ask my sister-in-law and my sister what was happening, wouldn't dare ask my mother anything that embarrassing." When asked whether she had had any expectations about sex, she replied, "No. I just . . . whatever we had together was very nice. But it was just as nice lying beside him, squeezing and hugging. But not to say that . . . Geez, wouldn't you have thought maybe my doctor would notice something was wrong if there was a prosthesis there? Wouldn't you have thought?"

Wouldn't you have thought Betty might have had questions about Billy herself? How did he deceive her and the other women with whom he was sexually intimate? For one thing, he never removed his underwear. It was always dark when they coupled, and none of Billy's women ever put her hands on his genitals. Commented one, "You just never got out of line with Billy. You didn't touch Billy." Billy looked as though he had a penis under his clothes, however. Betty remembered all the shopping trips on which she accompanied Billy, watching the tailor measure his band uniforms for alterations. Billy was very fussy about the fit of his clothes. "He was short, had a twenty-nine-inch inseam," she said. "I recall the tailor asking, 'How do you dress, sir?' — first time I'd heard that word — and he'd say, 'I dress left.'" The tailor thought Billy had a penis, and Betty thought he had a penis when he made love to her. He wore a jockstrap under his shorts, which felt firm against a woman's body when they lay close together, and, Betty explained, "Billy always wore a rubber he would strip off and toss away after we made love. So that's what he felt like, a man wearing a rubber." What sexual satisfaction did she think Billy got? "Must have been the satisfaction of kissing and fondling. When you've had that, you're almost home!"

"Who cares to define/What chemistry this is?" asks a song that Billy's trio used to play. "Who cares, with your lips on mine,/What ignorance bliss is?" Kissing a woman all over her body, insisting on the dominant role, devoting himself to her satisfaction, Billy was an active lover, Betty said. Did he conceal a dildo in his jockstrap? Or did he use another technique, laying his thumbs together back to back to slip inside her when she was ready for orgasm? How little we know! Like a magician, Billy had rehearsed so long and well that his legerdemain was completely successful. Only the pleasure was real, and only one question can be answered now: did Betty know? No, she says today. Never.

Yet Betty was no novice to sex. "Yes, I have certainly enjoyed my men," she said. "When I wanted a lover, I took a lover." In Billy she found such a ready partner that she finds it hard to believe the claims of celibacy that Billy's fifth wife, Kitty, made on nationally televised talk shows after his death. It certainly appears that Billy's own desire was aroused, enhanced, possibly even liberated by the directness of Betty's appetites. A wife of one of the musicians they traveled with later remembered overhearing their lovemaking through the thin walls of motel rooms. "He and Betty used to play some of the wildest games!" she said. "They'd be rompin' all over the bed having fun. Billy was sensual, loved to cuddle and kiss."

Aside from the sexual attraction, playing the dominant partner in what was thought to be a heterosexual couple was surely another important ingredient for Billy in this attachment. Billy was older, more talented, and better educated than Betty, who looked up to him. Their life revolved around Billy's work, but he made her feel a part of it. Betty recalled that after Billy had bathed and put on his underwear, he would invite her into the bathroom while he shaved. Yes, he shaved every day before going to work. She would sit on the toilet seat, chatting, while he prepared for the show and helped her choose the clothes she would wear to the club. Her poverty enlarged the scope of his role as provider. Billy loved spending money on a woman, and in fact, the more Betty needed, the better it must have made him feel to spend it. And the less he had, the more he spent, just like his father.

If Billy's emulation of G.W. contributed one stream of feeling to this bond, the need to correct an old injustice may have contributed another. It is possible to discern in Billy's relationship with Betty a working-out of the oldest problem in Billy's emotional history: abandonment by the parents, which left the children in free fall. In marrying Betty emotionally, if not legally, Billy was fitting himself yet again into a family that had been abandoned by a father. He gave as good as he got in this family, giving his energy, his glamour, his classiness, and getting the attentiveness of both a sexy young girl and a fun-loving mother. Lula Mae was part of the package in this relationship, and Billy remained in touch with her long after he and Betty split up. He sent snapshots for her photo album, studio portraits inscribed to "My Best

Mom," the LP recordings he made in the 1950s, cards on her birthday well into the 1960s. Betty's confidence in Billy's masculinity made it possible for him to add to his repertory the gratifying role of the good son. (Interestingly, Billy's desire to play the role of a man was surprisingly common among American women in the postwar era. In a poll conducted by *Fortune* in 1946, 25 percent of the women queried said they would prefer to be men if they could choose, while only 3.3 percent of men said they would prefer to have been born as women.)

Billy and Betty and Troubles spent a honeymoon year in San Angelo, working at the Melody Club and living in a funny half-built house that George Mayer found for them. "It was pretty from the front, but there was no roof over the hallway and no back porch," Betty remembered. The band's drummer was already living in one room that had a roof over it. Billy and Betty took the other, and "when it rained, we'd open the door and sweep the rain right out the back!" The house, so like a stage set, brought out the practical joker in Billy. He escorted a Shetland pony into the living room and photographed it wearing a straw hat.

For several months they lived like campers, Betty recalled. "George and his wife would buy some food and we'd buy some food, then cook together at their place. Kid, that was a blast! That was a ball!" Their earnings were meager. Then Betty took a job at the Roosevelt Hotel, where lodging was part of her pay, and she and Billy moved briefly into a room of their own. At Christmas, Billy gave her something she'd always wanted and had never before been able to afford to keep, a little black mongrel puppy. She named it Boots Liu, and it made the grumpy older dog, Troubles, start living up to his name. Shortly afterward, June arrived to check up on her dog and spent four days with Betty and Billy. "June said she had visiting rights," Betty explained. "I just wished she would get the hell out of my life!" She said she held her peace about it, though. "Well, I was pretty young. At that time of life, you don't really have a viewpoint."

When the job in San Angelo ended, in mid-1948, Billy and Betty returned to Joplin, and Billy spent a year struggling for a foothold. Joplin as a city seemed to be undergoing a collective sobering-up. Camp Crowder had been closed, a change that emptied the nightclubs of multitudes. Servicemen were returning to claim their old jobs and settling into long-delayed family life. By 1950, Joplin would no longer be touted as an urban playground but rather as "the gateway to the Ozarks for thousands of vacationers," and by the late 1950s urban renewal had begun a methodical erasure of the sites associated with the business of pleasure.

The music business too was taking a new direction. The big-band era was over, undone by economic factors, including a cabaret tax imposed on nightclub patrons during the war, and by a twenty-seven-month strike against recording companies instigated by the musicians' union. During the recording ban, the most creative instrumentalists formed experimental ensembles that focused on improvisation. "Bebop" emerged in 1940–1942, as a revolt against the commercialization of jazz by big bands, which focused on making dance music. By the time the strike was over, jazz was a different kind of entertainment. Vocalists, not bandleaders, had become the stars, and the cognoscenti sat down when they listened to it.

For musicians like Billy, who made a living impersonating the commercial trendsetters of the big-band era, the future lay in the formation of a trio or quartet. Big bands were now a losing proposition financially, but there were still audiences for Billy's music — jazz-inflected dance music and romantic and novelty vocals. So when Billy heard that a new nightclub was opening on the outskirts of Joplin, he approached the owner with a proposal for putting together a quartet as the house band. He had in mind a saxophone player named Lew Raines, just out of the air force, a local musician named Tommy Keene on bass, and a young drummer from Oklahoma City named George Ronconi. The owner accepted the deal, but only if the boys would help keep decorating costs down by helping to paint the interior of the club to his specifications. Raines remembered that "the owner's wife wanted a Chinese theme in the doggone dining room. We had to cut out pieces of wallpaper and paste them on, these watercolor things, trees and all. Billy and I painted red and black until we couldn't see straight."

The place was called Hidden Acres, and they played six nights a week for thirty-five dollars a week apiece. Raines felt that that was reasonably good money. "Union scale was five dollars a night, and we didn't have to travel," he explained. Playing dances, they tried to strike a balance between popular entertainment for the crowd and improvisation for the musicians.

To satisfy those with less cultural jazz taste, why, Billy'd throw in one of those comic songs, and that would get everybody back to listening. One of Billy's favorite ways to get 'em back was to sing "Get Along Home, Cindy." He'd start off, "I went down to old Joe Clark's/and found him sick in bed/I put my hand down his throat/and pulled out a chicken head./Get along home, Cindy, Cindy . . ." And people would pop up and say, "*What* did he say?" Well, he had about nine thousand verses of that. And the other song I will remember, "Playmates" — "Look down my rain barrel/slide down my cellar door" — I never hear that song that I don't think of Billy.

Well then, just as soon as he got 'em listening, we'd slip into one of the things *we* liked to do. We took great pride in playing things like "Body and Soul," "Perdido," jazz tunes that Count Basie and Duke Ellington and the old Jimmie Lunceford band used to do. That was the real meat and potatoes to us.

Then, when we'd finished playing at a club, nothing delighted him more than to go someplace where everybody could sit down and play.

Like most band jobs, this one didn't last long enough. By the end of 1948, the owner of Hidden Acres had fired the quartet and replaced it with one piano player, and then only on weekends. Billy made a living by picking up work where he could. For a while his quartet appeared regularly on station KFSB in Joplin, broadcasting a "silly little act" that Betty's kid sister, enthusiastic about having a celebrity in the family, listened to. The only surviving recording of a Billy Tipton Quartet comes from this era, including Billy's arrangements of "Flying Home" and "Yesterdays." Billy also began giving music lessons. The manager of Hidden Acres, Norm Wilson, hired Billy to teach piano to his son Terry. "He would come to the house with his wife, Betty, to give me piano lessons for an hour once a week, when I was about fourteen or fifteen," Terry said. "Not jazz, just the normal music, for ballroom dancing."

Billy also reluctantly went back to playing dance music amid the din of pinball machines at Gladys's Heidelberg Inn. One night a band-leader named Russ Carlyle came through Joplin for a one-nighter at the club owned by Gladys's rival, Minnie. Carlyle and his thirteen-piece band had quite a reputation in the Midwest, partly because Carlyle himself was a vocalist, in the style of Bing Crosby. Billy heard that Carlyle was looking for a tenor saxophone player and sat in that night at Minnie's. Carlyle recalled, "The minute Billy started playing, I was happy with him." Billy joined the band on the spot, and for several months traveled a wide circuit that included Wichita, Topeka, and Memphis. "I had a lot of things going," Carlyle said. "Billy did a great job and gave me no trouble, so I paid no attention to him." But one interaction stayed in his memory.

> Billy would come up to me once in a while to tell me what he wanted to do — I always asked the men what they wanted to do. I said, "You know, you're a young guy, and you're interested in music, and you play very well. What would you like to do *besides* play music?" He said, "That's all I ever want to do." He said he was planning to form his own jazz group.
>
> I think he knew a guy that hung 'round there, played different jobs, good friend of his — Jay McShann, a jazz pianist, made recordings. Black guy. Billy liked him, kinda talked about him. "He's all right! A piano man." Billy just kept telling me that's what he wanted to do, that's all he wanted to do.
>
> We talked about jazz, and I said, "You know, you've got to be very good at that." I told him that this is not really a business — you can be shut off in one minute, especially going into jazz. You know, that's a tough road to go.

Billy did not, strictly speaking, go into jazz, but into the entertainment business, which was adjusting to the collapse of the big bands. A well-managed swing-oriented trio or quartet could find steady work, especially if the musicians were willing to back other acts and could provide a floorshow of gags, sketches, and specialty numbers. By the end of 1949, Billy had settled on the way of life that would support him for the next decade. He would continue to focus his energy on managing his own ensemble, and he would flourish. These decisions were pragmatic, but they seem also to have been motivated by deeper urgings. The jazz historian Jim Merod, reflecting on the hardships imposed by Billy's lifelong disguise, offered the view that "the compulsion at work in Billy Tipton's odyssey was in large part the tug and allure of the jazz life itself. Playing music of this kind at a superior level offers a sublime self-overcoming. Billy's act looks Whitmanic — he affirms a vivid life of self-invention against implacable odds."

Moreover, managing his own group made Billy less vulnerable to accidental encounters that put the masculine identity at risk. It ap-

Lew Raines at Hidden Acres, Joplin, 1948

pears that he had begun to value the advantages of social normality, such as those in his relationship with his mother-in-law, and he had begun to pay the costs of maintaining them. For the first time, the woman in his life was not an ally but a liability in his efforts to pass, for she too needed to be kept quite literally in the dark. When Billy traveled with Russ Carlyle's big band, he left Betty at home, out of earshot of gossip and questions. Nor did he discuss his personal life with other musicians. As far as Carlyle knew, Billy was a single man. Yet his past had a way of catching up with him in Joplin. Hiring Lew Raines for his quartet is a case in point. While they were fulfilling the contract to redecorate Hidden Acres, pasting Chinese motifs on the walls, Billy and Lew got to talking and discovered that they had both lived in Enid,

Oklahoma, and it dawned on Lew who Billy really was: Dorothy, the jazz piano player who lived in that house on Maple Street that Lew used to pass every day on his way to school. They talked through the night, and Billy told Lew that he had decided this was the only way he could get work as a musician. Describing his own attitude toward Billy's masquerade, Lew said, "You see, Billy's love for music, Billy's feeling toward those who made music with him, was overwhelming. I wish I could be so centered, so focused. There was only the pure and total satisfaction of sitting at a keyboard and having people listen, join in, participate — that was satisfying beyond description. He was a great entertainer. And that was the only time it was ever mentioned between us. I kept that secret until the day he died, in spite of many temptations to talk about it with musicians from the Joplin days when we met up later."

Now that Billy's secret has been exposed, some of his Joplin acquaintances claim that there were always people who knew but did not tell, as Lew Raines surely knew and did not tell. None, it seems, held Billy's fakery against him at the time. Why not? Raines believes that those who might have seen through Billy's disguise were not required to consider the sexuality of his relationships with women.

Billy was intelligent enough to know that if he shared part of his life with a female companion, that gave it respectability and stopped the rumors and the gossip. He was married to June first, though I use the term "married" loosely. Then Betty, a very attractive blonde, a buxom thing. Dolly Parton could have been Betty's clone! Yet I cannot truthfully tell you that I ever saw Billy demonstrate affection with either of his wives. I can't ever remember anything but pleasant conversations between them, can't remember him hugging them, kissing them, touching them. I don't believe Billy did that. Whether they were married to Billy or not, they had no *physical* attachment to each other. [The women] were quite content that Billy would be a good companion, would be a provider. Back even in the forties, right after the war, people had been on rations, you couldn't get certain food items — we just got used to sharing things. So it just worked out. June didn't have a place to stay, Billy did have a place to come and stay. Whether they got married or not, I have no idea. Whether Billy and Betty got married or not, I have no idea.

Even Raines's mother, who had known of Dorothy's family in Enid, forgot what she knew about Billy's past. "My mom would say to me, 'Gee, why don't you invite Billy and Betty down?' Mom didn't even remember that Billy was not Billy. She accepted him as a boy. No, Billy and Betty would drive down to the farm and have Sunday dinner with us. And it would not be uncommon that we'd finish a job and Billy'd say, 'Come on by and we'll get Betty to scramble some eggs.'" Was this sexy, fun-loving guy with the buxom women in his life a lesbian? As Raines said, "No, no — no no no!" Yet Raines could not resist making a little joke at the end of this uncomfortable line of questioning: "Billy didn't want to come out of the closet. He was happy to be out of the house!"

Billy was obviously fortunate in his friendship with Lew Raines, but these kindhearted stories should also stand as cautionary tales, reminding us of how little we know. By 1949, Americans were again able to purchase homes and change jobs and buy cars and take vacations, and people were on the move again. Living in Joplin, near the territory she had traversed as a cross-dresser, Billy was *always* in danger of discovery, or at least of rude and jarring encounters.

People remember that Billy began suffering from an ulcer around that time. Whether because of worry about his safety or just from an impulse to try another way of life, Billy decided to leave the Midwest. His old pal and favorite partner, George Mayer, had called to say that he had urgent reasons to leave Texas. George's beautiful new wife, Margo, was a little more pregnant than she should be, and they wanted to get out of town before she began to show. George had signed up with a booking agent in Portland, Oregon, who was offering steady work in a six-state territory that stretched from Eureka to Seattle, Bozeman to Reno. All he needed was a couple of musicians. Would Billy join him? Yes.

PART IV

Rising

1949–1958

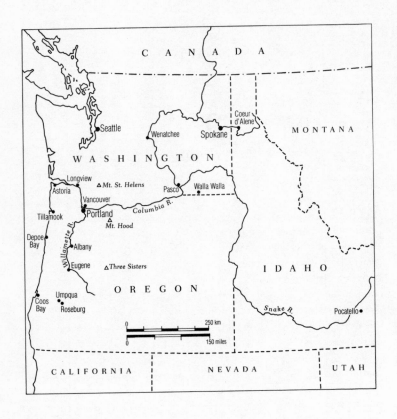

· II ·

Mobility

1949–1953

STRAIGHT MAN: Where do bad girls go?
BILLY TIPTON: Most everywhere.
　　　　　　　— "Gee Quiz," circa 1955

THE CITY of Portland, straddling the confluence of the Willamette
River with the Columbia, lies on a deep harbor a hundred miles from
the Pacific Ocean. Portland ends abruptly at a bridge that crosses the
Columbia River into Washington State, where wilderness begins again,
threaded by the highway winding north toward Seattle. The yellow
leaves of occasional poplars and maples shine against the evergreens
late into November in this damp climate, alleviating the gloom of the
rain-bearing clouds that stream constantly in from the Pacific toward
the mineral imperturbability of the Cascades: Mount Hood, as shapely
as Fuji, the blasted face of Mount Saint Helens, then the cone of
Mount Rainier.

These sparsely settled tracts of monumental scenery were the desti-
nation of Billy and her act in the summer of 1949. Even today they
put in perspective the daring of Billy's high hopes and the thinness
of her veneer, and how much maintaining that veneer required effective separation from the communities where she was known. Portland
was a terminus of the old Oregon Trail, which originated near Kansas
City. It was still a frontier as far as show business was concerned.
Jazz musicians had been shuttling to the West Coast for years, of
course, pulled by movie contracts. Hope for a summons from Hollywood lurked in the ambitions of every musician Billy ever played with,
but Hollywood drew musicians only to expel them, and a jazz culture
had been slow to develop in the West, even in the hip cities of Los

Angeles and San Francisco. The war in the Pacific changed that to some degree, as the establishment of military bases and defense industry up and down the coast increased the demand for entertainment and nightspots proliferated. By the late 1940s, a couple of large booking agencies were threading the scattered grange halls, bars, nightclubs, and resorts into a network of venues that could sustain a group of obscure ensemble players such as George Mayer's Sophisticated Swing Trio.

Billy knew little about the Northwest except what George Mayer told him in a couple of parsimonious phone calls, and George himself was more enthusiastic than informed. But if George said the agency could promise a month of steady work that would pay the expenses of a nice trip to the coast for Billy and Betty, why not go out and take a look?

Of course Billy had to buy a car for the journey. Like G. W. Tipton the race-car builder, Billy Tipton had a passion for cars. For the move west, he would accept nothing less than a La Salle like the one he'd wrecked in Corpus Christi, a model to which he was stubbornly loyal. It didn't bother him, Betty recalled, that the engine on this particular car was in poor shape. When he arrived to pick her up from her mother's place, the whole family gathered around. "That La Salle was big as a boat, gray and silver, a '41 convertible as long as this front room and loaded with everything they owned," Betty's sister recalled. "Billy and Betty just had room to sit." Betty's brothers scoffed at Billy for thinking he could get the La Salle over the mountains, since it looked to them like a car for picking up girls. But Billy put his girl and the dogs into it, said goodbye to everybody, and started off at sunset, to avoid the heat.

"Well," Betty recalled, "it wasn't long before we ran into ground fog, and the lights went out. We had those fixed, and got as far as Hutchinson, Kansas, which is a hundred and thirty miles west maybe, and the lights went out again. Then *nothing* was running. Needless to say, this was a car you couldn't find parts for — that's what my brothers warned. All the mechanics could find to put on was Chevrolet parts, and those didn't really work."

Billy was not fazed. Musicians' cars were always conking out on lonely roads at inconvenient hours of the night, and for Billy, what was under the hood held few mysteries. Billy's brother called this know-how a Tipton legacy: "It comes down through the family from Dad and probably from his folks too, that there isn't anything that can't be fixed. You just have to know how a thing operates. Dorothy wasn't a mechanic, but she had the knowledge — she picked it up as a kid, by tinkering." From Salt Lake City, Billy sent his mother a postcard completely devoted to news about the La Salle: "Made it okay so far. We're out of the high mountains. Had to put on a new fuel pump, buy a new tire, generator & regulator. Some fun, eh! Also a left wheel bearing. Will keep you posted. Take care of yourselves. Love, 'Stinker.'" Billy's way with automobiles was one of the things — along with his shaving — his former wives always mentioned after his death as grounds for assuming that Billy was a man.

Full of emigrant confidence, Billy and Betty dawdled along in their grand old touring car on two-lane highways, the hardened tracks of the old Oregon Trail blazed by the first white settlers. Forty-five years later, Betty still remembered their own expedition with joy. "I'm just a Missouri farm woman. I never thought I'd be anyplace but Missouri all of my life, before going with Billy," she said. He had a way of making theater out of their problems.

> Once, when we got up into the Rocky Mountains, we stopped for gas at a little country cabin in a pretty spot with three little lakes, in Montana. Saw some people over there fishing. Now, Billy wasn't very big and I wasn't very tall. Here goes this long boat of a car, two midgets and two dogs in it.
> We head up the hill and the car quit — something wrong with the carburetor. It was the altitude, Billy said. So we back it back down the hill to the station. He and the guys fiddled with the carburetor and we headed back up the hill again. Got a little further this time before it quit again. So we back down again. Billy figures something is wrong with the gas line or whatever. They fiddle some more. Finally, with the fourth or fifth try, we make it up the incline, and all the people are standing there applauding and waving. Billy takes off his hat and waves it at all the fishermen in triumph!

Betty and Billy wrote faithfully to Betty's mother back in Missouri. "Billy would always add a note to her about what we had seen and where we'd been, what we liked and what we did. I think Billy was as surprised as I was when we got to Oregon," said Betty. "You know, the big trees and the narrow winding roads with those big logging trucks grinding along on them. We weren't equipped to stay behind those trucks in low gear. We'd sit by the side of the road and try to coax the chipmunks to eat from our hands. I wanted one of them for a pet so bad! God, that was gorgeous country! When we got to the ocean we just sat amazed, watching the waves roll in." Best of all, it was now their home. Plains, rivers, mountains, the seacoast — all new to them, and a good agent in Portland paving their way with contracts.

Until Billy arrived, George Mayer's Sophisticated Swing Trio was an untidily ad hoc assemblage of temporary workers. George hoped Billy would help to stabilize the group. Their first job was at the Shalimar Room in Roseburg, Oregon, a town of sawmills and lumberjacks and beer joints. Roseburg was "not the kind of place where a swing band would optimistically stop," as a local historian put it, yet well-known musicians did play there from time to time, because Roseburg, half-way between Seattle and San Francisco, was a good place to lay over on the road.

The Shalimar Room was the classiest place in town, a pleasant little supper club with an entrance that looked for all the world like that of a post office. Since liquor by the drink was illegal in Oregon, customers brought their own bottles into the club and deposited them in labeled wooden cubbies, and a counter waitress would then dole out shots of whiskey with orders of mixer and ice. On Thursdays the local radio station broadcast live from the Shalimar Room, and — here is the reason Roseburg figures importantly in the life story of Billy Tipton — on four occasions someone made air checks of the George Mayer Sophisticated Swing Trio playing dance music.

Air checks are recordings of radio broadcasts. These particular performances were transcribed directly onto disks, which suggests that George and Billy were hoping to use them to scout a recording contract. On each disk, the announcer welcomes the audience to the "sumptuously furnished Shalimar Room." Behind his voice, the trio plays a smooth version of its theme song, "Sophisticated Swing," a golden oldie from the early days of the big-band era. Both George and Billy perform a couple of solos on each of the short takes, supported by an unidentified bass player. The music has an easy, practiced swing on such standards as "Flying Home," "If I Knew Then," "The Axe," and "Robin's Nest," and the effect is fresh and buoyant.

How did it feel to play music like this? Billy left no descriptions, but the jazz pianist Marian McPartland once told an interviewer about it: "Whenever I think of swinging, I think metaphorically. Swinging is like being on a tightrope or a roller coaster. It's like walking in space. It's also like a soufflé: it rises and rises and rises. The fingers and the mind are welded together. But it's dangerous. You have to leave spaces in your playing. You can't go like a typewriter. Sometimes I do, though, and I leave no note unplayed. It's hard to say what goes on in your head when you're swinging, when you're really improvising. I do know I see the different keys in colors — the key of D is daffodil yellow, B major is maroon, and B flat is blue. Different musicians spark you into different ideas."

McPartland, six years younger than Billy, has had a long, diverse, and distinguished career in New York. Billy is not really comparable to her, except in sharing the joy that McPartland describes as walking in space on the piano. A few such moments are held in the grooves of the transcription disks made in Roseburg. On "Flying Home," Billy engages with George's soaring Benny Goodman–like riffs as they trade solos over the strong walking bass line. Billy's piano playing on "Flying Home" is indeed like a soufflé: it rises and rises and rises. Norma Teagarden, listening to this recording, said with surprise, "Why, that sounds great! Say, she's a much better musician than I thought she'd be!"

Roseburg, Umpqua, Eugene; Depoe Bay, Tillamook, Astoria — those were destinations on the itinerary of the George Mayer Sophisticated Swing Trio in Oregon. They would then cross the Columbia River into Washington, to play in towns divided by rivers, such Longview/Kelso, which was logging country, and Pasco/Kennewick and Walla Walla in farm country, playing in Elks Clubs and VFW halls and lodges. Then they would go up to Spokane ("the heart of the Inland Empire," as the city slogan had it) and east through the rangelands of Idaho and Montana, north as far as Calgary, south as far as Pocatello. Billy called it their "turkey circuit." Arriving in a grange hall or a country bar, Billy usually found a piano that was out of tune or worse, with broken strings or missing keys. Betty recalled spending a miserable week in Great Falls, Montana, "way *up* there, and *cold!* We played in a little bar near the railroad station, one of those har-de-har bars full of miners and cowboys. It turned out they were expecting country music, and the boys didn't do country." After Great Falls, the trio insisted that anyone who booked them be able to provide at least a dance floor, and if possible have a grasp of the difference between country music and sophisticated swing.

In December of that year, 1949, George's young wife, Margo, gave birth to their son during an engagement in Lewiston, Idaho, and went to Texas to recuperate in her mother's home for a couple of months. By the time she returned to the Northwest with the baby, she had regained her svelte figure, and George finally permitted her to join the ensemble as its vocalist. The opportunity to sing with a band had been her private reason for getting together with George Mayer, she said later. Margo had grown up in the little town of Archer City, Texas, where the writer Larry McMurtry set *The Last Picture Show*. ("He was a local boy, and got it exactly right," she said.) Her father, who had made a fortune wildcatting in oil, wanted something a little better than small-town Texas for Margo and sent her to a women's college, where she studied voice. One night she went to a dance where George Mayer's band was playing. They met, and she told him she was a singer. "Why, my group is looking for a singer," said George. The next thing Margo knew, she was pregnant.

Margo said that when she married George Mayer, she didn't love him. "He looked like my ticket to ride," though, she said, and she saw that he was immensely talented, a crowd-pleaser who might very well make it into big nightclubs, maybe even into the movies. One of Mayer's stunts was to start a drum solo, then begin drumming on everything in sight: the wooden body of the bass, the top of the piano, then off the bandstand and out among the customers, drumming on the little tables filled with glasses and ashtrays, never missing a beat. During his solos on the clarinet or soprano sax he might fall to the floor and wave his feet in time while he wailed off a note-for-note imitation of Artie Shaw. He could pull his rubbery face into weirdly expressive shapes while singing his novelty number "Smoke, Smoke, Smoke that Cigarette." Painted on the bass drum was a caricature of him with a wide-open mouth — his impersonation of Cab Calloway. "Minnie the Moocher" was always the highlight of the floorshow.

These goofy antics put Margo off a little, but she had to concede that nobody seemed to share her objections. In any case, she saw that

George was very serious about his work. The band was all he thought about, a devotion that carried some costs. George suffered badly from stagefright. During the afternoon hours before every show he drank steadily from a bottle of vodka, and he would stop by a liquor store on his way to the club for a half-pint, which he would swig down just before hitting the stage, after costuming himself carefully. He was sensitive about his age, Margo said. She never did find out his date of birth but figured he was probably in his mid-thirties when she, age twenty, married him. George made himself look much younger by applying elaborate makeup, including base, eyeliner, and powder (in one publicity photo he appears to be wearing lipstick). "Took him longer to put on his face than it took me, by far!" said Margo. "When I'd tease him, he'd say, 'This is *acting!*'"

George directed Margo's act as well. Margo was a beauty, with wide-set eyes of clear, pale blue and black hair that tumbled in waves to her waist. She had the looks for singing romantic ballads, but George wouldn't allow any crooning. "He wanted to keep up the pace, he wanted bounce," she explained. "He'd always tell me, 'We're not artists, we're entertainers.'" A newspaper clipping of the quartet suggests the look George was after. Wearing a form-fitting off-the-shoulder gown, Margo shakes mariachis while George clowns and Billy and the drummer look on, grinning. "Shown in the act of performing Latin numbers," reads the caption. "I thought I was *in!* It was *happening!* I had a fantasy back then of being Gilda, in the movie. Rita Hayworth was glorious. I wanted to be able to capture people that way, take them into the *feeling.* Of course, Rita Hayworth said all the men she married thought she was Gilda, then woke up and found she was Rita. But, oh boy, dressing up in pretty clothes and singing with a band — that was another world."

Late in 1950, the Sophisticated Swing Quartet hired a new agent, Dave Sobol, who worked out of Spokane. Sobol was often able to book engagements of three weeks or longer, in larger cities with more urbane audiences, and to get the performers better fees than the competition did. The quartet's swankiest engagement was at the Boulevard Club, owned by Sobol, in the resort town of Coeur d'Alene, Idaho, just a few miles from Spokane. Gambling was legal in Idaho, and so was the sale of liquor by the drink, so Coeur d'Alene was a magnet for enter-

Dave Sobol at the Boulevard Club, Coeur d'Alene, Idaho, 1950

tainers. Sobol, now in his late eighties, doesn't mind telling stories on himself about the way he made money back then.

I had a gambling charge in Minneapolis. Got held up by an Omaha mob and got some bad publicity. We were sanctioned to gamble, you know. But Hubert Humphrey was the mayor of Minneapolis at the time. One day he called me into his office and told me, "Dave, we've got to close you down, I'm getting too much pressure."

About that time along came my old pal Allen Goldberg. He told me, "They're making so much money in that Spokane area you'd never believe." Wanted me to come out and take a look at the club. When I saw it had twenty-seven slot machines, I loved it. Guy was asking eighty-five thousand for the joint. We came up with about ten thousand apiece, borrowed the rest. Renamed it the Boulevard Club. Remodeled it with red velvet walls, real nice. I had four Japanese cooks. Served a dinner for two-fifty that today you'd pay twenty bucks for.

Well, we started going off the book in that place. I had a dollar machine that every time it got to two hundred, it got stuck. We cut a hole in the bottom of the machine and let the dollars go down into the basement. No more problems with the machine. Made a lot of money: eighty-one thousand bucks that first year, and that was a lot of money in 1945. I kept it five years or so before they outlawed the slot machines.

Slot machines brought in enough money to attract big bands. Playing three weeks of dance music at the Boulevard Club in 1951, George Mayer's Sophisticated Swing Quartet shared a spotlight with such luminaries as Billy Eckstine, the Ink Spots, and the Delta Rhythm Boys. For the first time, the boys were making good wages. As front man, George received eighty dollars a week, Margo recalled. The Mayers bought a yellow Mercury convertible, and Billy bought Betty a squirrel-paw coat. For the wives, though, the measure of a good gig was not cars and furs but a stopover long enough to locate a tourist cabin with a kitchenette, a sitting room, and a tolerance for pets, where they could settle in like suburbanites. In the trunk of their car, alongside their pots and pans, Betty carried a little cardboard box of family photographs and other items to give their lodgings the look of home. Billy would haul out his record collection and portable turntable. Betty would put doilies under the lamps and knickknacks on the bureaus. They would invite the other couples over for spaghetti on Sunday nights. Betty also remembered the difficulties, for a wife, of keeping the band's French-cuffed white shirts washed, starched, and ironed to Billy's satisfaction. The location, hours, and amenities of laudromats became a major topic of discussion among the women.

Absorbed in motherhood and in her work with the band, Margo did not spend much time socializing with the Tiptons. "We were — or I was — just aiming for simplicity," she said. "Of course we had baby Marcus, and we didn't have any money. George was sending half his pay every week to his ex-wife, as child support. Our life was music and moving and taking care of Marcus. But it suited me just fine." Nor was Margo much disposed to make a close friend of Betty, whose frank sensuality intimidated her. "Betty used to lie around their room stark naked, playing with her dogs on the bed," said Margo. "What a body! I thought she looked just like Sophia Loren." Baby Marcus brought the women together. Betty sometimes mentioned to Margo that she hoped to have a child, and both Tiptons enjoyed playing with Marcus and volunteered to look after him when the Mayers wanted time out. They often took him to town in his stroller, showing him off as if they were the proud parents.

Margo was sometimes uneasy about leaving Marcus with Billy and Betty, worried about their snappish dogs. One evening when Marcus was about two, he wandered next door to the Tiptons' motel room. Through the thin walls, Margo heard an eruption of fierce growling from the dogs, and she dashed into the room just as Billy yelled, "Don't worry, everything's fine, Marcus is okay!"

Billy had been dressing for the show. He was standing with his back to the door, wearing a dress shirt but not his pants, and Margo was astounded to see that he appeared to be wrapped from waist to thigh like a mummy, in bindings that crisscrossed his bottom. She backed out of the room, embarrassed, wondering whether something was wrong with him, something never mentioned, but she put it out of her mind. "You know, back then people didn't so easily talk about personal things," she noted.

Several years later she ran into some show people in Los Angeles who had worked with Billy in Oklahoma City. They told her that Billy was female, and a number of oddities fell into place. She remembered that Billy had occasionally grown a light mustache, which he would darken with dye for a while, then shave off. Since the mustache never looked very good, she had never figured out why he bothered. She also remembered the way rough customers could take offense at Billy's looks. One night in Coos Bay, Oregon, some rowdy sailors started yelling, "Pull down your pants and show us what you've got." Billy was cool and dignified, just told them to get lost. "Billy was a nice guy, not the kind to give anyone a reason to think a mean thought. The way he handled it, I now think it must have happened to him before," she said. "But I was so naive in those days, I didn't put two and two together."

Billy's partnership with George Mayer lasted into 1951, when George and Margo accepted a job in Hawaii. Billy turned down the opportunity to go with them and remained in the Portland area. Margo believed that Billy was tired of being under George's thumb. *She* certainly was. George had grown increasingly controlling and neurotic, she said.

Long before they met, he had laboriously learned to play arrangements by Benny Goodman and Artie Shaw and other recorded swing standards, note by note. He never did that anymore, and he never improvised anything, music or patter. When routines they were trying out for their floorshows fell flat, George gave up on developing new material and insisted that every show from then on be exactly the same every time. But he brooded about it. Driving home drunk after work one night, he started railing about his failures. "He said, 'I'm not a real musician — I can't play jazz.' Then he rolled down the window and threw out his clarinet! I like to have died — that was our livelihood," Margo remembered. "I didn't know his clarinet case was built for punishment. But George did, of course. It was all melodrama, just an act." George was also deeply upset by what he suspected to be a racially motivated incident in Coeur d'Alene. Their new Mercury had Texas license plates. One night they were pulled over by the Idaho State Patrol. Without much explanation, the officers manhandled George out of the car, cuffed him, and put him in jail overnight. It was a case of mistaken identity, but it left George shaken and depressed, ready to leave that scene. Maybe he thought that in Hawaii his swarthy complexion could pass for a suntan.

Was Billy sorry to part with George, or was he relieved? He had been coddling George for a decade and was used to George's moodiness. Nor had he seemed to mind letting George be front man. Billy was not a grandstander, and wasn't overly concerned about money or about being bossed around. But George's increasing artistic caution probably sat badly with Billy, who still believed in himself as a jazzman in 1951. Unlike George, Billy saw himself as an entertainer who was also an artist. The difference between these two showmen was the confidence of the improviser. George was defensive and anxious and consequently played by rote. Billy rehearsed his instrument, and his persona, in order to gain the freedom that mastery confers. With George out of the way, he would be in a position to develop new material and look around for compatible partners for an ensemble entirely dependent on his management.

Billy and Betty decided to go to Longview, Washington, a prosperous lumber town on the Columbia River fifty miles north of Portland. There they had become acquainted with an eccentric millionaire named Ned Berwin, a jazz aficionado who did a lot of his drinking at the Elks Club, where Billy often played. Berwin had built a dream house several miles out in the country on a ridge overlooking the river. His wife didn't like the location, so they had never lived in the house. Instead, Berwin used it as a retreat and as a showcase for his collections of antique jade and ebony. Caretakers lived in their own wing, and Berwin occasionally occupied a small studio out back. He offered Billy and Betty use of the rest of the house, rent-free.

For the first time, the Tiptons' home base was bigger than a motel cabin. Betty sent to her mother numerous snapshots of the things she loved about this house: the kitchen, with its separate pantry and its restaurant-size range; the staircase (shipped intact from Italy), which spiraled up three floors "without a single square step"; the illuminated glass cases containing Berwin's treasures that lined the dining room and the library; the deep carpeting, which intensified the silence; the wide sweep of river visible from the upper windows; the terraced garden where the dogs could run.

Billy too liked the place. Clearly, he could make himself at home anywhere, but at this moment, occupying a beautiful home supported the great expectations he had formed in the domains of G.W.'s wing-walking and Aunt Bess's racehorses. The view from Berwin's house may very well have felt like an outlook on prosperity to come. The world of entertainers, like the straight world, had its caste system. Billy expected to rise in it.

To fulfill this destiny, he would need to assemble a small group of men like himself, a trio or quartet of good musicians who were also entertainers, and put himself in charge. Billy's experience in the music business told him that success required total commitment. A strong ensemble spent all its time preparing and performing. No day jobs, no addictions, no exceptions.

Supported by the patronage of Ned Berwin and a job playing solo piano and organ at the Longview Elks Club, Billy had time to look for what he wanted, and it is reasonable to assume that the group he put together over a period of months in 1951 was what he was aiming for. In May he found Kenny Richards, a bass player and vocalist with a deep "Old Man River" voice. Kenny, who was twenty-five, had just graduated from Westlake College in Hollywood, training that provided a strong jazz background, and had taken a job that left him stranded in Longview when the leader of his band absconded with all the money.

The Billy Tipton Trio with Kenny Richards on the left,
Dick O'Neil on the right, 1951

Billy heard about his bad luck and proposed that they try working
together.

Kenny Richards was a lucky find. Billy experimented with a couple
of other local musicians before offering the third spot in the trio to a
young drummer, Dick O'Neil — a very surprising choice if skill was an
important qualification. Dick was untrained, though enthusiastic and
goodhearted. As another musician who later played with him put it,
"Dick was a drummer but not a musician. Once he got it, it was good.
You might say he had a lot of technique but didn't know what he was
doing." O'Neil concurred in this view. "I hardly knew my right hand
from my left. I learned on the bandstand. Now, Billy knew what to do
with his fingers. And if somebody was playing out of tune, it drove him

crazy. Didn't bother me. They were the musicians — I was just the drummer!"

Nor was Dick an entertainer. Billy tried to involve him in a number of routines he had worked up with Mayer, but Dick had no sense of timing. Billy finally gave up and started writing material specifically to accommodate Dick's personality:

BILLY: Hey, Dick, how long have you been playing drums?
DICK: Oh, about ten years.
BILLY: Well, I'll stick around. You ought to be through soon!

Why did Billy want Dick O'Neil? As O'Neil himself remarked, "Billy could have gone down to Portland in an hour and found a drummer that could do much better, maybe even sing." The answer seems to be that Billy, at thirty-six, had begun exercising caution in choosing whom he would keep around him. His sidemen would always be at least a decade younger than he and willing to take the role of younger sibling, the structure of leadership that most suited Billy. Dick O'Neil recalled that Billy actually called him "little brother," and Dick appreciated that. "I didn't have any brothers or sisters. After I left the trio, he used to call me up just to chat. Even to the last, he never forgot my birthday. I don't think he was so much interested in the talent. He wanted someone who'd be there on time, loyal to him and the group." Dick was twenty-three, and Billy's affectionate interest had a strong influence on forming the man he became. "This may sound funny, but I thought of him as always a gentleman. I noticed how he would help a lady with her chair, light a lady's cigarette. He taught me other things I wouldn't have noticed, too, like how to eat. Mother just cooked plain food, cooked vegetables way too long. My dad was just a millworker. I stayed with my parents while we worked in Longview, but as far as I'm concerned, I owe my way of living to Billy."

Kenny Richards also owed his way of living to Billy. When Billy offered him the job, Kenny was in a state of shock, not only from being dumped but from falling in love. On his first day in Longview he had met a local girl named Dolly, he recalled in a memoir he wrote for his family. "As I was unloading my stuff in front of the Elks Club, I saw this beautiful blonde coming across the street with her ponytail flipping in the breeze. This is where my life really started!" Billy arranged with Ned Berwin to hold the Richardses' wedding at the mansion and for the young couple to move into another wing of the house, along with their new boxer puppy and Dolly's daughter from a previous marriage.

With Berwin's enthusiastic encouragement, the combined menage of show people and pets formed a bohemian commune in the elegant mansion. The boys were away most of the time, because the trio usually spent afternoons rehearsing at the club, where they would grab a bite of dinner before the show. The wives usually joined them later in the evening. One night the gals strolled in unrecognized: chestnut-haired Betty had become a platinum blonde and towheaded Dolly a dark brunette.

Berwin was a frequent after-hours visitor to this commune, Richards recalled. "Ned kept his Jim Beam at our place. We'd wind up in the living room of our house, just relaxing. Social drinking, not getting loaded. We'd just sit around telling stories. Ned was a world traveler, and he'd tell stories about his adventures, true stories. Then Billy would chime in and take over. This guy just loved to hear Billy tell stories." Billy's style was what Berwin liked, what everybody liked. A good mimic, he could make comedy out of dialects and voices, but his real gift lay in his attunement to an audience. Billy could make a story last as long as listeners were with him, piling one absurdity on another until the momentum of laughter took over and people were collapsing in guffaws.

By 1952, Betty had been away from her family for two years and was lonesome for their company. Billy suggested inviting her little sister Loretta to spend the summer. Loretta was a shy, pretty girl of sixteen who hadn't seen much of the world beyond the town of Nevada, Missouri. Billy took her under his wing, as he often did with young people. In the postcards he mailed regularly, he called her Little Sister, and he always remembered her birthday with gifts of expensive clothes. That summer, he encouraged her to think about the future. He promised to send her to college when she finished high school.

Loretta loved Billy and was shocked by the publicity that followed his death. In the aftermath, she wrote a set of notes defending his good name, calling on her memories of that summer she spent in Billy and Betty's home in Longview. It was like living on the set of *I Love Lucy*, because of the way the ordinary life merged with their show business life, she wrote. Like the time Billy fell asleep under the sunlamp and burned his eyes — that could have been an episode in a sitcom. Or how he tried to teach her to play the accordion. She was "beginning to 'blossom out,'" and Billy made a running joke about her "getting pinched" as she tried to maneuver around her developing breasts. Then there was the night he decided to give her a taste of adult entertainment. Claiming she was eighteen, he smuggled her into a show at the American Legion Hall where the trio was booked and gave her ten dollars to play the slot machines. After she hit the jackpot and parlayed the winnings into $125 playing blackjack, Loretta said, Billy made Betty drive her home. Billy's sense of humor "was a fantastic asset to him in his business, and he loved to clown around both at the keyboard and away," she summarized, describing the way he would sometimes smuggle "antics" of their home life into his floorshows.

Loretta also emphasized traits that demonstrated Billy's masculinity. "Our memories are of a loving, caring man," she wrote. "He loved his pipe and cold beer — He smoked cigs at the clubs and would smoke cigars on his way home from work," this at a time when no woman she knew would smoke a cigar. Onstage, Billy "loved to perform skits where he was a fall-down drunk comic," though, Loretta added, "I don't ever remember seeing him drunk." At home he was a regular handyman, "a mechanic, plumber, and enjoyed mowing the yard. You name it, he could do it . . . I guess you could say I had him on a pedestal then and nothing now can knock that pedestal down," she concluded.

Loretta's defense of Billy's normality brings into sharper focus some of the ethical questions raised by his behavior. Loretta observed that Billy was *always* acting, "on the keyboard and away," yet she rejected the claim that Billy was a woman acting the part of a man. "Billy was a man," she asserted, twice, in these pages. What did she mean? That Billy's conduct was not only stereotypically masculine (smoking cigars and so forth) but also honorable, truthful to a cultural ideal we label "manly"? Loretta did not sort it out, and she did not permit the revelation of Billy's biological sex to influence her assessment of his character.

Billy's other former housemates echo Loretta's defense of his character. Recalling the way customers occasionally made disparaging remarks about Billy's "femininity," Dick O'Neil said in an interview after Billy's death, "I would almost fight anyone who said that. I never suspected a thing." Nor did Kenny and Dolly Richards ever doubt Billy's authenticity. "I really wish Billy had gotten away with it," said Dolly. When asked if he thought at the time that Billy was a man, Kenny replied, "Still do."

Billy's bandmates and their spouses have little to lose in expressing a generous-minded view of the deceitfulness Billy practiced during their lives together. Betty, the source of most of the details available about those years, occupies a more difficult position, as she is vulnerable to being thought a closeted lesbian, a stigmatized social identity in her world. Yet her views of Billy's character are surprisingly congruent with those of her housemates. "I cannot in my wildest dreams accept the fact I finally know to be true," Betty wrote after her first long interview for this book. "Perhaps it is my reluctance to let go." Floundering in embarrassment, she fell back time and again on the authenticity of feeling between them. "I am disturbed by my feelings and the love I had for the most fantastic love in my life. I wonder if my mentality is strong enough to survive . . . I have never *not* admitted to sleeping with, by, and enjoying the love that *was!* . . . I wish I could shout to the world how great Billy was as a person, friend, confidant, and a love. Just cannot express the personality he was. As you can see, [Billy] is still a he. Who is me — ?"

Because she desired Billy, Betty may be concerned with whether the love she felt was unconsciously perverse, for she believes herself to be entirely and naturally heterosexual in her desires. Her honest perplexity lays open the central mystery in Billy's story for the rest of us. What if *I* had met Billy at age eighteen, Betty's age when they became lovers? In 1957, I was as ignorant about the specifics of sexual intercourse as most of my girlfriends, and I did not know much about male anatomy. Would *I* have discovered Billy's secret? Or would Billy have discovered *my* secrets and, by requiring exciting kinds of privacy that gave fantasy the widest scope, elicited desire from *me?*

Significantly, Betty does not question Billy's motives or accuse Billy of wrongdoing. Feeling her way toward a moral judgment focused on Billy's actions — his caretaking, his empathy, his generosity — she arrives, as does her sister, at an insight about masculinity: that it is an enactment of a social identity for which biological maleness is only the customary qualification. Billy compensated with a talent for acting and a willingness to take big risks. Billy's goodness is not in question, for Loretta or Betty. For them, a good person is someone who acts good.

An anniversary picture, circa 1952

But how did Billy judge herself? Dwelling comfortably at the center of the household in Longview as a kind of paterfamilias, did she ever doubt the moral legitimacy of the ploy by which she dominated this group of dependents? The answer seems to be no. Apparently Billy too liked the character she had invented, this caretaker of dependent women who were conventional homemakers like her mother and her cousins, and of talented young men like her little brother. On the whole, society had reserved for men the privileges and responsibilities of playing music, of looking after women, of leading other men. Billy wanted those advantages, and took them by a bold but simple expedient.

Yet what had begun in 1934 as a strategy for achieving recognition as a musician had led by the 1950s to a tangled web of deceit that was full of risks for people close to Billy. The higher Billy had risen in the ranks of men, the more he needed the security of conveying a very conventional version of masculinity, which included a heterosexual marriage to a sexy woman. By the time he met Betty, Billy had learned not to confide in the woman on whom his safety depended. It may be that he had so thoroughly internalized the masculine identity he expressed that he felt no self-consciousness about claiming a privilege such as his marriage to Betty, with its adjunct roles of brother-in-law and son-in-law. To be sure, he had accepted to the full a responsibility for Betty's well-being and that of her family, and the better he succeeded, the more he had to give her. Betty's joy at living in Berwin's wonderful house was proof of how greatly she was profiting by his masquerade. As long as Betty was persuaded that Billy was a man, where was the harm?

By just such logic might Billy have rationalized the locked door behind which she climbed out of the shower in their beautiful home in Longview, dried and bound her breasts, and donned the genital gear that permitted her to play the role of Betty's ideal man. "Love is real now, it's ideal now" were words in a song often played by the Billy Tipton Trio. An ideal is a projection that feels real because it is so personally compelling. But Billy made a shrewd choice in choosing Betty as a partner, and it is the shrewdness that diminishes Billy's moral stature. And Billy's own mind cannot have been entirely at ease with the elements of fraudulent manipulation in her actions. There was that ulcer at work under the uniform — Billy's version of the knives on which the mermaid learned to walk in the fairy tale, the dues she paid for attaining her heart's desire.

One thing is certain: Billy acted these roles with a strong sense of purpose. He wanted to be a bandleader, and he did it. The trio clicked. "We woodshedded and built up a whole bunch of tunes," said Kenny Richards. "Then the Billy Tipton Trio replaced Billy solo at the Elks Club, supposedly for two weeks, and stayed about a year." As manager, Billy instituted firm schedules for rehearsals and a dress code. Publicity photos show Billy the bandleader looking sharp and trim in his white dinner jacket, having shed the avoirdupois that overflowed the piano bench in snapshots from his years in George Mayer's band. And by the time he was ready to take the trio on the road, he was making enough money to buy a new black Buick from a local dealer, one of his fans at the Elks Club.

All of the boys bought Buicks that year, 1952. In a scrapbook where he kept mementos of their travels, Richards labeled them "the Buick

Trio." They traveled a six-state circuit in caravans, three hundred to five hundred miles between jobs, each car loaded with gear. Betty remembered that the first thing into the trunk was Billy's collection of jazz records, which were nested in a big cardboard box and surrounded by boxes of dishes, pots and pans, extra bedding, first aid supplies, spare cans of motor oil, and a big box of sanitary pads — useful for filtering oil, Billy said.

They'd leave town on Saturday after the show closed, drive all night, check into a motel on Sunday, rest up, set up Monday afternoon at the next club, rehearse and check the acoustics, play the gig, then pack up late that night to make the jump to the next town and avoid paying for another night's lodging. "We'd often sleep an hour or two in a filling station waiting for a guy to open up — didn't want to run the chance of running out of gas," Betty remembered. "You get up in Idaho and Montana and the stations are far apart." The cars sometimes broke down. Richards remembered the time their friend the Buick dealer had a new transmission airlifted into some small town for Billy.

Hitting the outskirts of a city at 4:30 A.M., going from motel to motel, they sometimes attracted unfriendly attention from the police, who would follow them in a patrol car, eyeing the haggard drivers, the animals, the occasional broken window or ripped convertible top that no one had time to repair. "And of course we wouldn't stay in any motel that wouldn't take the dogs," Betty said. Kenny and Dolly Richards remembered how protective and tender Billy was toward the dogs. Troubles, the Pekingese that Betty had inherited from June, was now blind, and Boots, the little black mutt Billy had given Betty for Christmas the year they met, was high-strung and grumpy after her years on the road.

Once they ran into a rabies scare, coming back from the Tri-Cities in the middle of Washington to Longview, near the coast. As Kenny Richards recalled, "To get back to the coast in those days you crossed into Oregon, came down the Oregon side where there was decent highway, then crossed the bridge over the Columbia, the state line, into Washington again just after leaving Portland. Because of the rabies scare at this particular time, to get into Oregon, dogs had to have had their shots. Well, Billy didn't want his poor little old blind dog to have shots. So we came back home down the Washington side. I think it was right behind the last covered wagons! It was a terrible road — Billy and then us, dust flying, just to avoid going into Oregon." For Billy and Betty, the dogs were the children. In fact, Billy occasionally referred to them as "the kids" just to get checked into a motel. Sometimes it worked.

By the end of November, the Billy Tipton Trio was receiving invitations for return engagements from the numerous Elks Clubs and Eagles Clubs and VFW posts that were its mainstay, and it was moving up into jobs at the fancier resorts. Billy's old Joplin chum Bill Pierson remembers running into Billy in Reno that winter, at the New Golden Hotel, while he was working with a band at the Cal Neva, a smart new resort at Lake Tahoe. They also had their pick of the local venues, and often returned to the better clubs and hotels in Portland and Spokane for extended engagements. Yet even steady work with a well-managed band did not bring in a reliable income. Betty remembered, "Maybe we made $350 a week, divided three ways. I know we always paid the booker ten percent, then ten percent to the union. Then you had traveling expenses." They didn't save much money, though occasionally they'd lie low between jobs. "Billy liked to go fishing. We played a little tennis. On Sundays we might get together and play cards. We didn't go out to relax, because that was his work. Lord, they worked hard!" said Betty. "Everything Billy did was 120 percent. He could stay up all night working on an arrangement or a song. That was his way."

Billy and Betty were together for seven years, but she left him in 1954. People who knew them thought she left because she was interested in other men. The trio's agent, Dave Sobol, noticed that her flirtatiousness made heavy weather in the marriage, especially while the Tiptons were living in Longview. "Now Betty was a beautiful girl — boy, she was pretty. Billy'd be playing somewhere and she'd go out with somebody else, then go home with Billy." One of the wives who traveled with Billy and George Mayer for many years thought that "Betty was a cute little dickens, but too young to be anybody when she got together with Billy. But when Betty got to fooling around all the time — she'd flaunt it, *flaunt* it — Billy was hurt. He was too nice to women." Lew Raines thought that Betty had always gone out with other men, from the time the Tiptons lived in Joplin, and why not? Billy "didn't care what Betty did as long as she was a good companion to him."

Talk to Betty today, and she possesses the warmth and good looks for which people remember her forty years later. She is carefully made up, her shapely hands are manicured, and her laugh is low and sexy. When she talks about Billy, she laughs a lot. "We had so much fun," she says. "He was just such a neat guy! I'm sure he thought of *himself* as a man too. Imagine Billy trying to grow a mustache! God!" But she waves aside stories about her unfaithfulness. She and Billy were very happy together, she says, but the life of a "road wife" began to wear her down.

> I did like to dance, and there was always someone around to dance with. So what? And I always had a table at the club — what else is there to do? You can't stay in the hotel all the time, so you'd get dressed up and go out. We'd dress up, Kenny's wife, Dolly, and myself. It was fun to see your husband up there playing and people applauding, getting a bang out of the show. Then going out to breakfast afterwards, or to somebody's house, or to a jam session. All the musicians would get up there and jam until seven or eight in the morning. It was fun, a way of life. You could only cook so much, clean so much. Those little-bitty pots and pans! Those doilies I'd set around in the motel room to make it look like home!
>
> Oh, I have lots of good memories. But you know what they say: when you get to the seventh year, that's a breaking point. I guess I was getting tired of him being gone all the time, tired of being alone most of the time, tired of trying to work or find something to do with my hours. Then my father got sick in Texas, and they called us home. Daddy lingered and lingered, and we stayed down in Texas. Then I went up to Joplin and thought, Well, I'll just sit here a while.
>
> I didn't want to go back to Longview at that point. I must have had a wild hair in my ass! So I rented a house in Joplin. Then I got lonesome and said, "This is no life for me." I called him and said, "I'd like to come home to you." He said, "Nope, you made your bed, now lie in it." Whatever he said, he meant — it was that pure, that simple. "Nope" — that's exactly what he told me. I said, "Okay, if that's the way you want it." Of course I bawled a lot, but he meant it.

A short time later, Betty married. The gynecologist who had checked her out after her "miscarriage" when she and Billy were trying to conceive a child had been wrong when he told her she was infertile. She had five children in quick succession and then shortly after the birth of the last, her husband died. It was one of her sons, in fact, who broke the news to her in 1989, when he saw a television news story about

Billy's death and called to ask, "Mom, did you know Billy Tipton was a woman?"

When people pester Betty about things that are none of their business, she is a good sport. Asked whether the sex felt different with the father of her children from the way it felt with Billy, she answered,

> That's the goddamnedest thing to try to explain, to put the feelings into words. Attraction and friendship — those are the basis for love. I'm sure there was a difference in size, and a difference in a lot of things. There's a difference between lust — pure sex — and love. Between gentleness and unadorned passion. I can't say that passion wasn't there with Billy, because it was.

> But if somebody would have told me that when I reached this point in life that was how it *really* was, I would have booted their ass from here to noon. My god, my brothers would have killed me if they'd thought I was married to a woman! You weren't allowed to cross the line — any line! You didn't cross the line with Spanish, you did not cross the line — it was not allowed.

> Now, forty or fifty years later, you see these cross-dressers all the time on TV. You can certainly tell. Even on TV. I can look at a person and say, "Gee, that's obviously a woman." *Why couldn't I then?*

· 12 ·

Making It

1954–1958

> Remember, you are doing the act all the time, on stage
> and off. You've got to live the part, you've got to *wear* it.
> — Billy Tipton to a young magician, circa 1986

FRIDAY, the twenty-ninth of April, 1954: the Billy Tipton Trio is ending a night at the Candlelight Club in Albany, Oregon. A few couples are swaying to the ballad drifting from the subdued piano when a door at the back of the club opens and rainy air freshens the room. Billy feels, before he sees, the surge of curiosity — excited whispers, then applause. The Duke Ellington Orchestra has just filed in for a nightcap after playing a dance at the Albany Elks Club. Albany, like Roseburg, is a watering hole on the direct route to the San Francisco jazz scene. Everybody in town knew that Ellington was playing at the Elks Club that night. Nobody expected him to show up at the Candlelight afterward, but it is his birthday, and the Candlelight is the only place open at this hour. The management rapidly musters a celebration and a camera. Lights go up, drinks are poured. The Duke obligingly shakes hands with well-wishers, poses with his arms around the shoulders of the musicians, then sits down at Billy's piano.

Enlargements of these snapshots fill the opening pages in a scrapbook in which Billy Tipton was tracing the upward trajectory of his career as a bandleader. Duke Ellington was the greatest jazz celebrity in the world, yet the turkey circuit was paying some of the bills in his life too. The image of Ellington's suave, smiling face above Billy's keyboard provides the hopeful preface to a volume that eventually bulged with press clippings and publicity photographs of other well-known entertainers: Eddie Cole, Nellie Lutcher, Patti Page, Eddie Peabody,

The Duke's birthday, April 1954:
Dick O'Neil, Duke Ellington, Billy Tipton, and Ron Kilde

Rosemary Clooney, the Four Freshmen, the Four Knights, the Lancers, the Sportsmen. These glossy trading cards sometimes carried warm inscriptions. "Best wishes to my very good friend. Don't reduce too much!" wrote Eddie Cole, brother of Nat, who was apparently Billy's confidant on the subject of slimming. "These 4 weeks have been all too short, hope we meet again real soon," wrote the Lancers. And what were Billy's aspirations at the height of his career? The scrapbooks hold clues. Billy wanted to share a circuit with headliners such as Duke Ellington and Patti Page. To appear on televised variety shows, as did the Ink Spots and the Four Freshmen. To land the recording contract that would bring these other goals within reach.

During the years between 1954 and 1958, Billy's ploy to gain success as a musician finally paid off in a big way, and more than ever before Billy used her skills as an actor to free herself from the burden of behaving like a woman, the better to perform as a musician. Pasted into Billy's scrapbooks are newspaper ads and publicity shots that coincidentally illustrate the point that women musicians were enlisted almost solely for their sex appeal. When the Billy Tipton Trio headlined at a nightspot called the 3-D Club on a show with two musicians called the Pheby Sisters, the ad carried a head-and-shoulders shot of the boys, telegraphically captioned, "Clever floor shows and fine vocal harmony and solo work. A truly unique ensemble of musicianship and showmanship." The Pheby Sisters were shown three-quarter-length in a shot emphasizing the businesslike corsetry of their strapless gowns, a pose that required holding their clarinet and trumpet several inches below the waist. "The attractively wardrobed Pheby Sisters present an act abundant with talent, beauty and professional composure," promises the ad — don't worry about those low-down instruments.

Billy was in costume too, of course, but his clothing signaled that he was to be taken not so much as a man but as a medium. His "fine solo work" embodied the spirit of swing and summoned the listener's identification with its familiar words and melodies. Billy's repertory still consisted almost exclusively of hits from the 1930s and 1940s. Except when playing requests, he rarely drew from the current Hit Parade, and he never, ever played rhythm and blues or rock and roll, which he loathed, as did many of his peers. No, he continued to put his signature as a jazz musician on certain old standards: "Exactly Like You," "All of Me," "The Way You Look Tonight," "I May Be Wrong," "It's Only a Paper Moon." Just as his technical skill was required to bring these words alive in the feelings of audiences, his secret was expressed in the lineup of titles — a hidden reserve of emotional complexity that found outlet only in Billy's art. It was the performer's life that enlivened an improvisation. "Many people forget that jazz, no matter what form it takes, must come from the heart as well as the mind," said the jazz pianist Mary Lou Williams in an interview. "I can never admire a robot pianist whose runs flow straight from his studies instead of his feelings. Regardless of what technique he may have, a jazzman must be able also to tell a story."

To *tell* a story by animating the well-known melody with eccentric or deeply personal feeling, to *find* a story hidden until now in the lyrics: this is the improvisor's magic touch. Customers often drove through miles of black and empty rural silence to reach the neon-lit entrance of a lounge like the Candlelight Club or a fraternal organization such as the Elks or the VFW. They were provincials, but their taste had been refined by the jukebox at the local bar, by the movies, by the radios in their cars and kitchens. Billy knew it wasn't his trio's name but a private kind of yearning that brought such customers through the door, and he knew what fantasies were stirring as they settled into a drink in the dim light. "It's only a paper moon sailing over a cardboard sea. But . . ." Most of the customers had been young when they absorbed those lyrics. The world had been at war, at a distance that intensified ordinary life, making private love stories feel like episodes in a bigger drama. Now they were middle-aged, sitting in a roadhouse festooned with foil icicles hung up during the holidays, "a Barnum and Bailey world, just as phony as it can be." But. A song's insistent melody could pierce a listener's forgetfulness and bring back, in snatches, whole episodes of youthful happiness and sadness, which the song's firm lattice of measures held magically intact.

The artist in Billy could catalyze the song's promise: it wouldn't be make-believe, said the song, if you believed in me. In the trios he formed, the melody belonged almost exclusively to Billy. The bassist and drummer were rhythmic adjuncts. Billy's fingers lagging behind or pushing ahead of the beat, Billy's voice hovering over an emphasis, awakened the song's emotion, burnishing its familiarity, altering and releasing it in the moment. Before she had mastered her instruments, Billy had known what it was to be pierced to the heart by a song. Now the power was in his hands and voice, connecting strangers to their own deepest emotions. That's why Billy rehearsed his trio constantly and attended so closely to the details of their dress. Nothing should interfere with the magic. In his own eyes, in retrospect, nights like this formed the apex of Billy Tipton's career, endowing his life with inexhaustible satisfaction.

Billy's artistic aspirations were difficult to achieve. The trio lost its drummer when Dick O'Neil came down with appendicitis and went home to Longview. As a replacement, Billy called Ron Ronconi, a drummer who had played with Billy and George Mayer off and on since the Joplin years. Then, six months later, both Ronconi and Kenny Richards walked out on Billy to join a female trumpet player the trio had been backing. Richards explained, "We had stayed on the road far too long doing our silly crazy-hat acts and going back into the same stupid places. Our agent, Dave Sobol, would put a bad group into a place, then he'd be hurting to keep the club, so he'd put *us* back in. This was getting old. As the last straw, Sobol had booked us into Las Vegas in the spring, in 1954. All of a sudden Billy lowered the boom on us, said Dave had reneged. He didn't want to split the fee with the Vegas agents. We had been working toward this date for many months, fine-tuning the group. It was a threshold into the big time, and we were ready — impersonations, continuity great. So we blew our stack." Richards had a point, for Las Vegas was a talent showcase. But Billy was loyal to Dave Sobol. And Dave was the big, bossy type, so Billy had no stomach for conflict with him. Yet this double defection put Billy on the spot. Sobol had the trio booked solid right through the summer months, when work was hardest to find in the Pacific Northwest, since loggers and farmers were too tired for dancing on summer nights and cities were few and far between. He had to fulfill those contracts.

Musicians were hard to find in this sparsely settled country. With just two weeks in which to get another band ready for the road, Billy returned home to Longview and looked around. To replace Richards, he reached out to Ron Kilde, a string player recently discharged from the army. A child prodigy on the violin, Kilde had spent a year on the road with the Horace Heidt radio show before getting drafted into the Korean War, but he had never played a bass. No problem. Billy knew enough to show him the basics. Billy also contacted Dick O'Neil and found him ready to rejoin the ensemble as percussionist.

The trio Billy formed in March 1954 eventually achieved a level of professional coherence that Ron Kilde described as "unconventional" in the territory where they worked. But it began as a farce. "I had a day to learn the mechanics of the bass," he recalled.

The next day we started rehearsals. We were trying to start out on the road with forty songs that we could do vocals on, in unison. I typed up the words on little five-by-seven cards — the army taught me to type — and wrote the chord symbols over them. I'd lay them out on the top of the piano so I could read them. The latter part of that week we opened in Pasco at the Elks Club, fifteenth of March, 1954. Our opening day. We stayed there two weeks, rehearsed every day. Went on for a two-week stint at the Richland VFW and stayed five, and rehearsed every day. Went from there to Albany, Oregon, and stayed five to seven weeks. From there back home to Longview, played the Elks Club. Then up to Canada — Calgary, Banff. That first week of learning songs we were running back and forth between rehearsals and fittings for uniforms — suits, really, but it was very important to Billy that everything was just so. Our ties had to be alike, our shirt collars the same style. I guess we were ready — we were on the road for seven years!

The trio's snazzy wardrobe required a room of its own. Billy had now traded his black '52 Buick for a brand-new '54 Roadmaster convertible, white with a black top and a trailer hitch. Every member of the trio pulled a twenty-five-foot house trailer. Eventually the boys carried eighteen sets of clothes for the bandstand alone, clothes they never wore on the street: a cream suit and a rust suit (eight changes, switching tops and bottoms), a dark blue suit and a pale gray suit (eight more), plus a tux and a white dinner jacket. Everything matched, down to the links in their cuffs and the tacks in their ties. Billy would write out for each week what they were going to wear every night on the bandstand, so they could play for a month and never wear the same clothes twice. Given that they shopped in small towns, Billy's fussiness about clothes made for a few difficulties. "We'd go into a store and say we'd like to look at silk and mohair suits," explained Kilde. "What size? Well, a 40 short for Billy, a 46 regular for Dick, and a 38 long for Ron. And to try to buy three neckties alike is almost an impossibility." And they all had instruments to carry. Billy even had a little white piano — not a toy, a miniature — which he used in comedy routines.

By the end of the summer the trio was a tight operation, with everybody rehearsed to play more than one role. On extended engagements they would sometimes add a female vocalist. (Dick O'Neil tried to veto this development, according to Ron Kilde. "Dick complained to Billy that he didn't like working with a girl because he couldn't fart on the bandstand.") Billy kept publicity photographs of his favorite singers in his scrapbooks: Lea Ross, Mona Manning, Beverly Jean Clays. Another act they backed frequently was a magician named Dell O'Dell, billed as "the Funsation Femagician." She traveled with a menagerie of animals, Kilde recalled — "Rabbits, of course, but also a couple of chickens, two skunks, five monkeys. She'd turn them all loose in a motel room and they'd really take the place apart. Billy loved it. They made his dogs look good by comparison."

Billy was an exacting manager, Kilde said. "For example, we never took a draw, an advance to cover food and motels. Many an owner would say that we were the only band that didn't want a draw. We treated the trio like a strictly legitimate business. Same with drinking. We never drank until the last intermission of the night, so it didn't affect our playing or our judgment. A lot of times we'd drink after we were through playing, though. Like that night at Ellington's birthday party. We were staying at the motel next door. You had to cross a low fence to get there. More than one of us had to stumble over that fence and crawl back to the motel, Billy included! But when it came to working, we were strictly business."

Another of Billy's rules was that no member of the trio could hold a day job, because they had to spend the afternoons rehearsing new arrangements and floorshows. Before television completely saturated the market, nightclubs were the last outposts of vaudeville, and the trio generally performed two variety shows every night. They would play an hour of dance music first, take a break, then do a show, more dance music, then another break and another, completely different show later in the evening, to keep the customers drinking. "A half-hour show uses up a lot of material," Kilde commented, so the trio spent most of its afternoons working up new routines. Kilde remembered that a typical show would include a "Jukebox Saturday Night" medley of impressions of groups such as the Ink Spots and the Four Freshmen, followed by a couple of solos. Kilde's shtick was the strolling violin. "I'd start off with something that was relatively serious — say, 'Golden Earrings,' 'Autumn Leaves.' Then I'd do 'Hot Canary' — that was a favorite. Then I'd go into a hoedown on the violin, while Billy would jump in and slap the bass. Kind of a throwaway-type thing, but a rompin,' stompin' hoedown always went over real well."

Especially popular were the impersonations and parodies of celebrity acts that Billy called "musical nonsense." An entertainment sheet reported that the "rubber-faced antics of Tipton draw laughs as he and the group go through their impressions." These included an Andrews

Sisters number with wigs, a routine based on Elvis Presley's "Hound Dog," a parody of Ella Fitzgerald's rendition of "A Tisket, a Tasket," and a spoof of Rosemary Clooney's "Jambalaya" (which the trio performed as "Jam Bowl Liar"). Their most elaborate gag was based on a silly song from the 1930s, "Goofus." Kilde and O'Neil each had fond memories of that act.

KILDE: You've seen that picture of us looking at ourselves on television. That was our "Goofus" act. We each had a miniature instrument.

O'NEIL: We'd start out playing our regular instruments, then Ron would slip out in front with a little violin with a Ping Pong ball on the bow. I had a little drum snapped to my belt, and Billy had a little piano. One by one, we'd move out front playing those instruments.

KILDE: At the second break Billy'd go back to the piano and Dick would go back to the drums, and I'm still out there playing this little plastic violin into the microphone.

O'NEIL: Ron would be watching this Ping Pong ball as I'm standing at the drums and Billy at the piano. We'd start picking up the tempo, going faster and faster, and finally he can't keep up . . .

KILDE: And I'd have to get back to the bandstand and get to my bass. Sometimes it was a real bear to get back there. Might be a valance in the way, or a pipe, or the stage might be high and I'd have to jump up. We worked the crowd to where they could see the suspense coming up there: how am I going to get back to the bass?

Billy was the one who wrote the material and played the comic, assigning the sidemen the role of straight men. Frequently, the double meanings in the jokes were lost on everybody but Billy. He liked to play a medley of tunes from the musical *Oklahoma!* that included "Everything's Up-to-Date in Kansas City," a song about a burlesque dancer that would have invited a double take if audiences had known Billy was in drag. Equally risqué, for Billy, were the jokes about homosexuals he wrote into his act:

STRAIGHT MAN: Do you have a fairy godfather?

BILLY TIPTON: No, but I've got a cousin I'm not sure about.

The "Goofus" routine

Looking back, every musician who ever worked with Billy recalled occasions when somebody in an audience made belligerent remarks about Billy's manhood, but the musicians themselves never doubted him. Billy had them firmly under his control. A manager was a manager, it seems.

In 1956, as the new year opened, Dorothy Lucille Tipton, born in 1914, had just turned forty-one. But Billy Lee Tipton, who claimed 1919 as his birthdate, had just celebrated his thirty-sixth birthday. He was in his prime, and the year ahead was to fulfill at last the expectations that motivated this complicated double life. It was to bring a record contract, the musician's legacy to posterity.

Only in retrospect do we see the peaks and the turning points in a life. Retrospect makes it vividly clear that Billy, drawing on the thin resources available to him, spent the first half of the 1950s working steadily toward this moment of success. By 1956, the trio, now stabilized and seasoned by months on the road, was receiving good word-of-mouth reviews from both customers and managers. The bookings had improved too. No more one-night stands at what Betty called "har-de-har bars." The Billy Tipton Trio now appeared at better hotels, such as the Ridpath Roof and the Sillman Hotel in Spokane, at nightclubs such as the Tropics and the Embers in Portland, and at resorts and country clubs along the Oregon coast. Upcoming were new engagements in Nevada, where casinos ran nonstop entertainment seven days a week. During the winter months the band jumped from Elko to Ely to Winnemucca, then on to Lake Tahoe and finally to Reno, where it opened at the Riverside Hotel in a show headlined by Patti Page. It continued for eight weeks in the hotel's cocktail lounge, an ideal spot for ensemble playing, but the boys had their hearts set on Las Vegas. Still awaiting a summons, Billy saved a copy of *Jack Cortez's Fabulous Las Vegas Magazine*, with a corner turned down on the page where a columnist raved, "Looming on the spotlight horizon as a threat to many established musical groups is the Billy Tipton Trio. They recently concluded a 15-week stint at Elko's Ranch Inn Hotel . . . The boys are young and have a fresh slant on bandstand entertainment. We personally think they would be a good get for one of our local spots."

Like everybody else, they wanted to get to Los Angeles too. Nevada was the western gold rush territory for entertainers, but the heart of the jazz scene was on Central Avenue, a few miles from the distinctive urban sprawl of downtown Los Angeles. In June, the trio's itinerary took them at last to a little string of clubs in southern California, stretching from Palm Springs to Pico Rivera. Between club dates, Billy went into L.A. to check out the jazz.

He went alone. Neither Ron Kilde nor Dick O'Neil shared his passion for jazz, nor his curiosity about other musicians. Billy looked young, but they *were* young, still in their twenties, with ideas about music and culture shaped by the marketing of records and movies, and they were entertainers with few illusions about their talent. They liked the business, at least for the time being — liked the girls, the drinks, the spotlight, the aura.

But Billy was still pursuing the dream of making it in jazz somehow, and major-league jazz was happening in Los Angeles. For the past half-dozen years, Billy Berg had been bringing such stars as Charlie

Parker and Dizzy Gillespie to his club on Vine Street. Other nightspots, such as the Tiffany Club, the Haig, and the Lighthouse at Hermosa Beach, were thriving. New record producers, including Les Koenig at Contemporary and Richard Bock at Pacific, were defining the distinctive sound of West Coast jazz. During the same weeks that Billy was hanging out in L.A., his fellow Oklahoman Chet Baker was making recordings with the alto saxophonist Art Pepper that must have attracted Billy's attention. Perhaps he heard Baker live in 1956. Baker, a trumpeter, was a jazz celebrity, as was Pepper. Baker had recently been profiled with the baritone sax player Gerry Mulligan in *Time* for introducing "cool jazz" to the West Coast, representing the way swing could be modernized without losing melodic clarity. Oklahomans tended to keep track of each other, and it is likely that Billy Tipton kept an eye on Chet Baker's style and the tunes he sang that were in Billy's own repertoire: "There Will Never Be Another You," "But Not for Me," "My Funny Valentine." (At the opening of a documentary film about his life, Chet Baker's voiceover sounds eerily like the voice of Billy Tipton on tape. The intonations of Oklahoma followed them everywhere.) A superb ensemble player, the personification of all that was meant by "cool," Baker was also recognized as a unique vocal stylist. Billy hated the spastic rhythms and dense harmonies of bebop, but to the degree that he was acquainted with new directions in music, Chet Baker would have been a friendly persuader, a man who affirmed the tradition they shared. Chet could show Billy how to go forward.

But Billy was seeking to appease his love for swing and other old-fashioned forms of jazz when he found his way to the strip of gay jazz clubs along Ventura Boulevard between Encino and Studio City. At the C'est la Vie, he ran into the pianist Hadda Brooks, who was trying to revive a floundering career. The hip audiences at the C'est la Vie knew her records and had seen her on television — she was the first black entertainer to host a televised variety show — and in the movie *In a Lonely Place*, alongside Humphrey Bogart. Regarding her work at C'est la Vie, she explained, "The gays weren't accepted in those days. They could not get big entertainers to come to their clubs normally, but there I was, the Queen of Boogie! They were absolutely going to support me." Billy introduced himself and for the next couple of weeks was a frequent customer. Brooks thought Billy was a man, and she did not think he had come to check out the gay scene. "He paid no attention to anybody but me," she said. He just bought drinks and chatted. "He didn't talk about his personal life. We talked about what songs we liked." After Billy showed up several nights in a row, Brooks invited him to take the piano during her breaks. "There was enough to go around," she said, smiling, and it was "a nice gesture toward a fellow musician." Billy's manner, she noted, gave nothing away. "There were never any antics. He played swing jazz and never talked to the crowd." After a pause she added, "He is what you would call an actor."

Luck finally kicked in for the Billy Tipton Trio during a week-long gig at King's Supper Club in Santa Barbara. When the local TV station gave them fifteen minutes on an afternoon broadcast, they were heard by a talent scout and offered an audition by Doshay Records Corporation in Los Angeles. Under the label Tops, Doshay produced a line of generic "easy listening" LPs with titles such as *Music for a Lonely Night, Themes from the Movies,* and *Holiday in Italy.* Distributed through department stores, Tops "ultra-phonic sound high fidelity recordings" were sold alongside the playback equipment on the home furnishings floor, for $1.49 apiece. They were also stocked by dime stores.

The trio's first recording session took place in July 1956, and the album was released later that year with the title *Sweet Georgia Brown.* The result was a nice ensemble job, with Billy's piano working delicately on the top end and opening brief solo breaks for Kilde's walking bass on up-tempo tunes. On "The Man I Love," Billy injects a quote from "Rhapsody in Blue." While recording at a studio at Capitol Records, Ron Kilde recalled, "a gal who had been standing in the sound booth came out and said, 'Gee, you guys sound great.' And guess what? It was Ella Fitzgerald!"

Carl Doshay liked the tapes and followed up with an exclusive one-year contract, renewable, with royalties at two percent on the retail price. Twelve sides were to be recorded annually, with all rights reserved for the company. "I believe we should be able to do a very nice job for both of us," wrote Doshay. The trio returned a month later to cut a second record, to be titled *Billy Tipton Plays Hi-Fi on Piano,* with Billy's photograph on the album cover. Neither Ron nor Dick took solos, and neither is acknowledged on either of the LPs. On this disk, Billy opens the twelve-tune set with a lacy virtuoso arrangement of "Can't Help Lovin' Dat Man," hitting his stride in swinging versions of

Billy Tipton Plays Hi-Fi on Piano

"The World Is Waiting for the Sunrise," "Christopher Columbus," and "Blue Skies." After the recording session he posed for the cover, seated at the piano. Two sexy female models in low-cut blouses illustrated "Can't Help Lovin'," while Billy, in coat and tie, performed Dat Man.

When Carl Doshay sent Billy the contract, he asked him to provide "a complete autobiography" for use on the record jacket. As show people in the 1950s, musicians occupied the low end of the celebrity scale. But as the swing era faded into legend, its artists gained stature as subjects for movies (in the heydays of swing, of course, they had appeared on the bandstand playing music). *The Fabulous Dorseys* (1947) and *Young Man with a Horn* (1950), inspired by the life of Bix Beiderbecke, were followed by *The Glenn Miller Story* (1954). Nineteen fifty-five saw the release of *Love Me or Leave Me*, a biopic starring

Doris Day as the torch singer Ruth Etting, *The Benny Goodman Story,* and *Pete Kelly's Blues,* featuring Ella Fitzgerald and Peggy Lee, and 1956 saw *The Man with the Golden Arm,* in which Frank Sinatra played a drug addict trying to make it as a drummer. These films have in common the structure of a nut, in which the kernel is the performing life and the shell is made up of the pressures from the straight world. Music is shown to be a risky but ennobling business, and musicians are a crazy but lovable species that inhabits a parallel universe.

Billy had recently been fitting his own history into such genre terms for the entertainment magazines that advertised the trio's appearances. "Tipton has worked steadily in the Northwest since he arrived from Texas," claimed a squib in a monthly distributed free through hotels in the Portland area. The next issue corrected the record. "Billy Tipton, leader of the trio that closed at the Tropics Saturday, July 26, says he's from *Missouri,* not *Texas,* as stated in last month's issue of this mag. Well, anyway, before organizing his own group he toured Texas with another trio and somewhere along the line picked up a nice southern accent." Missouri, the "show me" state. Maybe another of Billy's private jokes. (Once Billy turned up in an Elks newsletter as "Milly Tipton.")

When Billy talked about the old days with the band members, he focused on his early days as a nomadic musician, rarely on his childhood home life. Ron Kilde recalled that Billy "had mentioned his dad being an inventor, rounding the back of the buses and trucks to create less wind resistance. Used to talk about his mother, how she would never shop for bargains, would shop for items in department stores, always pay too much for things. That's the type of person she was. Didn't talk about brothers." Billy never referred to his parents' divorce, and said that he grew up in Oklahoma and that Enid was his home town. "I guess he mentioned Kansas City, said he played saxophone there. Billy said he had learned all the piano he knew from Jack Teagarden's sister. Said that he was playing in a band when Norma Teagarden offered to teach him piano."

So when the chance came to put himself on record as a star, how did Billy tell his story? This is what he wrote:

Billy Tipton is the lad pictured on the front cover between the pulchritude. (As Bob Hope would say, "Pulchritude, that's highbrow for gorgeous gals.") But there's nothing highbrow about Billy or his superb musicianship on the eighty-eights. He's an Oklahoma boy, to be precise, who was born in 1919.

As a youngster his family moved on to Kansas City, Missouri, where he studied at the Horner Conservatory of Music after graduation at Southwest High School. He continued his schooling at Oklahoma A&M Junior College, where he also did some sax tooting between studies.

It was after getting out of college that his piano playing really began in earnest when he took a job in a small and smoky honky-tonk in Oklahoma City. The fans thought him "the most" right from the start, and moved him up to a much wider audience at Radio Station KOMA in Oklahoma City.

Next came a series of "going places" jobs that began with Scott Cameron's band, a midwestern favorite of the '40's, then two and a half years at Joplin, Missouri's Cotton Club and again back to radio, this time at Station KTWO, Springfield, Mo. By this time Billy had played enough piano and gained an amount of superb skill, feeling and imagination to rank him among the greatest. His top talent has been displayed from coast to coast in many of America's smartest supper clubs, such as Ciro's, Hollywood; College Inn, Chicago; Latin Quarter, New York, and many others.

TOPS Records is proud to include Billy Tipton among its outstanding roster of artists. We know you'll thrill to his relaxed treatment and interpretation of this choice group of all-time favorites.

These paragraphs, fewer than 250 words, are all we are going to get from the horse's mouth, and show mainly what Billy thought was worth concealing in print. His age, of course. He had been using the birthdate 1919 for years and still looked boyish, and a five-year difference would have been both credible and easy for him to remember. He also wants us to know that he's not one of the longhairs ("nothing highbrow"), but he's not an Okie either, so he gives himself diplomas from Kansas City's elite high school and music conservatory, with a stint in college thrown in. Was this Billy's way of distancing himself a little bit from his days with Louvenie Perkins and the Western Swingbillies? Maybe for the same reason, he lopped several years off his time in Missouri and avoided any reference to Texas. The sleek, wavy-haired poster boy on the album cover looks as if he just might have played at Ciro's or the Latin Quarter, though Billy never had gigs in New York, Chicago, or Hollywood.

Buried in the hype, though, is the professional ideal Billy *was* reaching for through the masquerade of a "lad" pictured with "pulchritude": "superb skill, feeling and imagination to rank him among the greatest" jazzmen. It was what his whole life had been about since leaving Oklahoma, and it was never closer than the day he fashioned this word portrait for the back of a record jacket.

Billy sent copies of these albums to the mothers in his life. He sent them to Betty's mother, Lula Mae, inscribed "To My Best Mom," though Betty had already married another man and was now pregnant with her third child. And of course sent them to Reggie, the only person who knew what it had cost to arrive at this moment of success. Reggie wrote, with a maternal glow, that she considered the album with Billy's picture on it much better than its predecessor, *Sweet Georgia Brown* — probably because his name was on the cover. "My how you have improved since your last record. I've played and played it over and over. I feel so very close when I hear you. I know it's your darling fingers on that record. Hard work, long hours in a dark dance hall, sleepless nights, and worry. But you never complained. God bless you, my darling."

Looking through Billy's professional scrapbooks, no one would ever know that during these years on the road he had lovers, or that he was rarely alone. Almost immediately after Betty left to visit her sick father, early in 1954, Billy installed another woman in his life. Her name was Maryann. She and Billy met at the Balboa Club in Coos Bay, a resort town on the Oregon coast and a regular gig on the Tipton Trio's circuit.

Maryann was thirty-three — just Billy's age, she thought, and just Billy's size. "With Billy, I had to wear flats. I'm five foot four and he wasn't much taller than that," she said. Like Betty, she had a large, upcurving, full-lipped mouth, dark curly hair, beautiful hands, and an eye-catching figure. Maryann had never been married but was the mother of a son — the result of living in a navy town during wartime, she said. She was Jewish, which to many people seemed exotic in a comfortable sort of way. It went with being a good cook and a deft manager of money, in the minds of people who remarked on it. She kept dogs around her too, and that made Billy happy, for Betty had taken Boots along for company when she left town, and Troubles had long since died. Maryann's favorite dogs were little Pomeranians, easy to travel with.

Maryann with Tippy, one of her Pomeranians, circa 1955

Maryann was attracted to Billy immediately. "You know how enter-tainers are," she said. "He flirted and I flirted back. Then we danced. We did that for . . . I guess he was there for a month." During the band's last intermission each evening, Billy would buy her a fancy bar drink, a "fuzzy navel": peach schnapps stirred into orange juice. ("I never liked the taste of liquor," said Maryann. "Just the effect.") Then Billy would feed the jukebox. They fell in love to a slow dance tune, "The Nearness of You." Most musicians never become good dancers, but Billy was an exception, light on his feet and quick to learn new steps. Then Billy would take her home. "I sure did fall in love," Mary-ann said. "I'm sure I even loved him as a person all these years. I've got pictures here of him, and that one on the record album. He was a doll. Real wavy hair, I loved it. He was . . . well, how shall I put it? The first time we danced, I noticed he seemed to have a permanent hard-on. I just thought, 'Lucky me!' And," she added, "he will always be 'he' to me."

Billy's friends knew that Maryann was a call girl when she and Billy met (Dick O'Neil said she was "a classy one"). Kenny and Dolly Richards remembered visiting the house where she worked. "Yes, it was right on the water in Coos Bay. Almost like a boathouse, with keys hanging on the wall! She was one of the higher-ups." Obviously, Billy didn't care. Forthright sexiness suited Billy very well. During an interview for this book, Maryann didn't want to talk about her life before or after the days with Billy, but she did say that she liked spending money on expensive gifts for him. Shortly after they fell in love she gave him a diamond ring, which he wore right up until his death. "Five stones set in a diamond pattern in yellow gold," she explained. "I had some money of my own at the time. By the time Billy left me, I didn't have a thing." She laughed.

When Billy and the boys moved on to their next job, Maryann moved with them, and everybody began referring to her as Mrs. Tipton. Only the band members and their wives knew that she and Billy weren't married. She felt that the other women looked down on her for it, but she never particularly wanted to marry Billy. "I was happy the way I was. I played it from day to day. I have to admit, living with Billy was a fun way of life." On the road, her job was feeding people. Like Betty, Maryann was clever at improvising meals and domestic comfort. In the early days of the trio, before the younger guys married, she prepared a daily communal dinner at five and served it in whatever motel room she and Billy were sharing. Both Dick and Ron were impressed by the meals she could conjure on a hot plate: chicken and dumplings, stuffed peppers, spaghetti.

Since Maryann was a mature, sexually experienced woman when she met Billy, how could she possibly have failed to notice that Billy wasn't a man? When asked, she replied, "Because he had a prosthesis, I guess. He never explained *that* he had one. And I never knew. I don't know how he got *his* kicks. I've often wondered about that since . . . You never, ever went in when he was in the bathroom. So I never knew, because he just had it on all the time. Can you think how miserable that must have been during his period?" She confirmed that her feeling about him sexually was that he was a man and that he was a good lover, but she refused to go into details, saying, "If he'd have wanted people to know, he would have told them!"

Maryann's husband, with his wife and their new Buick

Maryann did try to explain what their intimacy was like, however. "You know, he got the stuff [for his chest bindings] and I sewed them up," she said. "I never dreamed he was hiding his bosoms. No. And I look at Billy now, he was very much a woman in his build. Sort of a fat little lady." When asked whether she did his laundry, she said, "I did his white shorts. But then, he always had what they call . . . I keep wanting to say G-string, but when they play sports. [A jockstrap.] Yeah. But see, he'd always have something else to put on right away. You never saw Billy without any clothes. And you couldn't feel anything because he looked flat-chested. He should have been flat-chested. You know, if you bound them in and never lifted them up, you'd be flat too." She said that one simply didn't touch Billy, but went on to explain that "he hugged, you betcha. What I mean — you just never got out of line with Billy. But he hugged and kissed and did all the normal things." She too was led to believe that he had pain from an old accident — "I think he said a rib never healed right or something" — but he never talked about any injuries in the pelvic area.

Once Maryann joked that she ought to use her background as a nurse to do a little research at a medical supply store, to try to find out what sexual device Billy must have been wearing all those years. The question had been on her mind ever since an interview got her thinking again about the past. "Honey," she remarked, laughing, "I can hardly wait to read your book. I thought it was a penis."

Billy was evidently not a "stone butch," a lesbian who satisfies her lover without expressing any sexual excitement herself. Presumably the disguise itself was sexually exciting to Billy, and she may have positioned the dildo to stimulate her clitoris. Or perhaps Billy's "love-map," to borrow the sociologist John Money's expressive phrase, was that of the voyeur who has gained illicit access to the object of lust. But it is a mystery how Billy could have kept the required gear hidden during the years on the road, living in motels and trailers where there was little space in which to hide anything. Maryann insists that Billy was forceful in protecting his privacy, and that what was habitual in his behavior also came to seem natural, as is common in married life. She said that she could not remember any particular habits he had, "Just, his habit was 'Stay out of the bathroom when I'm in there! That's my private place.' I respected that. When he went in there, the door was locked and that was it. You know, what you don't see somebody halfway do, you just don't worry about. Once it's taken for granted."

So Maryann and Billy settled into life on the road together. But this relationship was different from Billy's previous marriages. Maryann was a homebody. She would attend the trio's opening and closing nights, but since she didn't drink much and didn't want to dance with anyone but Billy, nightclubs bored her. She preferred spending the evenings in their trailer, listening to the radio while doing her needle-work, with the dogs for company. Later, she came to think that was why she lost him.

After the release of *Sweet Georgia Brown* and *Billy Tipton Plays Hi-Fi on the Piano* in 1956, Carl Doshay wrote enthusiastically to Billy that he hoped soon to offer the trio a contract for a series of singles on Spots, a new label the company was spinning off "primarily for the exploitation of new artists through radio." The LPs were given flattering notice in the March 1957 issue of *Let's Go!*, the monthly magazine of the entertainment industry for the Pacific Northwest. In September the trio made the cover of the *Seattle Greeter*.

Songwriters began sending Billy tapes to consider for use on his next album or in a floorshow, or to pass on to a local disk jockey — anything. The boys began describing themselves in their publicity notices as "recording stars." According to the only royalty statement on file, 17,678 copies of the records had been sold by the end of 1957, and Billy had received an advance of $440 and an additional $31.28 in royalties. Though neither Ron nor Dick received any payment for the recording, good jobs suddenly became available in places they hadn't played before. Billy bought another new Buick.

But by 1958, success was causing a minor identity crisis in the trio. If they were really going to become recording stars, they needed a sound of their own. Billy bought a tape recorder and began capturing some of their rehearsals. The tapes show that the boys were experimenting with unison vocals, in the style of male singing groups such as the Sportsmen, regulars on *The Jack Benny Show*, with whom they now shared billing at Nevada resorts. In April, during a long engagement at the Embers in Portland, they linked up with Trudy Mason, a vivacious blonde who was performing a takeoff of Mary Martin's role in *South Pacific*. She added her act to their floorshow and her voice to their trio. Billy was by then preparing for their best booking ever: four weeks at the brand-new Holiday Hotel at Reno, to be followed by another recording session in L.A. On one of the tapes, Trudy and Billy do ten takes of a fast-paced "Lover (When I'm Near You)," trying out some complicated harmonies.

Arriving in Reno, the boys found an enthusiastic feature story about them in the industry newspaper *Reno This Week*, more evidence of the impact of ballyhoo about the records. But it was their slick professionalism that won over the Holiday Hotel management, which offered them the position of house band after only a week. The hotel's dinner theater was scheduled to open with Liberace the following week, with stars of similar magnitude booked through the year, and the job would more than double their salaries. Ron and Dick were elated. The trio was broke and road-weary by now, and increasingly aware of the hazards of the trade. Road accidents were a way of life, and also frequently a way of death, for traveling musicians, and Ron had smashed up his car and trailer the preceding year.

But Billy said no. He had been talking to Dave Sobol, he explained, who wanted to base the Billy Tipton Trio in Spokane. Sobol also wanted Billy to join the agency, to book the musicians. Billy was interested in accepting *that* offer. He felt like taking a day job and settling down.

What? He didn't want to be house band in this beautiful new location, at twice the salary they were making on the road? He didn't want to share a stage with Liberace? He didn't want to go down to L.A. and make the four new records Tops had offered? For heaven's sake, why couldn't he settle down in Reno?

No. He wanted to go to Spokane. He was stubborn, he was boss, and that was that.

Unknown to Ron and Dick and Trudy, an increasing number of incidents were showing Billy how easily his past could thrust through the veneer of his persona. Many entertainers from Oklahoma City had known Billy in her days as a cross-dresser, and many of them regularly traveled through Nevada to visit folks who had emigrated to California before World War II, like the Joads in Steinbeck's *The Grapes of Wrath*. They could easily be steered Billy's way by friends from the old days — by Non Earl Harrell, for example. She was regularly in touch with Reggie and would know how to find Billy if anybody asked. Others just ran into him by accident. While Billy was playing in Tucson, Lew Raines, who had been Billy's saxophone player at Hidden Acres in Joplin, caught his show at the Talk of the Town supper club while on furlough from the air force. "A poster on an easel was advertising the Billy Tipton Trio," he said. "When the guys came onto the bandstand, I said from the audience, 'Do you know "Playmates"?' Billy saw right away who it was. Got on the mike and said, 'I'd like to dedicate this next tune to a fellow who was with the original Billy Tipton Trio, now Lieutenant Lew Raines." Bill Pierson, Billy's wartime trumpeter at the Cotton Club in Joplin, looked him up in Reno when he saw a newspaper ad for the trio. He drove from Tahoe especially to see Billy, and was surprised to receive a cool reception: "Billy seemed real preoccupied. Just greeted me — 'Hi, Pierson, how's it going?' — and moved on." These were old friends, good friends, but who had Bill Pierson been talking to since Billy left Joplin? How safe was the secret with Lew? And these were only the chance encounters. Billy must also have known that his past would be thoroughly scrutinized by the kind of employer who was running a casino in Nevada in the 1950s.

Most worrisome would have been the threat of exposure by sophisticates who could see right through his clothes. By 1958, Billy had been outed at least once, according to a wife of one of the musicians who had traveled with the trio. "Well, I'm from California, and you recognize these things," she explained. "After I met Billy, I told my husband, 'I'm going to have to say something to you, honey!' I said, 'That's a woman!' He said, 'No he's not, I've known him for years.' Wouldn't believe me. Later I told Billy that I knew and promised that I would not discuss it with any of his friends. It is just no one's business. He was the sweetest person. He would never act up. But as I said, in California it would have been obvious that Billy was a woman."

Another woman said that to some observers, Billy's masquerade was obvious at first sight.

> I met Billy in Pittsburgh, Pennsylvania, sometime in the late 1950s. I had an act called Jean Shannon and the Brooks Brothers. The boys were gay. When my husband wasn't with us on a club date, they'd want to stop by the bars and meet their friends. Didn't matter to me — a beer was a beer was a beer. That's where I met Billy, dressed as a man. This was in a club where the gays were accepted. We went to see his trio sometimes in there, a very good trio. I was thrilled to hear somebody playing my kind of music. My friends said right off that Billy was passing, and that was the way it was.
>
> The next time I saw him was in Spokane, when my husband and I walked into the office to meet Dave Sobol, who had brought me in for a series of club dates. I saw Dave and his secretary, Gloria, and in the next office there was Billy, with a picture of the trio on the wall. When Billy looked up and saw me, I thought he was going to have a heart attack. But I just gave him a look that said "You don't have to worry about a thing," and from that minute forward it was never discussed.

Jean Shannon's dancing partner, Larry Martin, vaguely remembered meeting Billy too; he and Jean discussed it after Billy's death. "I saw Billy on the strip in Pittsburgh where musicians would go to jam after hours — saw him maybe two or three times," he said. "I recognized that Billy was passing. Maybe I saw through it because I'm gay but hadn't yet come out. Maybe I noticed the facial structure, maybe there were some mannerisms. It was more an intuition. We had a couple of drinks and some conversation, but I didn't bring it up with him."

These recollections cannot be completely accurate, since Billy's trio never went further east than Mount Rushmore and Billy was most likely never in Pittsburgh in his life. But memory is a blend of perception and inference. Jean Shannon's epiphany in Sobol's office sounds true, and probably it attached itself to another memory that explained and preserved it. And something like what Jean Shannon remembers almost certainly did happen to Billy, maybe more than once, and under circumstances far more threatening to his safety. As for those other people who knew but did not tell — well, they always did tell *somebody*. And Billy must have known they would.

This was the background to Billy's terse rejection of the big break that finally came his way in June 1958. The offer was not an opportunity to play jazz, it was a job backing other acts. Yet it was a door into the big time. Let us hope that Billy saw it as an affirmation of his whole career. Let us hope that when Billy turned it down, there was exultation in *her* heart as well as prudence in *his* judgment. Ron and Dick wanted to belong to a group that people would recognize. But Billy didn't want to be recognized. The more exposure he had, the more likely it was that somebody was going to come forward and say, "That Billy Tipton — I know her!"

At the time Billy just said that he couldn't break his contracts with the Omak Stampede in August and with Allen's Tin Pan Alley in Spokane that fall, booked long before. And once the group got to Spokane, Billy started settling for less and less and less. She had proved for more than twenty years that every talent she had was absolutely real, but by 1958, the drive to put a star named Billy Tipton onstage had gone about as far as it could go.

PART V

Settling

1958–1989

· 13 ·

Man's World

1958–1961

We're going to a town named shirttail — it's near the
county seat.
— Comedy routine, circa 1958

AFTER THE LAST level miles on the west plains, Highway 10 made a
bend leftward and downward into the city of Spokane. Around this
curve a panorama opened: a spreading cityscape, fissured by a river,
and at the city limits a low mountain range carved by glacial ice,
peaking in Mount Spokane, snowcapped for half the year. When Billy
Tipton made this descent on an autumn day in 1958, he knew where he
was headed. Winter and summer for the past eight years he had been
driving this road, accompanied by a changing cast of wives and musicians. New Year's Eve at the Monkey Room in the Sillman Hotel.
Opening night at the Ridpath Roof. Two weeks in the Matador Room
at the Davenport Hotel, another two at the Boots and Saddle. And
every winter the annual convention of the Northwest Mining Association at the Spokane Club, a blowout that culminated in an infamous
strip show called the Moose Milk Breakfast. Now he was about to
unhitch his trailer and settle down.

Rivers and mountains gave Spokane a natural grandeur that drew
people, but the squat, unlovely urban landscape had much in common
with the midwestern cities of Billy's youth and would have felt and
looked to him like home. Like Joplin, Missouri, Spokane serviced a
prosperous mining industry, and it also supplied farm machinery to the
agribusiness of wheat-growing in the surrounding Palouse country.
The chief entrepreneur of the conservative, male-oriented entertainment business that flourished there was Dave Sobol. And now Dave

had set before Billy an irresistible combination of opportunities: day work as a booking agent, managing the musicians in Dave's stable, and a one-year contract for the trio as house band at a local nightclub in which Dave was a silent partner. No greater prospect of financial security had ever come Billy's way.

Billy knew where he was headed, but did he know what he was *doing?* Abandoning the tribe! For the past twenty years Billy had been a citizen in the nation of vagabond entertainers. He crossed the border with a union card to work in what entertainers called the straight world, but the vagabond world was home. Billy lived on wheels and on the outskirts of town and never in one place for very long. Billy's family addressed letters to B. Tipton, care of his agent's post office box. ("One year we were lucky," Maryann recalled. "We moved only five times.") In that world, night was day, and most transactions were undocumented. Billy's marriages are an example. In the vagabond world, Billy's successive commitments to women were accepted as honorable, though illicit. In that world, Billy was listed for tax purposes as "self-employed," and as the lean earnings on his social security records suggest, many financial arrangements were off the books. For insurance purposes, he gave the home address of Dick O'Neil's mother, who lived in a low-insurance-rate district in Kelso, Washington.

During his twenty years in show business, Billy had gained the status of a pro and finally of an artistic director and business manager — trouser roles all. Billy had been greatly assisted, or, more accurately, blessed, in this undertaking by a disposition to take risks and a strong sense of entitlement. She was consistently daring and she was cheerfully optimistic about getting what she wanted. Without these character traits, how could she have persevered? Billy had *attitude*. But equally important to her success had been the institution of the theater, specifically of vaudeville. Itself a society with its own mores, which included a high tolerance for sexual ambiguity, vaudeville offered on-the-job instruction in the techniques Billy had to master for personal survival: impersonation, legerdemain, character acting, comic timing.

Yet Billy was performing under a number of constraints, some practical, some characterological. She avoided conflict that might lead to grudges, fights, injuries, and other risks of exposure, and possibly for that reason could not assert sufficient leadership to manage a band of musicians as talented as herself. The trio with the greatest longevity —

Tipton, Kilde, and O'Neil — cohered because Billy tolerated artistic shortcomings in order to maintain the position of boss.

Arriving on that autumn day in Spokane to settle down, Billy was about to change the circumstances of her life, to make it less risky and more financially secure. Yet she seems to have approached this new life less as a change of identity than as another role for which show business had been the training ground: impersonating a common man with an ordinary life in an ordinary place in Middle America.

The Dave Sobol Theatrical Agency was located on an upper floor of the city's one architectural monument, the old Davenport Hotel in downtown Spokane. Built in 1914 by Louis Davenport, a famous restaurateur, the hotel had been host to presidents and dignitaries. Its dining

Dave Sobol and colleagues: Dick O'Neil, Billy Tipton, and Ron Kilde, 1958

rooms and assembly rooms were spectacles of eclectic architectural exuberance. Ballrooms were called the Hall of the Doges and Marie Antoinette; salons bore such names as the Peacock Room, the Gothic Room, and the Orange Bower. An Italian Garden Room was decorated copiously with flowers at every season of the year. Most of this ornate decor existed only in memories by 1958, but to reach his office, Billy still walked through a luxurious lobby, cavernous as a movie set, where caged songbirds and a Moorish fountain made constant music and an ornate fireplace held burning logs even in the heat of summer. Stopping at the newsstand for his Lucky Strikes on the way out to lunch, Billy would pocket coins washed to near mint condition — one of the Davenport's special amenities.

These stagy surroundings supported the secret drama of Billy's transition into the life of a booking agent. Dressed in a coat and tie, hair trimmed short and neat, could she continue to pass as a man successfully while working alongside a female secretary and a male boss, day in and day out? Yes, it turned out. In Spokane, business was men's work. The Sobol agency represented more than a thousand acts, scheduling them into nightclubs, conventions, fraternal organizations, arenas, state fairs, rodeos, and regattas across thirty states and western Canada, Dave bragged — wherever short-term entertainment was required. The agency made its money by arranging multiple bookings within a few hours' traveling distance for the entertainers, whom it charged a ten percent commission. Billy booked musicians and Dave booked other kinds of entertainment, so they worked side by side but not together. Billy was the first subagent Dave had ever hired. "I saw that he was savvy, got on well with the club managers," Dave said. "And he was *honorable*. If he told you something, you could take it to the bank." Once Billy sat down, lit up, and started dialing the phone, it wouldn't have occurred to an observer that the person in a coat and tie was anything but a man, no matter how short of stature or high of voice.

Moving to suburbia was also in the script. Working on commission from 1959 on, Billy soon made about $1500 to $1800 a month, plus about $800 a month for the trio's nightclub work. He put in long hours for the money, occasionally adding a date at an after-hours club or a strippers' breakfast for conventioneers. Within a year he had enough cash to make a down payment on a home. The postwar housing boom was pressing the city outward in all directions, and in late 1959 he and Maryann moved into a tract house in an abandoned apple orchard in the farmland that lay just east of the city limits. Maryann, who managed their money, recalled that they paid $12,000 for the house, "a two-bedroom ranch-style, with a patio and lots of gadgets, everything brand-new." There was ample room for the "kids" — their three Pomeranians, Timmy, Tinker, and Tippy — and Maryann started talking about building a swimming pool. They bought a baby grand piano so Billy could practice at home, though with Billy holding a day job, the trio seldom rehearsed anymore.

The world Billy now lived and worked in was a man's world in every way. One local businessman remembered the customary division of labor in those days as "I make the living, and my wife makes the living worthwhile." The work day that started in an office often continued in a bar. "I used to spend eight hundred dollars a month drinking when a shot of whiskey cost thirty cents," he said. "That gives you a sense of the scale." When an important client came from out of town, business would last through dinner and maybe a show or two at a nightclub, followed by another drink or two at an after-hours place and then by a discreet phone call to a cab dispatcher. An ex-cabbie from the 1950s remembered that

> after the war there was a lot of money floating around. Drinking and carousing was the thing to do then. Bars at that time closed at midnight, so from midnight on, the east side after-hours places would be swinging. Bootlegging, you could get six dollars for a pint that would cost two-fifty in the state liquor store, twelve dollars for a fifth. Against the law, of course, but that was a laugh! Cab-driving at one time was pretty lucrative, with the side money. I'd be making four hundred dollars a month where others would be making two hundred fifty dollars at straight jobs. Oh yes, this was a good source of income.
>
> Another side business we had was acquiring women, pimping! There were four of us working: the dispatcher of the cab company, the cabbie, and two girls — a four-way split. But that was a limited clientele, because the east end of Spokane was full of whorehouses. They were legal, controlled by the state. Finally closed them down, probably early 1950s. One madam in town was friendly with all of the upper echelon. I swore they'd never close her down, but by god, they did. She was a nice old lady, drove a Chrysler.

This was a crooked town. Cops were paid off. The newspapers would report the raids, but what they didn't report was that nothing closed down, the cops just got paid off. One cop I remember — stop you for driving too fast, he'd flat-out tell you, "The faster you go, the thirstier I get." What he wanted was a bottle. A whole different breed of people then than now.

The nightclubs and after-hours spots were for men only by custom, whereas private clubs were segregated by policy and were associated in one way or another with doing business, which is why they are now illegal. The Spokane Club, the Spokane Country Club, and the Athletic Round Table were the prestigious social clubs where civic leaders and businessmen met for lunch or social hours several times a week. Wives were invited only once a year for a fancy party. One club was so elite that only its members knew that it existed. Sometimes called the Prosperity Club, it was nicknamed the Ham and Eggers, because that's what the members ate at the end of a long Thursday night. One member recalled how his father, a prosperous businessman, initiated him into the world of men by introducing him to the Thursday meetings.

"Boys' Night" would start at noon, with everybody out on the golf course. A hundred percent attendance was required, and no other commitments tolerated. After the game and a round at the nineteenth hole, the boys would retire to the basement of the Spokane Club, a kind of dungeon room, the more clandestine the better. The meetings were always the same. Drinks were donated by a member each time, so there'd be a round of applause, followed by storytelling, mainly travel stories or jokes. This was the home away from home of the city fathers, the place to get away from the office and have a good time. These guys were there for hardcore fun. No politics, no issues. Anybody gets up with a business proposition gets booted out of the club. Of course, you'd be sitting down with the people you'd pass elbow to elbow all week in the round of your occupation. You'd get to know them, they'd get to know you, and it mattered. If things needed straightening out, you could catch up with them later.

After drinks, people might go off in little groups to a nightclub for dinner and a show, maybe an after-hours club — Sam's Pit, Mother's Kitchen. Maybe arrange a rendezvous. The Pine Shed was another place. Guys used to call it "Menopause Manor" — older women were always around waiting for somebody to ask them to dance. Occasionally entertainment would be brought into the club for an evening. Mainly the entertainers were male too.

My father used to get home in the wee hours Friday morning, but it was part of the code you were on the job again as usual next day, no matter how ferocious the hangover.

According to a regular at these clubs in the old days, "There wasn't much cheating on the missus. Mainly we got together to drink and talk about sports. I recall a columnist from Los Angeles who got stuck in Spokane covering the hockey league, said to me, 'Spokane is the kind of place that rolls up its sidewalks at nine o'clock — in the morning.' That was about right. We had so many blue laws in Spokane we had to organize private clubs just to keep people off our backs."

Segregation by sex operated in Spokane like a law of nature. In a community so regulated by convention, a woman might be able to pass as a man more easily than in places where the actual gender diversity of the world was more visible. And in fact Billy had a predecessor in Spokane.

This was Alberta Lucille Hart, M.D. Her story is known because her early struggles to undertake a man's profession caused her such despair that at age twenty-six she underwent psychoanalysis. During her treatment she wrote copious notes about her background, and these were later published by her analyst in a disguised case history.

Hart, born in 1892, grew up in Albany, Oregon. She described herself as an outstanding high school science student. Drawn to medicine, she enrolled at Stanford University, where, as the only woman in her pre-med course, she "had a rather severe initiation." She received her medical degree from the University of Oregon in 1917. Hart had always been sexually attracted to women, but considered herself entirely normal until she began reading the medical literature in psychopathology. Having diagnosed herself as "an invert," she resolved to seek a professional and intellectual life in the guise of a man. She wanted to undergo a hysterectomy to sterilize herself, partly as an act of social conscience, but mainly, she acknowledged, to eliminate the inconvenience of menstruation. Her analyst agonized over this decision before helping her acquire the medical treatment she requested, but he concurred that her ambitions could not be fulfilled within the constraints of existing social conditions. (Learning that Hart had married a woman who was "fully cognizant of all the facts," her analyst commented, "My protest was indefensible except on grounds of prejudice and a habit of thinking begotten of long years of conformity to social dogmata.")

After the hysterectomy, she renamed herself Alan L. Hart and embarked on a successful career as a radiologist. Dr. Hart also became a writer. In addition to clinical papers and a popular book on radiation therapies, he wrote four novels in which the main characters were medical men battling small-town ignorance and prejudice.

Dr. Hart was forty-four years old and living in Spokane when his first novel, *Doctor Mallory*, was published, in 1935. The *New York Times* gave the book a cautiously positive review ("Whether or not one approves of . . . socialized medicine, one must grant Mr. Hart the point of making an excellent case for it"). Billy Tipton was also forty-four when he adopted Spokane in which to conduct a more or less ordinary life as a man. A geographical coincidence draws together the stories of Alan Hart and Billy Tipton, yet once paired, they seem birds of a feather. As young women, they were sexually attracted to women and socially attracted to work reserved for men. Each was a self-confident pragmatist who intended to get what she wanted, and each devised a home remedy for the problem of being female in a man's world.

The case history of Alberta/Alan Hart was discovered and decoded as recently as 1976, by a researcher in the new field of American gay history. After Billy Tipton's death, some observers lamented that neither medical technologies nor cultural and political acceptance of homosexuality had been available to ease Billy's path. Yet the examples of Alan Hart and Billy Tipton provide historical information too specific to ignore. In each case, a fairly simple disguise provided conditions for the liberation of a distinctive creativity. Neither of them lacked for work, companionship, or sex. They were successful in the eyes of the world, and in the eyes of the people closest to them, they did no evil. Though Billy, unlike Dr. Hart, stopped confiding in the women he desired, being desired by Billy Tipton suited those women at the time, and as we have seen, they do not renounce him now.

Possibly, both Hart and Tipton benefited from the absence of widely disseminated social taxonomies by which they might easily be categorized. Dr. Hart's contact with a pathological term for her psychological disposition arguably caused her more harm than good. As far as we know, Billy did not seek self-knowledge by consulting diagnostic categories of this sort. Once her character had been organized within playing the role of Billy, role-playing itself seems to have taken over and provided guidance for behavior with its own legitimacy.

Looking at Billy Tipton in terms available in the late twentieth century, we see someone who fits the profile of the female-to-male transgenderist or female "gender blender," that is, a person with a female body but an indeterminate gender identity, a blend of traits that is not simply a femininity in disguise and is not a lesbian identity. Billy's success in this strategy raises the question of what it felt like to be on the inside of this performance. Did Billy, we wonder, feel like a man or like an actor? Only one thing is evident: Billy managed to suit herself/himself without disquieting others very much for fifty-four years.

By settling down in Spokane in the position of booking agent, Billy took a stride in the direction of economic security, but by working as a musician at Allen's Tin Pan Alley, he virtually abandoned his aspirations as a musician. At Allen's, the Billy Tipton Trio's main function was to back variety acts in three nightly floorshows. Allen's offered continuous entertainment, a "show going on anytime you come in from 9 P.M. to 2 A.M.," featuring lineups straight out of vaudeville: "Jack Brooks, pantomime at its finest. Tommy Bleeker, Your Host and MC. Myra Taylor, sepia song stylist. Kitty Kelly, Irish Colleen. Billy Tipton Trio, top recording stars." The showgirl might be an exotic dancer or a man in drag, since Dave Sobol alternated strippers with transvestites. The most notable act that Sobol ever took to Allen's was the Jewel Box Revue, a famous group of cross-dressers who advertised themselves as "twenty-five men and a girl." Which was the girl? The answer, not at all obvious, was revealed in a number called "The Surprise," when the master of ceremonies, Stormé DeLarverié, stepped forward to identify herself as a woman in male attire. Stormé joined the revue in 1955, following a career as Stormy Dale, female vocalist with a touring band. For her role with the Jewel Box she cut her hair, then began wearing men's clothing offstage. The very light-skinned daughter of a black mother, she made her sex as hard to identify as her race, and the ambiguity attracted questions that she never answered directly. "Some say sir and some say ma'am, and that's the way it is. I never change expression," she explained. In that era of gender fundamentalism,

Stormé's poise was bold, and possibly educational. The souvenir programs for the Jewel Box Revue billed the show as "family entertainment" and stressed that the artistry of impersonation was a venerable theater tradition reaching back to Shakespeare. The elegant Stormé gave off more complicated signals, as she was seductive and she was *now*. The Billy wannabes in the audience would have taken courage from her example.

Dave Sobol was the West Coast agent for the Jewel Box Revue and made money on them every time they went on tour during the mid-1950s. But that was before the Billy Tipton Trio became house band. By the late 1950s, little clubs like Allen's could no longer afford expensive productions such as the Jewel Box, for Sobol had been forced to close down his lucrative gambling enterprise. First the slot machines, then the lotteries, and finally the football pools, cardrooms, bingo parlors, and pinball machines had gone, the victims of pressure from politicians urged on by the community's religious fundamentalists. Even the Spokane Elks' low-adrenaline Friday night bingo game was imperiled. So Billy never backed the Jewel Box Revue, though he knew about the act. He was no doubt glad he never shared a bandstand with Stormé DeLarverié, who would have been hard to deceive.

Moreover, Billy — shamefully — often expressed disdain for the female impersonators that Sobol booked at Allen's. He made them, along with male homosexuals, the butt of jokes in his nightclub acts:

STRAIGHT MAN: Who was that lady I saw you with last night?
BILLY TIPTON: That was no lady, that was my brother. He always walks that way.

Another of Billy's jokes may have made a covert reference to hearings held by the House Un-American Activities Committee in Seattle earlier in the 1950s, when the search for Communists had had a way of turning into a search for homosexuals:

BILLY TIPTON: Did you hear the one about the little tugboat who committed suicide? He found out his mother was a tramp and his father was a ferry.

By these and other ploys, Billy distanced himself from transvestites and homosexuals in show business. Apparently he never played music in Spokane's best-known, perhaps only gay nightclub, Dorothy's. As one of its owners noted, though the club did a good business and attracted customers from as far away as Canada, "that kind of thing was not accepted socially or legally," and the manager needed to have "wonderful rapport with the police."

Despite his precautions, Billy did not entirely escape scrutiny himself. "Before I met Billy," one of the local musicians recalled, "I had been indoctrinated into the gay world. When I met Billy, I thought, 'There's something wrong here.' I didn't think about whether he was gay right away but noticed some things — never any sign of a beard, the pink cheeks, the high voice." This man accepted what everybody else in Spokane accepted. Why was this? "Well, the first test in show business is to look at who their friends are. Generally, if they are really gay, you'll notice people coming around who are less cautious, less discreet. But nobody ever showed around Billy. Some nights, going through the clubs, I'd see who he was talking to, and they were always people as normal as me. If any entertainer qualifies as normal!"

One sure sign of Billy's "normality" was a fondness for the coarse humor exchanged among the boys. The jokes that Billy wrote into his routines were risqué in the bland style of the 1950s, but the jokes he traded with male acquaintances could be repellent. A former trio member recalled, "One of Billy's favorites was about a guy in a theater. Everybody was starting to move away from a drunk because he smelled so bad. The usher came over and whispered, 'Did you shit your pants? Why don't you go clean yourself up?' 'Cuz I ain't through!' I heard Billy tell that to a lot of people." Another musician observed that no-holds-barred joking was a way musicians had of relaxing with each other. "Musicians can be really gross. You get conditioned to that. Many of the jokes in those days hit on blacks, Poles, women. Billy was just like the other guys."

Within two years of settling in Spokane, Billy had established a model middle-class life. Ironically, he kept it going by taking drugs for the first time in his career, "dexies" and "bennies," amphetamines that musicians used to keep themselves awake on the road or on the bandstand to counter road weariness. After a long day at the office, Billy went directly to Allen's, where he kept a change of clothes. After a brief early dinner, he would spend the hours before showtime rehearsing with the

new acts. Drugs helped keep him going but had a bad effect on his
moods. Maryann noticed that he was aloof and increasingly short-tem-
pered with her during the brief amounts of time he now spent at home.

Maryann urged Billy to invite the acts home with him after the show,
the way they had done in their little trailer, to unwind over a late
home-cooked meal and a few drinks. But Billy was too tired after his
long day. He had to be in the office early, and the performers didn't like
to make the long drive into the valley after work. So now the Tiptons
had a big home for entertaining but few guests. Maryann recalled that
Billy became irritable and withdrawn and criticized her for not being
more outgoing. "Oh, I went in every so often to see one of the acts," she
said. "But you don't sit in on somebody else's job seven days a week. I
thought I was doing a good job right here at home. I did the nice little
things that little people are supposed to do." But they didn't keep this
marriage happy.

One day Maryann took out the vacuum cleaner and noticed that
it was surprisingly heavy. Opening the canister, she found it full of
ashes from a fireplace. "I didn't have a fireplace," Maryann said. "But I
knew that one of the strippers had just bought herself a house — Billy
talked about it. And then I noticed Billy's clothes going out, a little at a
time. So I just, you know, put two and two together. And when I
confronted him about why he was leaving, he said I crocheted too
much! I said, 'Well, a poor excuse is better than none at all.' I just cried
and cried and cried and cried. I just didn't need that. After seven years
together!"

Yes, Billy had something like a seven-year itch (Non Earl had lasted
from 1934 to 1941; Betty, from 1946 to 1954; Maryann, from 1954 to
1961). The stripper who had caught his eye was a gorgeous, freckled
redhead billed as Kitty Kelly, the "colleen" in Allen's ad, also known as
"the Irish Venus." Kitty had been one of Dave's regulars for several
years. Based in Seattle, she came through Spokane every other month
or so for two-week engagements. She had been in burlesque for eight
years and planned to quit in three more, when she turned thirty, and
settle down in Spokane.

As bandleader, Billy felt a special obligation to look after the strippers, especially during the last floorshow, late at night when customers
might be drunk and rowdy. One of the drummers who worked with
Billy at Allen's recalled that quite frequently "guys would try to scrub

Kitty Kelly, the Irish Venus

out cigarettes or cigars on a stripper. Entice her over, use a cigarette to burn her leg, sometimes try to light their silken gowns on fire. I know one girl was burned to death when that happened, and many strippers carried burns on their bodies." Sometimes men would hang around after the show and try to stop a stripper as she left the club, so the musicians would wait for the girls to escort them to the hotel where they usually stayed. But Billy took more than fraternal interest in the volatile Kitty, who lived up to her feline nickname, acting adorable one minute, spitting the next. Her tirades against musicians who didn't please her sometimes escalated into screaming fits. Kitty had "a mouth on her," as one of Billy's trio members put it. Another remembered her as "a pretty good dancer, did the bump and grind like most strippers, but you didn't want to tangle with her or give her lip. She knew her way around." Billy took Kitty's tantrums as a challenge to his skills at soothing temperamental artists. Her rage had a lot of layers in it, one of which was an appeal for tenderness. For his own reasons, Billy was attuned to that. He could usually calm her down with a corny Irish joke.

Kitty said it was Billy who made the first move, coming to her dressing room one night after the show and surprising her with a kiss on the mouth. Another night he took her for a drive, parked in a secluded spot overlooking the city, and told her how he felt about her. "Billy had given no sign," she recalled. "Billy had no 'sidebar,' as we called it — did no flirting in the office — so I'd never thought about him. My only interest in Billy was as a working partner. We had a lot of fun onstage, in front of everybody." That night, Billy confided to her that he wasn't actually married to Maryann. "He said that he had a wife who was in the loony bin and so he wasn't legally married to anybody." But since everyone accepted Maryann as Mrs. Tipton, Kitty included, there wasn't much difference. "Anyway," she added, "I wasn't interested. For one thing, I was still in pain from surgery" — she had had a hysterectomy six months earlier, as treatment for cancer of the cervix — "and not ready for any boy-girl relationship. The thought of someone even touching me below was painful. Even going to the bathroom was painful." That night, Billy also told her his story about being injured in an accident that had left him unable to have the children he'd always wanted.

The growing attraction between Billy and Kitty was noticed by everybody they worked with. One band member recalled that Billy kept a room at a motel and offered it for his use when a girlfriend came from out of town; he thought Billy was meeting Kitty there. Dave Sobol, who was fond of Maryann, said he tried to talk Billy back to his senses. But Billy was besotted.

Why did he fall so hard? Was it because Kitty was a showgirl? Had Billy vandalized his self-esteem by giving up showmanship for life in the suburbs? Maybe he was projecting *Billy's* shortcomings onto Maryann when he criticized her for crocheting too much. Unlike Kitty, Maryann didn't know jazz, didn't know the unique high that performance could bestow. Dazzled by Kitty's attention, Billy might have felt the return of the suppressed jazzman he had been and that June and

Betty had fallen in love with. That's how it looks, given the way Billy pursued Kitty during her weeks on the road during the fall of 1960 by mailing her a spate of short, chatty, silly, sexy cards and notes addressed to Tiger. One card tells her salacious details about the sex life of his dogs. Another sets up a joke: "My typewriter has a contract in it and so I'm doing this by hand. I have been doing it by hand for some time, now . . ." When she returned, he bought her gifts. In December 1960, he wrote her a love poem.

> Deep in the valley of heartache, there grows the tree of despair.
> One dark, sunless day, a small bud appeared on the lowest
>   branch of this tree.
> Through the dismal, endless days, the bud continued to grow,
>   and a small ray of hope began to spread.
> And the whole tree was gradually illuminated in a beautiful
>   glow of happiness,
> As the bud spread from tree limb to tree limb.
> And the valley became a whole new and beautiful world to
>   live in.
> Could it be, that someone, somewhere, had said . . .
> "I Love You" . . .
> And really meant it?

The following June, he commissioned an oil painting, a fanciful portrait of Kitty that still hangs in her bedroom. About four feet by three feet, it depicts an idealized, full-breasted nude lying on a beach by the sea, blond hair spread over the sand. An oasis stands in the background, and behind it a volcano is erupting. As in Manet's painting of the courtesan Olympia, the woman's body is fully exposed to view, though her crotch is not detailed. Looking at the painting, Kitty commented, "A woman's breasts are Mama, motherhood, but the rest of a woman is private to herself." Billy's attraction may have been intensified by that split in Kitty, who deployed onstage a body from which she remained to some degree aloof.

In August, Kitty's mother paid a visit, just before Kitty left for a month-long engagement in Canada. "One night Billy showed up at my door with an engagement ring. He purposely made a date to see me while my mom was there," Kitty said. "The three of us were sitting on the couch, me in the middle. Billy reached across to my mother and took each of our hands. He said to me, 'Look at me.' Said to my mother, 'Would you convince her to marry me?' Then, if he didn't go down on his knees! Told me he loved me and wanted us to marry." It was after her return from that job in Canada that Kitty used her savings to make the down payment on a house, and Billy helped her move in, using Maryann's vacuum cleaner on the fireplace.

During this courtship, Maryann heard no rumors. Since she rarely went to the club, she saw little of the trio and nothing of Dave Sobol. Sure, she had watched Kitty's act and had met Kitty at Dave's Christmas party the preceding year. Kitty had even been at their house a couple of times. She was crazy about dogs, as was Maryann. But after the confrontation with Billy, Maryann stormed into Allen's and yelled at the boys, "Why didn't you warn me?" She later claimed that "Ron and Dick knew all along that Billy was playing around. Oh, I knew better than to bawl them out — they had bad consciences themselves. A wife is always going to be the last to know. But the way he left me was a terrible way to leave anybody. You know, I really thought we were going to stay together. But I didn't fight him. You stop and think. Kitty was sixteen years younger than I was. Billy, at that time, lied about his age and was older than he looked. For him, it was really something to have a young woman, with *that* body. They're all that way! My mother used to say, 'I'm going to spend everything I can of your father's, because if anything happens to me, I'm not having anybody else come in, some young girl, taking it all.'" "They're all that way" — men, she means, losing track of what she later learned about Billy. In that as in all other details, Billy got it exactly right.

Kitty was not a young girl, though. At twenty-seven, she had been twice married, twice divorced. Life in the burlesque theater had offered a refuge from a tough adolescence. Emotionally deserted by an alcoholic mother, bumped between juvenile custody and foster homes, raped and made pregnant in her early teens, Kitty had turned suspicious and standoffish. She invested her feelings in the costumes she made by hand and in the pets and plants she lugged around for company. She was proud of her body, but it never gave her any sexual pleasure, she now claims. "I have never had 'ecstasy sex.' I've never had an orgasm, as far as I know. After being raped, I don't think I was capable of it. If you are looking for the causes and the reasons that bring me to the point

Kitty Kelly backstage, circa 1959

where Billy and I could live together and me not know he was a woman, we're going to get into the emotional part."

Attempting to account for the emotions that anchored her in this relationship, Kitty summoned a vignette from mid-December 1961. She had been working a two-week circuit through Montana and Idaho. During her absence, Billy had settled things with Maryann and moved the last of his possessions into Kitty's house. "The morning after I finished the job in Boise," Kitty recalled, "I rushed to the airport with a box of Christmas ornaments balanced on my luggage. All the planes were grounded. After a whole day sitting in the tiny little airport lounge, I caught a converted mail plane out of Boise, got to Spokane very late. The Spokane airport was in a small one-story building then, with a restaurant across the road. I walked into the building, and from afar, under the lights, I saw this little figure off in the distance, heading toward me from the restaurant. It was Billy, coming to pick me up, grinning from ear to ear. He waited all that time for me! That's how life began with Billy, and this was the theme of my life with him. He had intuitions, a way of knowing what I needed."

Kitty claims vehemently that she and Billy were never sexually intimate. "Passion! I wasn't passionate — I would stiffen when anybody came toward me. The only time Billy saw me with my clothes off was onstage! Billy knew the rules. Arm around the shoulder, pushing my hair away from my face, a hand on the shoulder. More like comforting. He did play with my hair a lot, stroking. He loved the dimples on my bum, said he wanted to rouge them. I preferred hands always above the waist. To me, love and sex are entirely different. Love has nothing to do with sex. And I didn't want anyone coming up behind me — remember, when I had six-inch heels on, I towered over Billy! No passion. There was always a lot of laughter — everything was supposed to be kept light."

Kitty can't believe that other women had sex with Billy, either.

I absolutely don't believe there is any way in hell that he could have lived with a woman for any length of time with her not knowing. Give me a break. There's no way. You mean they never insisted he take his shorts off? It's not possible. Well, they could have had sex as two women. But I can't see any woman going to bed with a guy who doesn't take his clothes off. She'd have been better off sticking to the other story. I don't believe *any* of these broads who say they had sex with Billy and didn't know. There was no way they had the know-how! We all agree he wore a gadget. The thing would have been stiff, never go down. No. I don't think so.

Letters that Billy wrote to Kitty while she was on the road complicate this picture. During the late summer and fall of 1961, before they started living together, Kitty had several jobs that sent her out of town for weeks at a time. Billy wrote every day, sometimes more than once — miserable, yearning, sexy letters that counted the days and hours until her return, when they would move in together: "I do like privacy when I'm with you. We get sort of noisy, at times, Mommy. Huh?" A running joke in the letters has to do with "Percy" and "Hortense": "We could make a fresh start. But who wants a fresh start when they can have a lot of old hassles! Right? Right! Besides, we have to do everything the hard way. Speaking of hard ways — Percy sure misses Hortense. Will you please bring her home. He hasn't had a good talking to since last Friday. My back seems to be better today. Maybe by the time she does get home Percy should be able to really give her a going over!" On another day Billy sent a card with a writhing cartoon figure, hands crossed over the groin, under the captions "Ouch!" and "I think of you so much it hurts." "Percy and I need you," he wrote. "I'll be walking on three legs by the time you get home! MOMMA! . . . Hortense!!" Percy sent the message "Hortense — cum home!"

Billy's letters also mention propositions from other women. "I got a call the other night to come to the Davenport after work," says one. "This married woman, that I told you about, was 'pitching-a-bitch' but I told her, in no uncertain terms, that I was in love with a wonderful girl and I wasn't interested in anything she had to offer . . . Percy has been behaving himself. He gets 'twinges' every now and then but he doesn't want anyone but Hortense Hotbreath! Hurry home to me, my love, I need you so badly. Your husband, Billy." Another claims, "I have been behaving myself — had a few good propositions but can't go — I got a woman that would de-nut me if I trifled so better not take any chances. Can't afford to lose what I do have! My big ol' wife would beat me, wouldn't she, Momma? . . . Tell Hortense that Percy loves her and is faithful to her. And for her not to be too tired for a short conversation when she gets back."

Kitty dismisses these letters, explaining the references to Percy and Hortense as jokes, examples of "Billy's sense of humor — names he gave his fantasy about if Billy and I had been a normal couple having sex." Billy *was* obsessed with Kitty's body. After Kitty accepted the engagement ring he offered in that dramatic gesture with her mother as audience, Billy took a picture of her wearing it, then cut away all but her hand. He kept this odd little fetish in his office, tucked into a card he had sent her. He also saved handfuls of the long red curls she cut off that summer when she adopted a pixie hairstyle, à la Jean Seberg. Both of these trophies were found after Billy's death in the closet that held the history of his career.

Kitty seems to be telling the truth when she says that she did not know Billy was female. In the twenty-nine letters Billy wrote to her in 1961, he refers to himself only in masculine terms. "To me you are the most beautiful girl in the world and I'm a very lucky fellow to have you." "Tell those salesmen and Idaho hillbillies to keep their hands off my wife." In another letter Kitty gets advice about managing an oil-burning car from "your old dad." Annoyed when he learns that Kitty's ex-husband has visited her on the road, Billy growls, "Maybe some guys like for their women to support them. But I wouldn't be a 'douche bag shaker' for any woman!" Remorseful the following day, he explains, "You know that I worship you and that I am terribly jealous . . . I'm holding on to you — forever. When I get old and wrinkled you can tell them I am your father — what the hell!" "Oh my darling you are marrying an idiot," he tells her after a phone call, "but this idiot will do everything in his power to make you happy." Resenting their separation, Billy writes, "When the snows fall this winter we can stay inside where it is warm and snug and find out all the things that make a man and woman love each other." Billy signs his letters "Your husband," "Your Papa," "Your better ½," "Your lonesome old man."

About Percy and Hortense and Momma, Kitty is telling only a partial truth, but wouldn't most of us? After all, this is a story about Billy's life, not her life, and those were names that Billy gave *his* fantasy, which she apparently did not share. Despite Kitty's protestations to the contrary, Billy's letters make it clear that she lent her body to this fantasy, just as she lent the spectacle of her body to the fantasies of customers at Allen's. Kitty was Billy's last and greatest conquest. "I don't know how any of the other men in your life could have ever let you get away from them. You're all the woman I'll ever need. So much for this sex talk — I'm in bad enough condition — it has been 5 days since I have had any. Come Home!"

· 14 ·

Family Man

1962–1979

> Whither thou goest, I will go; and where thou lodgest, I
> will lodge: thy people shall be my people.
>
> Ruth 1:15

BILLY AND KITTY exchanged vows and rings before a justice of the
peace in Coeur d'Alene, Idaho, at 4 P.M. on Saint Patrick's Day, 1962, in
a private room at Templin's, a fancy restaurant owned by one of Billy's
business associates. It was a civil ceremony, but verses from the Book
of Ruth were read. After the wedding, Bob Templin threw a champagne
reception for friends in the business. At dinner, while the band played
"There'll Be a Hot Time in the Old Town Tonight," the bride ate lobster
and the groom ate steak. They spent their wedding night in Coeur
d' Alene, in room 5 at the Garden Motel. Or so it says in a satin-bound
wedding keepsake signed by the officiating justice of the peace.

The wedding was never registered, and the signature of the justice of
the peace was forged. But Kitty says that she left all the arrangements
to Billy and believed that a legal marriage had taken place. Nor did she
notice that the official-looking "Certificate of Marriage" that they kept
among their personal papers carried no serial numbers or other anno-
tation of bureaucratic attention and contained significantly different
information from the satin-bound keepsake. Handwriting comparisons
show that Billy forged all of these signatures, but in retrospect it appears that at least three people — the justice and the witnesses —
colluded somehow in this deception. Kitty says that they were Billy's
acquaintances, people she knew only slightly. All of them are dead now.

Billy's choice of Coeur d'Alene as the site for their ceremony suggests that he knew Idaho to be a safer choice than Washington for his
risky undertaking. Couples usually married in haste in Coeur d' Alene;

quickie weddings were one of the local industries. Billy and Kitty were in no hurry. They had been living together in Spokane since December 1961. Deciding to wait out a tactful "divorce period" in consideration of Maryann's feelings, as he put it, Billy chose Saint Patrick's Day 1962 as auspicious for his wedding to the Irish Venus. This gave him time to find out whether the ceremony he arranged would result in a binding contract. Quite possibly, this marriage was legal in the state of Idaho, and by extension, in the state of Washington. A frontier attitude skeptical of lawyering was evident in the Idaho Code, which held that couples were legally married if they said they were. Even a marriage conducted by a fraudulent official was valid if "consummated with a full belief of the parties so married, *or either of them,* that they have been lawfully joined in marriage." The code, in 1962 at any rate, did not even specify that the couple must be one man and one woman. If proof of the marriage was ever required, Kitty's claim to ignorance of any irregularities would be enough to affirm its legitimacy, and to protect her if Billy's sex should be exposed.

Nobody seems to have doubted the validity of the marriage at the time, least of all Kitty. She kept a photograph album commemorating their first days and months of married life. Black-and-white snapshots show the newlyweds at the Athletic Round Table on their wedding day, and a rumpled Kitty in bed with their dogs the next morning. Color snapshots of a party at Allen's the following week show Dave Sobol, Ron Kilde, and Dick O'Neil toasting the bride and groom; they remember Billy saying over and over, "Just look what I took away from other guys!" Other photos keep track of Kitty and Billy settling with their family of dogs into their new home. Billy made himself, once again, a most agreeable son-in-law. On Mother's Day he wrote to Kitty's mother, "Everything is going fine. Sure love my girl."

Billy was acting under false pretenses but in good faith when he said "I do." Letters he wrote during their courtship attest that he was deeply committed to Kitty. "I fell in love with you the way you were and was given an added reward when I found the real you," he wrote, "a wonderful person, decent and honest . . . I love you with everything that is in me, and I only hope that I can make you happy for the rest of my life." "If I spoil you a little and love you with all my heart, it is because you are something I have waited for all my life." The way he regarded this commitment may have been reflected in the biblical verses he

Kitty's husband, 1962

chose as a reading to sacralize their vows: "And Ruth said, Entreat me not to leave thee, or to return from following after thee: for whither thou goest, I will go; and where thou lodgest, I will lodge: thy people shall be my people, and thy God my God. Where thou diest, will I die, and there will I be buried: the Lord do so to me, and more also, if aught but death part thee and me." These words had been adapted in 1954 for the lyrics of a popular song, "Whither Thou Goest," and no one would have questioned their use in a wedding ceremony. Yet Billy might have chosen them for another reason: Ruth was pledging herself to another woman.

Two months after the wedding, the newlyweds were puttering in their new house one day when Kitty fell off a ladder and crushed several vertebrae, an accident that required immediate surgery. Billy, deeply worried, wrote to her mother, "The operation was a spinal fusion. The tail bone had been jammed into another vertebra just like you would smash your fist into the palm of your other hand. The nerves were almost severed. The doctors give her a 50-50 chance to regain all feeling. She was paralyzed on the right side from her hip to her knee." Kitty was confined in a body cast for the next couple of months, and although she recovered completely, physical separation from Billy remained a way of life. "We slept in the same room but didn't share a bed," she explained. "Billy had weight on him; I needed a bed to myself. We shared a bathroom. Yes, we locked the doors, and we didn't think it was unusual. Just because I used to do what I did for a living didn't mean I didn't need my privacy."

What kind of loss was this for Billy? Kitty said that they had never shared a bed, whereas Billy's letters suggest otherwise. (Writing to Kitty in December, he had joked about sleeping with their dog Buster: "He's a pretty good bed pardner. Not as good as you, but he sure can snuggle, too.") In any case, Billy was forty-seven years old when he married Kitty. The first twinges of arthritis were stiffening his finger joints, and the first hot flashes of menopause may have already begun signaling the change of life. Kitty had reignited Billy's sexuality — there is no question at all about that — but when she began putting physical distance between them, was Billy at least a little bit relieved? To retire from the field of intimate heterosexual conduct, honor intact; to relax the vigilance imposed by the secret — these must have been some compensation for accepting the sexless marriage Kitty claims they had.

Indisputably, Billy's love for Kitty was very deep, and it endured for many years. Six years into their marriage, when Kitty was being treated for an ulcer, Billy put into a letter his gratitude for the life they shared.

My Darling,
It has been a long time since I have written a letter to you. About seven years ago, I believe — That is a lot of years to let pass without renewing the acquaintance of a love such as we had. The years have a habit of lulling one into a false contentment and causing one to neglect to say and do the real important things. Just lately it was

brought to my attention, rather abruptly, that I have been guilty of just such conduct. I am truly sorry for this. I have loved you with all my heart for these past seven years. There have been times when I didn't like you or some of the things you did, but I have never stopped loving you for one moment. You are instilled so deep in my heart that you have become a part of me. It would be difficult to imagine life without you. In our seven years together we have seen much hurt and much pain, both physical and mental, and we still cling to each other. Just when it looks like circumstances will separate us, you touch my hand or I touch yours and we cling together, tighter than ever.

Right now, I know you are having a fight within yourself. All I can do is stand by and watch and wait. If you need me, I'll be there — If you don't need me — send me away. But I do want you to know that you are a part of me — you are my love — and when you need me or want me, I'll be there to touch your hand and feel you cling to me and with God's help I will be able to give you the strength you need.

You are my life, my love —

Your husband,
Billy

If Billy was satisfied with a marriage devoid of sex, perhaps it was because he had another aim in marrying Kitty: to raise a family. Once Kitty had recovered from her back injury, Billy began pressing the issue of adopting children. Kitty thought they would be turned down by official agencies. "Billy's age, our past, our lack of money — I didn't think we'd have a chance." But Billy pursued the subject on his own and one evening came home with news. Someone had contacted him on behalf of a woman who wanted to put a child up for adoption immediately after its birth. Their lawyer worked out an agreement with the mother, Kitty explained. "I saw the signatures of Billy, the mother, and the lawyer. Later I found out that these were not legal papers. Looking back, I see that he took a big risk. His identity could have been discovered at any time."

The baby, a boy, was born 19 October 1963, and a few days later he was taken to the Tiptons' home by the person who had done the match-making. Kitty recalled that Billy arrived home from work shortly after-ward. "Billy walked in in a light-colored London Fog raincoat. I will never forget this. I picked up the baby and brought him over to Billy. The look on his face! Just for a minute, it was like a mother's ecstasy.

Mother, father, and first son, 1963

Billy sat down with John in the rocker. Didn't even take off his raincoat. Just rocked him and rocked him. To build a family of his own was Billy's hope then." Billy chose the name John Thomas, both names from the Tipton family. A patient and devoted father, he shared the evening rituals of feeding and bathing before leaving for his nightclub work and gave John his last feeding after he returned at 2:30 A.M.

For two years John was the Tiptons' only child. Then, around Christmas in 1965, Billy told Kitty about the plight of a woman he had worked with off and on, an entertainer who was badly alcoholic. Her toddler had been placed in foster care, and was being neglected. This child was virtually the same age as John, a mere six weeks older, and had flaming red hair, just like Kitty. Wasn't it time to give John a brother?

Neither Billy nor Kitty was prepared for the sight of the little boy, and Kitty broke down and wept when she remembered his arrival on Christmas Eve. "He was delivered in a snowstorm by two strangers, a really unhealthy-looking, frightened child accompanied by a paper bag

Father and son, 1964

and a grungy yellow stuffed rabbit. His head was shaved and there was a note talking about his food. It was four thirty in the afternoon. I called Billy and said I had to go shopping immediately — everything about him was filthy. I took him to a store and outfitted him, brought him home and bathed him. Throughout the whole process the child hadn't said a word. When I set a plate of food in front of him, he attacked it. I hadn't realized how hungry he was."

Billy named their second son Scott Lee, Lee being a family name that had passed into Billy's own stagename from his father's sister Julia Lee. It took many months to make Scott part of the family, Kitty remembered. He was slow to learn to talk and to be toilet-trained, and he had serious health problems, including petit-mal seizures, which required drugs, and rickets, which required braces for his legs for three months. But once he began coming out of his shell, he was an infectiously happy child "with a marvelous giggle." Dave Sobol recalls that Billy and Kitty were terribly proud of their boys. At Christmas the year after Scott's adoption, Billy gave the Sobols a studio portrait of the pair, each dressed in jacket and tie, inscribed "To Uncle Dave and Aunt Rubye from Scott and John Tipton."

In 1967 the family expanded once again when a third boy came to live with them. This was Bobby, the twelve-year-old son of a local musician who was a friend of Kitty and Billy's and who was going through a clamorous divorce. Bobby was a member of a junior hockey league sponsored by the Athletic Round Table. Kitty became its chief volunteer organizer, taking over the league's bookkeeping and fund-raising as well as chauffeuring Bobby to hockey practice. She discovered that she enjoyed getting out of the house again. "My two kids were little, not in school, so they were involved too. Bobby taught them skating. The whole thing grew!" She laughed. "Animals, kids, we were an affectionate, close family unit. Always touching, hugging. Close. And Bobby fit right in. He was a jewel and a doll and a wonder."

Kitty has poignant evidence of Bobby's gratitude, a letter he wrote a year after moving in with the Tiptons, nominating Kitty for "Mother of the Year": "I would like for my Mom to win, because I think she deserves to. She is really my foster mother and I have two little foster brothers that are both adopted. She loves us all and helps me with my home work. She gets up early to take us to practice hockey and works for our hockey teams. She washes our clothes and keeps the house clean and cooks every day. Mom stayed with me when I had my tonsils out when she could have gone to San Francisco free to see Grandma. Sincerely, Robert Calicoat."

To keep track of family appointments, every year Kitty bought a big wall calendar and entered extensive information on it, including the mileage for Billy's out-of-town engagements, the children's medical diagnoses, and the dogs' birthdays. These calendars indicate that Billy was still playing music regularly right through the 1960s. The Billy Tipton Trio was no longer a house band anywhere but played on weekends only, mainly dance music at the Sillman Hotel, the Fairchild Air Base Officers' Club, the Elks, or the American Legion. Occasionally Billy

An ad hoc Billy Tipton Trio, circa 1963,
with Dick O'Neil and Terry Donoghue

would play a nightclub, backing strippers at the Kon Tiki, or would put together a show for conventioneers, with jugglers and tap-dancers and vocalists. Sometimes he would solo at a piano bar, taking requests.

Billy now improvised his trios. This was easy to do from his chair at the Sobol agency, where he could line up the gig and the musicians with a couple of phone calls. Once in a while he still called on Dick O'Neil, but he most often worked with two younger sidemen, Marvin Richter on drums and Ben Tessensohn on bass. Sometimes he replaced the bass with a trumpet, which was more effective for backing nightclub acts.

Billy also began scheduling one-nighters out of town for his trio again, in order to make personal visits to the regional clubs into which he booked bands. Maintaining the loyalty of managers became crucial with the advent of rock music, which was rapidly changing the entertainment business. Almost overnight, the jazz ensemble had become obsolete. The jazz pianist Don Asher described the shock of his own first encounter with this kind of competition, at a popular nightclub called the hungry i in San Francisco: "Out of behemoth speakers the size of small garages the otherworldly roar emerged like voltaic belches from the massed mouths of bottlenosed whales — an implacable vortex of sound that engulfed, lifted and spun our world away as effortlessly and irreclaimably as Dorothy's Kansas farmhouse." In Spokane, Dave Sobol hired a kid named Mike Cavender to handle the rock groups, which neither he nor Billy could tolerate, and segregated the offices to keep Cavender's longhairs out of sight. Billy experienced the change as a steady erosion of his commissions.

He turned to Marv and Ben as younger men who shared his passion for jazz and swing and who looked up to him as a veteran of the golden age. Ben recalled that jazz survived in their work mainly in the form of musical allusions, "things we do unconsciously. We'd find ourselves making little jokes, little references. Billy was a hell of a musician, and a hell of a reader — read all the charts right off, and carried tons of stuff in his head." Another musician who played bass with the trio during those years, Kyle Pugh, elaborated: "Billy was a creative ad-libber. You'd listen for it, good things happening musically with the chords and progressions. Being tight."

Ben Tessensohn recalled that Billy's years in the business made him a good MC, and a quick study with all kinds of acts. "Often we didn't have much time for rehearsing shows. We might have from four to six to go through all the music with them. The singer would come with charts. He'd play and I'd play, and we'd look at each other — oh, boy! Then Billy would say — he was always very tactful — 'You know what? You have a marvelous voice, but this arrangement doesn't do you justice. Do you mind if we change it? I'll show you.' He'd turn to me, say, 'Ben, let loose!' Then we'd get into it, and the singer would say, 'Wow!'"

Marv and Ben were usually the sidemen Billy took with him on gigs out of town. One time something odd happened, and each of them remembered it after Billy's death. Marv described it this way:

> Normally when we were on the road, Billy booked a room for himself. He would be in and out, promoting his business as a booking

agent. Billy made quite efficient use of his time on the road that way. Having his own room, he could just go out and come back, independent of us.

This particular night, we were all pretty wired after the job, not wanting to just go home to bed. Went out and got a hamburger or something, kind of relaxed a bit, then back to our motel.

Ben and I went into our room and Billy went into his room. For some reason there was something I had to ask him, about our schedule or the like. Our rooms were adjacent. Went out the door to Billy's room and noticed that the door was ajar. Instead of knocking on it, I was starting to walk in — got one step and stopped because I saw a nude body in there, and I saw that it was a female body. Standing up. I didn't see the face, just saw the breasts and the front portion of the body. I was astounded. I stopped short and thought, What's going on? Billy's got a girlfriend! We knew Kitty, we knew the family. I always felt that Billy was a very true person who would not cheat. So it was kind of shocking, frankly. I just stopped short. Obviously, I'm not going to walk in or knock on the door. I just spun around and went back to the room. He didn't see me. Now I know it was Billy undressing, and why the door was ajar I have no idea.

I went back and said, "Ben, I don't know how to tell you this, but Billy's got a girl in there!" Ben said, "You're kidding!" I said, "No, I'm not! Did you see him talking to a girl, getting excited about a girl?" Because musicians on the road do run into that kind of thing, it's available to them. That's life. Ben said, "No! Maybe you and I would goof off, but not Billy!"

It was so out of character they didn't know what to think. They just forgot about the incident until they met again at Billy's funeral.

Most of the jobs Billy played during those years brought in only a small income, between twenty and thirty-five dollars a night, topping out at about fifty dollars. A fairly complete account of his earnings as both a musician and a booking agent is available for 1967, the year Bobby Calicoat joined the family and added a tonsillectomy and hockey equipment to the household expenses. Billy claimed $832 as income from playing music and $10,116 from the Sobol agency in commissions. Since he worked long hours and seemed to be making a reasonably good income, it is likely that much of his pay was off the books. But Billy was not aggressive about collecting money from the bands, unless he was pushed to do so by Dave Sobol. Kitty recalled that one year he calculated he was owed $8000 in uncollected fees. Nor was he willing to look after his own career interests when it required standing up to Dave. A letter Billy wrote to Kitty before their marriage reported a typical example of Billy's way of dealing with bosses. Under Maryann's influence, he had acquired a small portfolio of stock along with his suburban lifestyle, and he was preparing to sell some in case he had to pay back taxes. "I talked to my attorney this morning and he said that he had come to the conclusion that the club is responsible for the tax and not I. Won't [Allen] Goldberg [owner of Allen's Tin Pan Alley] be surprised. I haven't told Dave yet, either. Allen will owe for two years and Dave for just one year. I'll probably end up paying for the whole thing. My luck, you know. Oh well, it's only money." Faced with Sobol's bluster and Goldberg's tough-guy attitude, Billy would fall back on soothing. "If I said 'Jump!' Billy would say, 'How high?'" Sobol acknowledged.

Yet the Tiptons lived well. Kitty's mother, Carrie, had married a merchant seaman, who sent them handsome gifts from his travels, including a fur coat from Hong Kong for Kitty and a suite of living room furniture from the Far East. Billy bought a big motor home and a piece of property at nearby Deer Lake. He and Kitty liked to fish, and wanted to teach the boys when they were old enough.

Kitty ran on high octane all the time. Every holiday or family anniversary required designing and baking a special cake, and every change of season required changing the color scheme in household accessories. Once the children started kindergarten, she joined the PTA and began helping out with field trips, raising money, shuttling children who needed rides in bad weather. In many of these activities she had the welcome assistance of Carrie, who moved up from San Francisco with her husband in 1967 and bought a house a couple of doors from the Tiptons'. Carrie had been a very young mother, only fifteen years old when Kitty was born, and neglectful. In middle age she began attempting to compensate. Good-natured and relaxed where Kitty was irritable and driven, Carrie gave ballast to family life and also shared the child-rearing.

In 1969 Bobby Calicoat rejoined his father, and the Tiptons decided to adopt another child. This time the process was instigated by the expectant mother, an entertainer who knew the Tiptons and knew

Billy at the barbecue, 1963

something about how John and Scott had been adopted. She contacted Billy early in her pregnancy and arranged to deliver the baby at a hospital in Oregon under Kitty's name, Stella Marie Flaherty Tipton; the father named on the birth certificate was Dee L. Tipton. The baby, another boy, was born 17 November 1969. This one they named William Alan and nicknamed Little Billy, which added stature to his father, who now became Big Billy on Kitty's calendar.

Carrie drove with Kitty to Pendleton to pick up the newborn at the hospital. They found him in terrible distress, as he had become addicted to drugs in the womb. They worried about his survival for days after arriving home in Spokane, Kitty recalled. "I slept with his crib next to my bed and kept my hand on him all night in case he went into convulsions. He had to be incubated twice: for a week shortly after his birth in November, then for two weeks in January for projectile vomiting. He couldn't keep any food down; he had a defective valve in his stomach."

Carrie worried with Kitty through the touch-and-go of William's earliest days of life. Virtually a next-door neighbor, she took charge of the children when Kitty needed her. Shortly after William's arrival, Carrie and her husband divorced and sold their home, and since the Tiptons had decided they needed more living room, they pooled resources with her and found a spacious two-story house with a big garden on a handsome tree-lined street in one of Spokane's best neighborhoods, on the south side of town and near a large park. For the first year of William's life, Carrie and Kitty had rooms downstairs with the baby, while Billy and the older boys had rooms on the top floor. Carrie remarried the following year and moved away, but she returned to the family a few years later. Altogether, she spent four years living in the house with them. She believes that the family was strong and stable when the boys were young, "a regular Brady Bunch." "Each of us had a chair in the sitting room," she said. "Tipton liked to stretch out on the couch in the evening. We bought the kids turtle pillows and they'd lie in front of the TV. The message would come on the screen: 'It's ten o'clock; do you know where your children are?' We'd feel happy that we were all home together."

Once established in the family, Carrie made herself useful to both Billy at the office and Kitty at home. Where Kitty was highstrung, Carrie was easygoing. "I tried to enforce the rules by making jokes," she said. "They were real boys. John was a daredevil, loved risk-taking. Scott had no conscience. But I never had any trouble with them. We just kept our sense of humor." When fighting broke out, she would bump their heads together.

Carrie regarded Billy as a good friend and was glad to comply with his request in 1971 that she be written into the codicil of his will as the children's guardian in case he and Kitty died. She thought she knew him very well. Privately, Carrie seemed to think she knew him better than Kitty knew him, but she too seemed genuinely astonished, after Billy's death, by the discovery of his sex. "Believe me, for him to completely fool us all was odd. Yet I didn't notice a thing," she said. She concurred in Kitty's description of Billy as "a very private person who

Kitty Tipton with *(clockwise from top)* John, Scott, and William, circa 1972

closed doors behind him," but that did not seem peculiar to her. On the contrary, it showed what good manners he had. "When he'd come downstairs in the morning to let the dog out and make coffee, he'd be dressed in shirt and trousers. I never saw him naked. But there was certainly no prudishness about him." Carrie enjoyed his raunchy jokes and the nightclub patter he shared with her when the children weren't around. She remembered too that the kids liked to take a "fun run" nude through the house at bathtime, and that Billy encouraged it. But he taught them to knock and wait before opening a closed door.

Billy had more closed doors in his life than anybody in Spokane knew about. One of the benefits of his office job was a filing cabinet in which he could sequester mail from his family. Billy didn't talk much about his folks, so Kitty knew only that Billy's parents had been divorced and that he wasn't in touch with his father. She thought Billy had a cordial but distant relationship with his mother. In fact Billy remained in close touch, sending gifts on birthdays and holidays to Reggie and her husband and paying occasional visits. Lynn still called his stepdaughter Dot, though he tactfully addressed the envelope to "B. L. Tipton," as did Reggie, whose letters always greeted Billy as "darling" and often referred guardedly to the disguise.

Notably, Reggie's letters reveal that she accepted without criticism the presence of women in her darling's life. Several times she mentions Non Earl, Billy's first girl, who still lived in Oklahoma City. Succeeding letters inquire politely after Billy's other wives. As Billy and Kitty began adopting children, Reggie asked after them as well. Typically, her emotions are cloaked in references to money, and like the speeches Eugene O'Neill wrote for the mother in *A Long Day's Journey into Night,* these references often end up reversing the roles of parent and child. Consider this excerpt from a thirteen-page letter Reggie wrote shortly after a visit from her son Bill.

> My Darling,
> I'm late, I know, please forgive me. I just never seem to have any time to write, when I'm so very tired I can't think. I first want to thank you for the five dollars you sent Thanksgiving . . .
> Brother brought his girl friend home the Sat. before Thanksgiving. They stayed all nite. I sure don't care for her . . . had a hard cry when he left. He won't listen to me . . . We are barely getting along now. It seems to me he'd realize I'm not young. And if he'd even once in a while say, Mother here's $5.00 get someone to help you, or even do some little thing at Xmas or my birthday, it would make me so happy. I am always telling him how wonderful you are to me. He never says anything. Well, Darling, I guess I told you this because I'm so hurt. Way deep inside. We'd never have moved to Oklahoma City, but I thought he and I would be closer together . . .
> By the way I hope I haven't waited too long to write about Xmas . . . I have my heart set on Hartmann Caravan. It's expensive, but it will be the last I'll ever get. The Caravan Poudre case, or cosmetic case which is the same. Cost $45.00 . . . I've saved $25.00 on it, so if you just send me $5.00 or $10.00 I can manage. I know you have planned

to give me something and that would be wonderful. No more than
$5.00 or $10.00 — please. You need every dime you can make. You
never know when you can work in this kind of weather or when your
car will need working on. Also big bills to pay. So let's be sensible. It's
hard to buy clothing as one never knows the size to get. And it just lays
around unused.

I'm sending you some money for your Xmas, and birthday. Ha! Ha!
they sure come close. Now you know what you need and your size.
Maybe you would like a garment carrier for your clothes to hang in
the car, since you travel so much. They are real handy. Or something
for the car. I don't know your size and it's really hard to buy shirts, or I
thought of a new robe. But I think you could get it better than I . . .

Well Darling I must say bye bye for now I've got to get a bite to eat.
I haven't eaten since breakfast some toast and coffee and now it's 7
P.M. So bye bye my little one. Be careful and drive slow. I'm so worried
about you. Merry Xmas and I'll write soon again.

Love

Mother

Reggie's appeals for money and sympathy seem to be directed toward
Billy's masculine traits. He is a traveler, where she is a homebody; he is
a wage-earner, she a dependent; he has a size and shape too different
from her own to be surmised. Notably, Billy is the *good* son in Reggie's
life, in contrast to that other one, Little Brother Bill. But Reggie almost
always reinstates Billy's feminine identity at the end of her letters, and
her memory of mothering Dorothy. "Hope Kitty and little boys O.K.
and they have a merry Xmas . . . I get your baby pictures out, and think
back to those years when I held you in my arms."

Reggie's last illness nearly blew Billy's cover. One day in the fall of
1971, the Tiptons' telephone rang and a voice with an Oklahoma twang
demanded to speak to somebody at that number named Dorothy. After
a bit of back and forth, whoever answered the telephone called Billy to
the phone. He was told by Aunt Cora that Reggie was gravely ill. Billy
said he would go immediately to her bedside. The source of this interesting story is Cousin Eilene.

Mother [Dorothy's Aunt Cora] never did accept Dorothy's passing, and never would call her Billy. Mother would always say, "Oh,
why does she have to keep this up?" When Reggie was sick with her

last illness, Mother went to Oklahoma City and found her needing care. Lynn had died a year earlier, and she was alone. Bill [Dorothy's brother] couldn't leave his work in Kansas City to look after her, and Reggie refused to go to stay in Bill's home.

Mother got fed up and very angry and decided to call Dorothy in Spokane. She dialed the number Dorothy had given her and asked for Dorothy Tipton. The woman who answered said, "Resting, can't be disturbed." Mother got riled up and said, "This is the number Dorothy gave for an emergency. Who are you?" The other person said she was his mother, and Cora said, "Well, I'm standing right in Dorothy's mother's house and I can tell you, you're not her mother!" So Dorothy was called to the phone.

Was it Carrie who answered the telephone and called herself Dorothy's mother? Did she keep this episode to herself? Kitty says she never heard about this phone call. The information came to light only after Carrie's death, but the story sounds plausible, and shows how permeable the boundaries between Dorothy and Billy had become once Billy Tipton had a permanent address, a listed telephone, and a big family.

Billy flew to Wichita, where Reggie was hospitalized, but it was Dorothy who stepped off the plane, a middle-aged woman in a pantsuit, having changed nothing but her role. At the hospital, it was Reggie's daughter who took her hand and wept and who embraced the brother she hadn't seen since he was a teenager with a trumpet in his hand. Dorothy was now fifty-six years old and Bill was going on fifty, but Reggie, seventy-five, was an enduring link between them. Dorothy and Little Brother said goodbye to her together. Dorothy alone was with Reggie when she died.

The obituary in the Wichita newspaper stated that Reggie's survivors included "two sons, W. T. Tipton, Blue Springs, Mo., and Dorsey L. Tipton, Spokane, Wash." Dorsey, not a name Billy Tipton ever used, was a family compromise, and only family members attended the small funeral. After a brief service, the mortician turned to what he thought were Reggie's sons and asked, "Will you boys help carry the casket?" Billy, shorter than Bill, struggled under the load. The memory of this sight still saddens the cousins, Madeline and Eilene, who were there with their own children and their mother, Cora. Billy placed a standing order with a florist to put flowers and greenery on Reggie's grave at Christmas and Mother's Day every year. "Dorothy did love her mother," said Eilene. That she wasn't acknowledged at the funeral as Reggie's daughter and couldn't grieve without hiding behind her disguise seemed to them a high price to pay. But was this sad for Billy? Hadn't she been the man in the family when the original Billie Tipton had left Reggie in the lurch? Hadn't she been the ongoing connection to the happiest time in Reggie's life? Hadn't she maybe been the kind of daughter that suited Reggie best, a piano-playing good-time girl?

The death of their mother did not bring about a renewal of comradeship between Dorothy and Bill. This disturbs him now, but at the time he shared the Tipton family outlook that it was "not right" for Dorothy to go about dressed as a man. Bill's wife, Doris, commented that Billy's look was not at all outlandish. "You could have taken her for a man or a woman. She had on slacks and a straight jacket — a leisure suit — and short hair, but lots of women have short hair." Bill contradicted this. "No, she was very mannish, masculine. I didn't condone it and still don't," he said. "I kind of admire her for what she pulled off, but at the same time I hate that she did it. It's not the normal run of life to do something like that. I believe she could have done better, broken it off at a later time and straightened up." But he understands what was at stake for her. "She was known all over the country. She'd have had to start completely over with her work, and her music was her life. I always say, 'That was Dorothy's life.'"

But Reggie's death did revive the close friendship Billy had shared with her two female cousins. Billy, Madeline, and Eilene now began writing regularly to one another. The cousins implored Billy to visit them in the Midwest, and in 1975 Billy found a way to accept their invitation. All three of Billy's sons were planning to attend a big week-long Boy Scout encampment in New Mexico during July, and parents were included. Billy told Kitty that he would drive her and the boys to camp, then continue on to Kansas, where something about his mother's estate required attention. Kitty was disappointed not to have the whole family together, but looking back, she said, "I now know why Billy opted not to stay with us. We were housed in tents. Billy would have had to go into men's washrooms, take showers — there were hundreds of scouters there, and these facilities were pretty open. I can just imagine him panicking at the thought. I can see now how he routed us around problems, but it never dawned on me at the time." Apparently she was kept in the dark about Billy's transactions with the

Tipton family too. She never met or spoke to Billy's brother until after Billy's death, and she never learned of the $5500 check Billy received for the sale of Reggie's house after her death or, later, of the $3300 Bill Tipton sent after selling a piece of property in Oklahoma City — property Dorothy had been given long ago by the aunt for whom she was named.

Billy's visit to Cousin Madeline's home in Wichita in July 1975 provided the occasion for a reunion. Four of Madeline's six children congregated in the family home, and Eilene came with her husband from their cattle ranch in Oklahoma. Dorothy was dressed, as always, in men's clothing. To prevent anybody from slipping up and calling their visitor Dorothy, they didn't gad about; mainly they cooked enormous meals and gossiped around the table. Madeline remembered that Dorothy "seemed perfectly at home with us, and giggled a lot, bubbling over all the time. She was happy, cheerful, the life of the party, quick to give a comic turn to people's sayings. All of my kids liked her — all of their lives they had known about her. And she loved talking about her own kids. She was crazy about them."

Madeline and Eilene had been itching with questions they didn't feel they could ask Dorothy in front of the men, so the cousins found a way to steal off for a slumber party. They talked about Dorothy's father, who was very ill. One of his legs had been amputated as a result of advanced diabetes, and he was not expected to live much longer. Dorothy had not seen G.W. since his marriage to his third wife, in the late 1930s, and had never met G.W.'s wife or the son of that marriage, her half-brother. "His family is ashamed of me and won't let me go and see my father," she said. They talked about her health worries too. "She said that she thought she needed to have a checkup, thought she might have emphysema," said Madeline. "Eilene and I wanted her to see a doctor right while she was visiting. We'd go get her a secondhand dress. You know, she'd never had a Pap smear, as women should." Eilene asked as tactfully as possible how Kitty fit into the picture, and Dorothy knew what she was getting at. "Kitty knows all about me," Dorothy told her, "but there's no hanky-panky. I have a room upstairs with the boys, she has her own room downstairs. I'm straight!" And how in the world did she handle the problem of using a public men's room? "She said, 'I never go if there isn't a door,'" Madeline recalled. And menstrual periods? "Okay, we asked about that!" Eilene laughed. "We asked for a lot of details. She said she had to manage it 'very, very carefully.' She had to

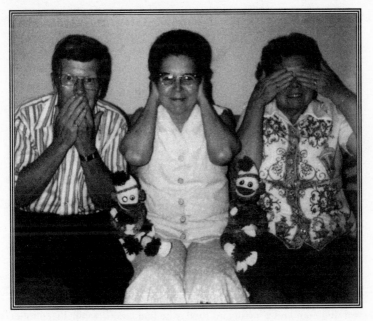

The Three Monkeys, 1975

be alert at all times. We asked her how it was going through the change of life and she said, 'Just like you, only I can't show it!' Oh, we asked questions! And she answered, and we all laughed about 'em."

Sometime during the weekend the cousins spent together, one of Madeline's daughters came by and snapped a photograph of them goofing off. Lined up on a sofa, Dorothy, Madeline, and Eilene panto-mimed the story of the three monkeys who speak no evil, hear no evil, see no evil. And indeed, Dorothy kept her own counsel where the cousins were concerned. She never confided that she had had fe-male sex partners prior to Kitty, women who had traveled with her as wives. The cousins were quite distressed by newspaper stories pub-lished after Billy's death that quoted Betty and Maryann's acknow-ledgment of sexual relationships with Billy. Eilene said, "I'm just a provincial farm woman. I can't even conceive of it." And Madeline concurred. "We thought she gave up everything in a normal woman's life, for her music."

You might say that it was duplicitous or cowardly of Dorothy to mislead these loyal, affectionate cousins. But you might also say that it was not merely pragmatic, it was generous-minded to spare them embarrassment over things that, as Oklahomans, they all might have considered nobody's damn business. Homosexuality carried a stigma even among the entertainers with whom Billy worked. How would it have affected the cousins' husbands to learn such news about this cousin by marriage, whose physical appearance and bohemian line of work already seemed so outlandish to a number of family members, including Dorothy's own brother? What would Madeline and Eilene have felt about it, deep down? Dorothy did not put their affection to any test greater than the discreet protection of her disguise, and she visited them only once. Yet with Reggie gone, Dorothy apparently needed to reaffirm these relationships with Madeline and Eilene, to preserve a sense of continuity with the otherwise invisible half of her split identity. The cousins provided an outlet for the expression of her womanhood, just as Reggie had done.

Back home in Spokane, Billy led another kind of double life, as a working man and a musician. By day he had an office job, like a lot of other dads, but after dinner and a nap and a shave, he turned into a glamorous entertainer right before his sons' eyes. "When he got dressed up to go out, put on the black silk suit and the butterfly tie, Billy would glow," said Kitty. "He so loved performing. He was always clowning around here at home too, putting on floppy hats, hats with earflaps, pulling funny voices to sing 'All I want for Christmas is my two front teeth.' He'd be playing a serious song and then just bust in on himself with a goofy routine." William remembered Billy playing a romantic song he'd written for Kitty, "Red Hair and Green Eyes," and teasing her, which tickled the boys. "Mom would sometimes get pissed off, and he'd play a funeral march — Da dada dah da da da da da da da-a. A game he played on her emotions." "And every now and then he'd ask me to do a dance," Kitty broke in. William continued, "Yes, Dad would be noodling at the piano, and when Mom walked down the hall he'd play the bump and grind. Mom hated that. Another thing he'd do: start playing 'Puff the Magic Dragon' and deliberately hit sour notes to get her attention. She'd yell at him, but it was a game. He'd play the piano all the time — lightning in his fingers!"

Billy Tipton's fifty-fifth (fifty-ninth) birthday, 1974

Kitty's photograph albums show how the family saw itself in the mid-1970s. "We were so *normal*," she marvels. Here's Billy in a barbecue apron, there's Billy and the kids with a pony, Billy driving the motor home, Billy on a camping trip with Scott and John's Boy Scout troop. The patrol leader recalls that Billy was on the Troop Committee and participated along with the other dads in camping trips, though "while the rest of us would be sleeping on the ground in tents, Billy would go camping in the motor home." Scads of photos show all three boys and both parents at scouting events, and Kitty's calendars indicate that she was active in major, ongoing volunteer work for which she was presented the Boy Scout Council's highest service award. There are photos of Scott and John as altar boys at Our Lady of Fatima Catholic

Church, and of William's First Communion. One shows Billy receiving a lacquered box with a collage of family photos and the legend "This Is Your Life, Billy Tipton," a joint project of Kitty and the boys for Father's Day 1975. A big glossy photograph shows William, age seven, being presented with a citation for a watercolor painting he made in school, which was selected from among three thousand entries to appear on the 1978 calendar of the Northwestern National Life Insurance Company. Also in the albums are many photos taken at Christmas. "The kids looked forward to picking out decorations for the Christmas tree every year," says Kitty. "Going to midnight mass, opening presents on Christmas morning — those were things we always did together. Even that last year, the Christmas before the family broke up, Billy clung to these traditions."

Why *did* the family break up? Kitty's short answer: "Billy was gutless." Living upstairs with the boys, Billy took sides with them against her, Kitty believed, forcing her into the role of disciplinarian. Somebody in the family had to lay down the law, but when the boys broke the rules, Billy wouldn't back her up. He babied them, protected them, lied for them. "Billy wouldn't let them grow up. Everything he did for them kept them from maturing into men — they couldn't develop their own strengths. Billy never wanted them to have to bear the consequences of their actions, never wanted them to be punished."

Most kids get in trouble, of course, but the older Tipton boys were double trouble. Nearly the same age, they were also a pair, a left and a right. Neighbors remember them in complementary terms: "X was the one we worried about; Y was the one who did things." "Y was the more immature; X was mature beyond his years." "Y was the kind kids would pick on; X would take exception." "X was never quite as devious as Y." John and Scott were described as neighborhood bullies, but teachers recall them as the reverse, "the kids that were always picked on." One of their classmates, looking back on their school-days together, commented that their reputation for badness may have been exaggerated. "They were the first to break the rules. But you have to bear in mind, the school we attended was right out of *Ozzie and Harriet!*" Maybe the problems were partly in the eyes of the be-holders.

During the later 1970s, Billy's arthritis worsened and he grew reluc-

Merry Christmas, 1977! Billy on the left, Kitty on the right

tant to play the piano. The Tiptons began having money troubles. Their comfortable way of life began to falter, and they gave up the lot at Deer Lake and the mobile home. Kitty went to work to help support the family. "The kids started needing braces, needing their eyes corrected. Two of them had to have eye surgery, and I had heavy back surgery. Like most agents and musicians, Billy didn't have a retirement plan, and we had to buy private medical coverage. The nest egg started to run low." Kitty took part-time jobs, aiming for work hours that coincided with the boys' schedules. John and Scott had paper routes and also helped out by minding William during the summer. Despite the atmosphere of cooperation, "little things started happening" that worried her, Kitty recalled. "We still had scouting together. Family life didn't come to a standstill, but John and Scott were doing badly in school. I couldn't put my finger on what was wrong."

Kitty's mother, Carrie, thought that the change in family life was a natural result of the boys' growing up, "a battle of boys going into their teens and playing one parent against the other. Kitty being the strong one, Tipton took the role of letting the kids get away with murder." But Carrie's judgment glides past the brutalizing episodes in Kitty's own experience of growing up, which would have made her the last woman in the world capable of mothering teenagers easily, even under the best of circumstances. During Kitty's own adolescence, one of her mother's boyfriends had pursued her sexually, and she had been raped at age fifteen by an older boy and then incarcerated as "incorrigible" when a pregnancy resulted. Along with a dislike of sex, she bore a bitter sense of having been ill used by the justice system. Now, in her early forties, she was faced with disciplining boys whose behavior brought to mind her worst experiences. Rigid, exacting, explosive, hypochondriac, worried about money, and really ill, she asserted her motherhood as control and called it discipline. And she asserted discipline by yelling.

Kitty's tirades were so loud they could be heard across the street through closed doors and windows. One of the children next door was afraid to be alone after school because of the violence of Kitty's explosions, audible across the narrow space between the houses, and always had a schoolmate stay with her until her working mother arrived home. Kitty seemed unaware of neighborhood disapproval and concern. Anyway, she could not contain her rage. Neighbors recall that she would rush from the house the minute Billy's car turned into the driveway and berate him for the behavior of his sons.

The last months of cohabitation with her sons, as Kitty tells the tale, were replete with betrayal by the men. One of the boys began getting into serious trouble with the law, using the other two as willing accomplices. The boy in trouble ran away, ran out of money, and called his father, and Billy helped him get back home. According to Kitty, most of this drama took place behind her back.

The family fell apart on a Saturday morning during the winter of 1980. The upper floor of the house was now the boys' territory, outfitted as an apartment with its own small kitchen, bath, and laundry room. The boys were responsible for the weekly cleaning. When Kitty went upstairs to check on their progress, she found Scott and John lounging around in the clutter. Now seventeen years old, they were both wiry young men, but to Kitty they were just bad boys. "I started yelling at them, and John and Scott came at me physically, Scott swinging with his fists. Little Billy screamed and ran into Billy's room. The cat leaped onto John's back. This distracted him. I grabbed Scott and got him off balance, shoved him down the stairs, grabbed John and threw him down. Both were dazed. I moved them down the stairs and out the door and locked it. I could see Billy sitting in his rocking chair in his room, just sitting there, with little Billy on his lap, saying nothing."

· 15 ·

Out and Down

≡≡≡

1980–1986

This has been my choice.
— Billy Tipton, conversation
with Madeline Byrd, 1983

IN 1962 Billy had pledged to be parted from Kitty only by death, but eighteen years later, the Kitty he had idealized was no more, and parenthood had divided his loyalties. Not that Billy didn't understand Kitty's rage. He knew about the emotional and physical violence that had formed her character, and recognized the source of the impetuous zeal with which she reacted to any threat, real or imagined. But Billy also remembered what it felt like to be a teenager abandoned by parents. He could not close ranks with Kitty against their children.

Nonetheless, he too had grown ineffectual in the role of parent. Ever since John and Scott had entered puberty, Billy had been vamping, just trying to get by. Billy had spent adolescence as a female, of course, in a household dominated by a strong woman, and her brother had been too young to help her now in understanding the adolescent male mentality. If she called upon her own memories, she probably identified with the boys' rebelliousness and the example of her father's abdication. After age twelve, Billy had never undergone a father's moral scrutiny or profited from a father's encouragement or a brother's proximity. Moreover, Billy hated conflict. Her entire disposition was at odds with the project of turning these rowdy seventeen-year-old sons into solid citizens.

So in 1980 Billy stepped down from the middle class and took the boys with him, retreating to the outskirts of town and to a way of life he had never shared with Kitty. For practical help, he turned first to Dave

Sobol. "Billy came by the morning after the fight and told me all about it," Sobol remembered. "Told me she didn't throw him out, she threw out the kids, two of them. I said, 'Where'd you sleep last night?' He said, 'A motel.' I put my jacket on and we went out to a mobile home place. Found a nice used one. I laid out eight thousand bucks. He fixed himself a nice place to live with the two kids. And he paid me back, over time." The Tiptons hauled their new home to a trailer court in the Spokane Valley, near where Sobol had relocated the agency. Billy had one of the tiny bedrooms, John the other, and Scott slept in the living room on a daybed. John and Scott were seventeen when they moved with Billy from picture-perfect Manito Boulevard, on the South Hill of the city, to Park Road, in the unzoned commercial sprawl of the Spokane Valley — just the age Dorothy had been when she left Aunt Bess's fancy home in Kansas City for the cramped quarters she shared with Reggie in Oklahoma City. The boys enrolled in a new high school, and they settled into new routines without much interference from Billy.

William was left behind with Kitty in the big house on Manito, with the whole upper floor to himself. Only ten years old, he had been kept out of earshot after the scene he witnessed from the safety of his father's lap. In his memory, the family explosion blends with the sudden eruption of Mount Saint Helens that same spring, when falling ash darkened the sky and disrupted all normal activity in Spokane for days. "Nobody could explain to me what had happened. One day I had a family. The next day it was gone," he said. As soon as school was out, Kitty, who was working in an office full-time now, sent him to join the Valley menage, where the older boys could look after him.

At first the all-male household felt like a summer camp. Billy was already an expert at living in close quarters with a lot of guys, and now he took up cooking, calling Carrie every day for tips. William recalled the enthusiasm Billy brought to his new role: "He got recipes from my grandmother and became a good cook — such as meat loaf, other ordinary things like spaghetti. Back home, his favorite food was chocolate pudding. But when we moved out, he gave up a lot of his habits, and that was one of them. He bought desserts, and he liked to make rice with sugar and milk. He even baked cakes on our birthdays. Nothing fancy, but he would slap something together, to celebrate. When he wasn't into cooking, we'd go out to Kentucky Fried Chicken or Chinese restaurants. We'd order chow mein, because there'd be a lot of stuff on the plate and we could split a meal."

As a homemaker, Billy made himself into a fairly good substitute for Kitty, but he remained passive in every other way, offering the children no guidance. In William's mind, that summer marks the end of childhood. "I missed my mother," he said. "Growing up, she was loving, energetic, protective. If somebody tried to accuse us, she'd defend us. All three of us. She was the power source, the drive in the family." Kitty had been attentive to William's education, signing him up for music lessons and art classes and supervising his homework. Billy had never involved himself with the kids' schooling and didn't do so now. Nor did he impose any house rules on them. William recalled that as soon as Billy left for work in the morning, "Scott would crank up the stereo. Then they'd jump in their cars. I'd come home in the middle of the afternoon and find everybody running around nude. Usually I spent the day alone. Got more and more into smoking marijuana. My brothers would supply me — I'd do things for them. I'd sit at home by myself and get wasted. Dad knew I was drinking with my brothers too, but he didn't see that there was a lot he could do. His usual response was to throw up his hands and say, 'Oh God, why me?'"

Why was Billy, who had been such a good manager of his band, so lackadaisical about managing his boys? Partly, it seems, he worked hardest at looking good, pleasing people, and motivating his sidemen. His business practices were geared to acquiring and fulfilling contracts, not to being pushy or demanding. When others were pushy or demanding, he was not good at standing up for himself, and his sons, it appears, intimidated him. William recalls him as "skittish and apprehensive" around them. The lifelong traits of avoidance that had handicapped Billy's work life now disabled his home life. He would grin and bear it. Carrie recalled that Billy used to call her every morning from his office to complain. "I was a sounding board for his problems," she said. "But he didn't want to *do* anything about them, just wanted to keep the boys wrapped in cotton. I would tell him, 'You've got to stand up on your two legs and say no to them!' That wasn't much help, I guess." William said, "Dad wanted our love any way he could get it. He was just too nice."

Over the next twelve months, Kitty saw no signs of improvement in the boys' behavior. Billy, buying time, hoping the kids might just grow out of their rebellious phase and permit the family to reunite, offered soothing reassurances. "I'll try harder. You're right, I know you're right," he would tell her. A pair of catastrophes during the spring of 1981 wrote an end to this standoff. In March, Kitty's car was rear-ended. The accident severed a nerve in her back and left her lame, so that she had to wear a brace on her left leg in order to stand upright. Her recovery was slow, and she needed help getting around, since she was confined to a walker. Her situation might have led to a reconciliation with Billy, who was too softhearted to leave her without support — he might have returned with William, leaving the older boys on their own — but in June, John was involved in a spectacular motorcycle accident that broke both his legs and ended his high school education. Billy spent much of each day and evening at the hospital for six weeks, in anguish over John's pain and worried that he would lose the use of his legs. The coincidence of these accidents spurred Billy, once again unwillingly, to choose between people who needed him. He chose his sons, and Kitty asked for a divorce. Kitty says that she left the details to Billy and their lawyer. She recalls that the divorce was final in September 1982, though she cannot find her copies of the papers. (No documents were ever filed officially, and the lawyer is dead.) Two years later, in June 1984, Kitty remarried.

With his tiny residence occupied by a pack of large, surly children, Billy made the office his refuge. The Dave Sobol Theatrical Agency now occupied shabby offices in a converted two-bedroom home in the Spokane Valley, quite a comedown from the days at the grand Davenport Hotel, when the agency had handled over a thousand acts and seventeen cruise lines and booked entertainers in thirty states. The shag-carpeted front office where Dave held court had formerly been a small living room, and Billy and the two other agents, who handled the rock music Billy wouldn't touch, had cramped offices that were formerly bedrooms. The location was good, though, on an arterial road that linked Spokane with the Idaho state line. Idaho had lenient liquor and gambling laws, and entertainers passing back and forth across the state line would drop by the office for a cup of coffee and be served up Billy's Satchmo impersonation — "Well, hellooo, Dolly" — along with his joke of the day. One of his friends said that Billy could build up to a puny punchline with a narrative that became a full-scale theatrical event lasting fifteen minutes. If Billy wasn't schmoozing over coffee, he was on the phone, often to members of bands he had booked who had retired or taken other jobs. Billy was a one-man repository of their mutual past and a shrewd collector of information about the business, such as it was. His closest friends observed that he seemed content with his life those days, just keeping up his connections.

One of the people who dropped by the office whenever she was in town was Billy's former wife Maryann. Now a widow living in a mobile home in Portland with two dogs, Maryann had a pension, owned a nice car, and liked to visit her old friends in Spokane. Billy counted as an old friend. At the time of their separation, Billy, remorseful at leaving her unhappy and financially strapped, had agreed to pay for Maryann's training as a practical nurse. "I stayed mad till I started going to school," she said. Several years later she ran into Billy while he was visiting Kitty in the hospital. Maryann said she took an ex-wife's pleasure in going out for coffee with Billy while his current wife lay groaning in a hospital bed, suffering from ulcers. They continued to stay in touch after Maryann married a railroad man and moved to Oregon.

When John had his motorcycle accident, Billy turned to Maryann for medical advice, worried about how much pain medication John was taking. Maryann visited Billy and the boys several times during the summer of 1981, bringing home-cooked food for all of them and treats for John. William recalled that it came as quite a shock to meet one of Billy's ex-wives: "He'd never even mentioned her before!"

By 1982, Maryann and Billy were regularly on the phone with each other. In letters, Maryann said she was contemplating a move back to Spokane. She hated the weather in Portland and was lonesome for her friends. Maybe she could bring her mobile home up from Portland and park it near Billy's? "I would want grass around it for my babes" — her two Pomeranians — she wrote in June. "We have a lot to talk over . . . Will wait to hear from you."

Maryann drove up to Spokane at the beginning of June 1983 and spent a week with Billy and the boys. Back in Portland, she wrote Billy a letter reflecting on some of the issues raised by her visit: "I couldn't take the kids fighting all the time. It's as I told you, if I moved to Spokane I would have my own place. Even if it weren't the boys it would be that way with Kitty there. I realize they'll always come home at times . . . I hate living alone. Sometimes I get so depressed I cry. I'm not saying I couldn't be happy with you. I'm sure I could if we both worked real hard at it. It would be a different love. You can never take back a yesterday."

In August she made another visit. Billy met her literally halfway, taking the Greyhound to Pasco and driving with her and the dogs to Spokane, which gave them several hours on the road, as in the old days. Maryann remembered that they had fun together, and Billy seemed happy to be with her. When they took a break and wandered into a shopping mall, they found a piano on display, and Billy played for her. His fingers were stiff with arthritis, but his voice was still strong and sweet. After her return to Portland, Maryann wrote warmly, "You know honey I finally figured out that of all the people you really needed me the most."

Billy agreed, and he began to press the issue of living together. As Maryann explained later, she felt very cautious about making a home with Billy again as long as the boys were with him. "Billy and I would come back to the trailer and find those boys having a knock-down drag-out. Billy would say, 'We'll wait out here till they're through.' See, he acted helpless, as if he couldn't get into his own house! After being on my own for a while, who the heck needs teenage boys that hate each other?" There was another issue too. Billy was still wearing his wedding ring — on his pinkie now, but she thought this indication of his attachment to Kitty promised trouble for any new woman in his life. Or any older woman, for that matter. So they didn't reach any decisions, just let the matter hang between them.

What did Billy want from Maryann? Possibly, at nearly seventy, he was ready for the comfort he had walked away from when he was approaching fifty. Maryann's skills as a nurse and her access to medications may have been important, for Billy was increasingly concerned about his ulcer and his shortness of breath. But Maryann was also a good companion. She had not lost her sense of humor or her trim figure, and Billy liked the way she cooked. She cheered him up. He even seemed to like the way she nagged him. He stayed in touch.

In late 1982, after forty years as a booking agent, Dave Sobol decided to retire, hand over the agency to Billy, and move to Arizona. Though business had declined, Dave was still booking acts for conventions and cruises, Mike Cavender was still handling the rock groups, and Billy

Billy at the Dave Sobol Entertainment Agency, circa 1986

was making about $10,000 a year booking bands. Dave thought the agency was in reasonably good shape, but he was tired of it. "I said to Billy, 'You pay the rent and send me $125 a month for use of the office equipment. As long as you've got the place and you've got the equipment, you're home free.' We shook hands and went to an attorney to draw up the papers and that was the end of that," Dave said. "I knew he didn't have any money. Billy never had a dime from the first day I saw him, spent everything he made. But I always liked Billy. He was good to me. I wanted to leave him something."

Dave's surprising gift recharged Billy's batteries. He moved proudly into the front office and took over Dave's big leather chair, and he renamed the business the Dave Sobol Entertainment Agency, dropping the old-fashioned "Theatrical." He needed the Sobol name for continuity, but he wanted to promote a youth-oriented image. "Most people want the bands that play the music of the past, but they don't want old people playing it. They want young people playing it," he told a journalist. "We give them what they want. That's the name of the game." Billy too had a game. The photograph accompanying this interview was a stunt postcard made up for the Billy Tipton Trio, in which Billy points to a mocked-up television broadcast of the trio's comic routine "Goofus." The card had been produced as long before as 1958, when Billy was forty-four going on thirty-nine, whereas now Billy was sixty-eight. Cousin Eilene, congratulating him on the new venture, hinted that it might be time for *Billy* to retire, but he replied that he wouldn't know what to do with himself if he wasn't working.

During the mid-1960s, Billy's client list held around two hundred names, but by 1984 it had dwindled to fewer than twenty. To build up the business, he hoped to attract local acts that could profit from the savvy he had gained in his long career as a nightclub entertainer. "My satisfaction is taking young unmarketable musicians and working with them so they are marketable," he had said to an interviewer back when he had been handling only musicians. In his new role, Billy shamelessly dropped the names of headliners from his days on tour, ranking himself with stars such as Patti Page, Jimmy Durante, and Rosemary Clooney, who had played the dinner theaters of Reno and Lake Tahoe while his trio was off in the cocktail lounges. But he lived up to his ambition. Once he signed up an entertainer, he would work closely with that person until the act met his standards. One such recruit was a young magician who called himself Barron Stringfellow. "I'll never forget the day I auditioned with Billy," Stringfellow recalled.

> I did the floating dollar bill. Billy closed the door and ripped me up — he'd spotted the string. Said he'd worked with great magicians such as Dell O'Dell and Mandrake. He had seen what they were doing from the back, and recognized all my tricks. "Kid, you have to create an air of mystery," he said. "Remember, you are doing the act all the time, on stage and off. You've got to live the part, you've got to *wear* it."
>
> Billy kept a notebook with jottings about the acts he booked. He'd often drop in to a club where one of his acts was playing a show, watch the show from the back. Wouldn't let you know he was coming. Later you'd hear from him about how it went. Always encouraging, but he let you know what the standards were. The things he knew!

Most of the artists Billy booked were making a living at something other than their art. A guitarist and keyboard player named Mike Brandon was typical. He had started a band called the Sidelines, to make the point that music was an avocation but a serious one. As he remembered, "The day I first contacted Billy, I said, 'Guess what, me and my brother have a band.' He said, 'You and everybody else's brother!' He agreed to book me once. A wedding, as I recall. I came in the following Monday to pay his commission, and he told me nobody had complained, so he took us on. With Billy booking us, we became the most-heard least-known band in Spokane! We played conventions and corporate parties and probably five hundred weddings. There are not too many people living in Spokane who haven't danced to my music — they just don't know it."

Brandon recalled that he and Billy hit it off right away, mainly because he loved to get Billy talking about the old days on the road with his bands.

A conversation with Billy when I dropped by the agency to pay my commission usually lasted over an hour. He was genuinely interested in what you had to say. He'd ask about how things had gone, and what you'd say would remind him of one of his stories. We shared a lot that was fairly personal — music, to me, is very personal.

I got so much enjoyment out of him telling me how he learned to play Latin music, or how he learned to play Chicago blues. All the musicians that had legitimate engagements throughout the community would meet at an after-hours club after their own shows, and that's where the music would really take place. You'd have all of these different influences coming together. He'd learned those rhythms and progressions from whence they came. He'd go into an after-hours club in El Paso and find the music entirely different from what he would find in Chicago, for example. In the middle of the 1980s, I was in the music business fighting the inevitable emergence of disco. I could never understand in my own mind why somebody would want to go out to a club and listen to *recorded* music.

By the summer of 1984, after managing the agency for a year and a half, Billy was deeply in debt. Brandon recalled that he seemed to be thrown by the logistics of managing his life and that he "always seemed to have some current crisis with a water pump that wasn't working or an incidental expense he couldn't handle." John and Scott had turned twenty-one, but Billy was still paying their bills and occasionally bailing them out of expensive kinds of trouble. Their grandmother Carrie, who was in close touch with Billy, said that "the boys took advantage of his good nature. Both were constantly running up debts that Billy would end up paying to protect his own credit." Billy's business records show a steady trickle of checks written to John and Scott, marked "loan" and "draw," while deposits dwindled. Commissions for the second quarter of 1984 averaged only $450 per month, against monthly office expenses of about $600.

Most of Billy's financial difficulties stemmed from an unwillingness to collect commissions from the bands he booked. Working alongside Sobol all those years, Billy may have produced commissions partly in order to please the boss. It appears in retrospect that for Billy, even an office was a stage. He needed an audience in order to perform; he wanted admiration and applause as much as he wanted an income from the role. From his clients he got applause only for playing the good guy. As a business attitude, this was disastrous. News got around that Billy was a soft touch for any kind of hard-luck story.

Marv Richter, the drummer who had worked with Billy until the trio was disbanded, explained how the musicians manipulated Billy.

> A group would be booked for a few days in one venue. Billy's commission should have been mailed to the agency on the next work day following the group's departure. But the group would need travel money to get to the next venue. They'd call and ask to keep Billy's fee as a loan. Billy might advance the group their fee, only to discover that the group never made the next engagement and so didn't owe a fee and didn't have money to repay the loan! If the acts didn't show, Billy would be out. Many of them were kids, somewhat irresponsible, unaccountable. Like all his friends, I was aware that he was having financial difficulties, but he didn't put that burden on anybody else — he was going to take care of things as best he could. I guess you could call him a man who had a motherly instinct. He was very concerned about *his* people. I tell you, the thousands of dollars that man let go out of concern about other people!

Mike Brandon added, "Billy knew absolutely every dime that everybody owed him. But he was so generous, so nice, so amiable, so nonconfrontational, he allowed people to take advantage of him. He earned money that he knew about but that he never got paid." "Oh well, it's only money" was Billy's refrain.

Floundering in unpaid bills and facing bankruptcy, he got a bright idea. Why should he not sell the agency to Mike Brandon, who was already a businessman, and return to working on commission? Billy talked it over with Dave Sobol. As Sobol remembered, "I said, Go ahead, it's yours, you can do what you want with it." Brandon was surprised, but the idea appealed to him. "I was kind of looking for something else. I guess it was part humanitarian and part capitalist. I saw an opportunity there to make some money. So we sat down and agreed on a price."

Looking over the accounts, Brandon thought he could see a way to shape things up. "I got a bad-debt list and went after the deadbeats with a collection agency. When Billy owned the agency, the business account was pretty much his personal account. The business account on any given day would have eighty dollars in it. I managed to get it up to about a thousand, so we could cash checks for people, that sort of thing. Working together, I thought we might bring in fifty grand. Actually, I don't think we ever made more than thirty-five grand. It was a pretty sleepy little store."

Selling the business did not put Billy on his feet, Brandon said. "Billy paid off a few of his debts and a few of his kids' debts. He reduced his expenses as much as he could, to live. For a few days he was caught up, but in a relatively short time he was back where he started. Only now *I* owned the business." Brandon pressured Billy to claim the social security benefits to which he was entitled.

> At the point where I bought the agency and got involved in his finances, I asked him about Medicare, social security, and the answers were always vague — he didn't want to, he didn't like to. Then at one point he told me that although he had a social security number, he had lied about his age when he got the card so he didn't really want to make any claims for social security because he was afraid it might get discovered. He said he had wanted to go to work and had needed the card and so had lied about it.
>
> My concern was his security. I knew that as soon as he left the business, the business would go away — there wasn't enough money to hire somebody to replace him. The selfish side of me wanted to keep him going to keep the business going. But I sincerely cared about him and really and truly did want things to be better for him. We went through the exercise of trying to get him to submit a claim on social security, but he absolutely refused, it was nothing doing.

Despite these problems, Billy's home life did improve. By 1985, John and Scott, now twenty-two, had moved into their own apartments. The trailer seemed roomy. William, who was sixteen, wanted a dog, which suited Billy just fine, and a black Labrador puppy joined the household at Christmas. They named her Sam — why not! — and the three of them settled into what William called "an unvarying routine," which it gave him great pleasure to recall, because of its ordinariness.

On a normal day Dad would wake up at 5 or 6 A.M., 7 on weekends. He'd get ready for work, drink coffee, and eat cornflakes — he switched from Wheaties to cornflakes when we moved to the valley. Dad worked nine to five, then he'd go to the grocery store. Every single night he'd buy five or six dollars' worth of dinner, usually a TV dinner for each of us. When he got home, I'd fix us a glass of iced tea and we'd drink that every night, summer or winter. Then he'd sit and do crosswords before cooking dinner. Later he'd go to his bed and watch TV, game shows — *Jeopardy, Wheel of Fortune* — or read a book. He loved Louis L'Amour. In bed by ten. Every morning when he woke me to go to school, he'd put black coffee and juice by my bed.

Weekends we would clean up. He'd do the laundry. Usually we went out to dinner on weekends, or to movies. Sundays were kind of neat. Early in the morning he'd take the Sunday paper and the dog out onto the patio and eat doughnuts and drink coffee. Sun shining, the sprinkler on the grass.

During that peaceful time together, Billy began making William his emotional heir. He had already made him his sole legal heir by updating his will when Sobol turned over the agency to him. After John and Scott had reached legal age, William was Billy's only dependent. But it was not until the older boys left home that Billy formed close ties with his youngest son. He had been casually teaching William to play keyboard and bass for the past several years, but now they sometimes went down to Billy's office, where he kept a piano, and jammed. It was Billy's only indulgence in playing music by then. "He had arthritis so bad that he wouldn't play for anybody but me," William said. "He'd start to play, then he'd stop and massage his hands or hit himself on the head and say, 'Oh, you dummy!' Get very disgusted with himself. He literally started to forget the music. One day he slammed the cover so hard he split the wooden casing. After jamming, he'd say, 'I don't have it anymore — my hands are gone.' But it wasn't true. Only the fun had gone out of it."

Loss of memory, loss of dexterity — the normal curses of aging — prompted Billy, now seventy, to pass on other legacies to his son. "Every day we lived together we'd sit and talk and talk and talk," William said. "He was interested in me, and I was interested in him. We got a lot closer than we had been before. Not only father and son — we got to be good buddies. He told me stories about his time on the road. About the Depression, the Oklahoma Dust Bowl, World War II, the forties, his travels all over the U.S.A. and Canada. To think about my dad's show business stuff blows me away now! Of course, later I found out that some of his stories were actually about his brother's life — being in the air force, for example."

William apparently was the one person in Billy's day-to-day life who paid close attention to the person across the table from him. Of all the people who shared their memories, William alone was able to summon details about Billy's habits and preferences and routines, his quirks and apprehensions — to convey what it felt like to share Billy's life within the complex blend of intimacy and privacy that a household provides. Perhaps Billy chose the women with whom he was intimate partly because they were not interested in paying the kind of attention that William paid to Billy. But of course Billy had not chosen William shrewdly, as he had chosen the women in his life. He rose to the opportunity presented by William's needs and William's love.

This peaceful home life ended abruptly, however, in the winter of 1986, when William was seventeen. "Because of my abundant drug habits, we stopped doing things together," William said. "Now I know that was a mistake, but at the time I was enjoying myself. But I started having mood changes, hanging out with 'stoners.'" William admitted that using drugs led to exciting criminal behavior that he wanted to conceal from his father. He secretly arranged to rent an apartment, and one day just walked out on Billy. "Not a pretty picture. Dad was hurt and wondered why I was so distant. And I felt bad about moving out. I was his lifetime companion." Billy of course drew back from opposing his son's wishes or intervening in his self-destructive way of life. That was Billy's character.

Yet, to look ahead, during Billy's last illness, it was William who cared for him as tenderly as a nurse, and it was William, arguably, who suffered most from the postmortem disclosure of Billy's sex. "The night before he died," William said, "I came to his place after my job as a dishwasher and prep cook. I worked at night. Got off at 1 A.M., drove his car home — I'd wrecked my car. Checked on him and found him asleep. I stood in his doorway for a while. I knew he was dying, I was just waiting for it to happen. I was working on a song for him, on a bass guitar." William paused. "Now I feel that though I knew him for eighteen years, I never knew him at all."

William was bound to feel that way. Yet in spite of the fact that a young person's sense of intimacy with a parent is almost always partly a delusion, there is no doubt that the emotional bond between William and Billy had a firm base of mutuality.

During the last eighteen months they lived together, Billy gave deeply of himself to William, and the content of what he gave perhaps offers an important insight into the character produced by this long impersonation. It shows us what Billy thought a son needed from a father. For William's sake, Billy produced an idealized image of masculinity made up of elements from the character of other Billy Tiptons she had studied and loved, namely, her father the aviator and her brother the soldier. They made a lineage worth passing on to their namesake, who would never know them in person. Despite the falsehoods imposed by her disguise, Billy had risen to the challenge of this relationship by paying attention, and was repaid by the surest sign of love, revealed in William's simple declaration, "I was interested in him."

· 16 ·

The End

1986–1989

> I always wondered why Billy was stuck in Spokane. He
> was a star — well, he could have been a star.
> — Barron Stringfellow, 1997

BACK IN NOVEMBER 1984, when Mike Brandon bought the Sobol
agency from Billy, the two of them spent a couple of days reorganizing
the office, which was still cluttered by cardboard boxes of files that had
not been unpacked since Dave had moved out to the valley from the
Davenport Hotel. "I'm talking about things like contracts from 1953!"
said Brandon. "We went through every box, categorized everything,
pruned it by about ninety percent. It was interesting to see some of the
names on those contracts. Sammy Davis, Jr., before he was famous,
had been one of Dave's acts — just one example. Of course, Billy knew
the inside story on everybody."

Billy also used the office to store personal papers and trophies of his
life in show business. These included two saxophones, one alto and
one soprano, the fishhorn he'd used in the act where he played piano
with his left hand, standing up, accompanying himself on the sax, and
a ukulele and a banjo. Uniforms from the days of the Billy Tipton Trio
hung on the clothes pole, still in plastic bags from the last round of
cleaning and pressing, and in covered boxes were the bow ties and
handkerchiefs and jewelry he had worn onstage, as well as an array of
cufflinks and tieclasps with piano motifs. Stacked in piles were the
leatherbound scrapbooks from his years on the road, and various fake
books, the musician's reference work of words and chords for popular
songs. Audiotapes of air checks from radio performances were stowed
in cardboard boxes, along with copies of the trio's recordings. Other

boxes held his sheet music, his joke books, his handwritten routines, and glossies of various Billy Tipton Trios. One photograph was a personal favorite, judging from the multiple copies in the files: a photograph of Billy, retouched to eliminate facial wrinkles, alone at the piano in black tie, wearing his diamond ring.

The closet also held a shrine to Kitty, the final trophy of Billy's career. In a filing cabinet lay a brown paper bag full of her marvelous red hair, cut off the year they became engaged, and a stack of the love letters he had written, which she had discarded and he had retrieved. He kept the copies of Kitty's publicity photographs that were on file in the Sobol agency: Kitty as a fan dancer, Kitty as an exotic in pasties. But he had also filched photographs from Kitty's own portfolio, including two topless shots that showed the mantle of freckles across her shoulders and the beautiful lift of her breasts. These mementos of their romance were locked in a drawer, but in a corner of the closet lay another relic: a dented hubcap from the Dodge Barracuda that Billy bought for Kitty at Christmas in 1966. William found it while cleaning the office for Billy and observed that it had been recently polished. "Dad was so sentimental it wasn't funny! He held Mom up like some kind of prize," he noted. Billy kept no photographs of his other wives, except in a few group snapshots pasted into the scrapbooks. In his filing cabinet he kept letters from his mother and from his cousins, and the few mementos of family life in Oklahoma City that had managed to survive the itinerant life he'd led since leaving home.

This closet and these file drawers, safe-deposit boxes for Billy's memory, were private. Billy was not garrulous about his past, and as much as possible he still surrounded himself with young people, welcoming any visitors that dropped by and keeping them in their chairs by continually filling their coffee cups as they chatted. Billy would chew Tums, for his ulcer.

By the end of 1986, Billy was again on his own in the office. After a year and three months in the booking business, Mike Brandon stopped fighting the inevitable and became the manager of a stereo store. Though he remained the agency's owner, his only involvement was to pay the bills and make the increasingly slim bank deposits, work he could accomplish in an hour's visit to the office once a week.

With Brandon out of the office, Billy was more than ever eager for visits from the young musicians he booked. One favorite was a guitar player named Doug Brock, who had been Billy's client since the mid-1970s. They shared a down-home connection, since Brock's father had been a friend of the country swing musician Bob Wills. "My dad had Bob Wills out to the house when the Wills band was in New Mexico and needed a place to practice," Brock said. "I started playing music myself as a consequence. At age thirteen I bought my first guitar, from Sears, Roebuck. When I first played music, it was country swing." For Doug Brock, Billy was the embodiment of a vanished era in the music business, and Brock enjoyed gassing with him.

He had a huge office chair he'd hop into, put his feet up on the desk, lean back with arms akimbo behind his head, and talk for hours. Billy liked to talk. He was electric, always jolly, enjoyable to talk to. He was an unusual agent — go to bat for you in a minute if you needed it. One time he sent me to Canada to replace a musician named Billy Allen. The owner of the place was expecting another Billy Allen type. He told me, "This is Tipton's mess-up." He got on the phone with Billy, and after a short conversation, the guy paid me for a week's work plus expenses, even though he wouldn't let me play — said the customers would not be satisfied. Billy was awfully good on the phone, in looking after the musicians' interests.

I remember another time I had a job in Montana. A massive snowstorm stranded me in Lincoln, on the way to Shelby. I went to a bar and called Billy, told him I was snowed in. He said, "Stay where you are and call me back in a few minutes." Pretty soon I called back and he said, "You're playing in that bar tonight. The band they're expecting is snowed in too — in Shelby!" We just traded places.

My strongest memory of Billy's appearance was how big the clothes were: big baggy white shirt, baggy suit with a wide jacket. He had plenty of advice about how my band should dress. Thought we should cut our hair. Told me, "I used to have long hair, but I didn't get any work until I cut it."

After Billy's death, Brock realized that Billy's crack about the haircut had been a joke. "It occurred to me that Billy Tipton should have gotten an Academy Award as the best actor of all time," Brock said.

While Mike Brandon was active in the business, he hoped to get Billy involved again in playing music. A fancy new motel had opened up out on the highway to the airport and had installed a grand piano in its cocktail lounge. Billy was excited about the piano, and Mike thought that might mean he would agree to play it.

I told him, "Here, the Ramada has a very quiet little lounge, nice clientele and so on, just go out there and sit down." They wanted dinner music from six to nine. He could be back home in bed by nine-thirty.

Billy absolutely refused, would not play in public. I finally realized that if he couldn't perform at his peak, he wouldn't perform at all. His fingers didn't have the mobility, the strength anymore. Performance was a real issue to him. Not just how does your music sound, but how do you look, how do you present yourself as a whole package. He was not in his prime physically, from an appearance perspective. I heard him play a little bit on that piano and on our piano at home, and he could easily have played in public, no problem at all. But he was very, very proud, and it was important to him that he be able to present the whole thing as well as he could. So nope, he wouldn't.

Billy kept in touch by phone with the musicians he had handled, whether or not they were still active. Younger show people were the beneficiaries. Though business was slow, Billy decided to put another man in charge of booking acts while he continued to look after the musicians. He asked the magician Barron Stringfellow to take it on. Billy liked to give Stringfellow advice, and Stringfellow rather enjoyed being mothered by Billy. "Yes," he remembered, laughing, "his own kids had more or less deserted him — the acts he had left *were* his kids! Mike Brandon, for example. Billy was really proud of him. Mike was working a day job, but he had one of the hottest bands around, a show band, working weddings and so on. But I hated to see the way a lot of the other guys were treating Billy. When I went through the books, I saw that Billy hadn't been collecting commissions, yet his bread and butter was the bands. Everyone *else* was number one."

Stringfellow worked in the afternoon, then changed into perform-ance clothes before leaving the office. If Billy was going out, they shaved together. "He preferred to use that bathroom rather than at his trailer," said Stringfellow. "It had a beautiful entertainer's mirror, with good lighting. We shaved side by side." Billy was full of stories about his days on the road, explaining how, in many a bar, he had often had to dress in a men's room where there was hardly room to turn around and where the entertainers could be walked in on at any time. "He gave me advice about stress: if you're an entertainer, the only way to reduce stress is get out of show business. But Billy never showed any stress. He would have iron-clad explanations for anything he did. I think he got away with all of it because of his air of confidence. 'Study the greats, like Mandrake,' he told me. 'You should see that man's *poise,* Barron!' Little did I know I was watching the greatest magic trick of all."

Billy was good at keeping up appearances, as Mike Brandon recalled. "He didn't have fancy clothes or new clothes, but the collars were pressed and everything tucked in, square with the world. That was true until the day he died. No, he didn't look like a poor man." But Billy's appearance was changing in those years. Photographs show that as he aged and his body weight declined and his hair thinned and his skin lost its collagen, Billy began looking less masculine. Doug Brock recalled that "a lot of the musicians called Billy 'that little old lady.' My band members would stay in the car when I went to give Billy the commission — they thought it was weird. Billy did look like a woman. Broad in the behind, with a hairless face and a wrinkle pattern you wouldn't see on a man. That and the high voice, and the small size. In my view, it didn't matter." Nor did noticing these physical characteristics permit Brock to realize that Billy *was* a little old lady.

But they did strike someone else as evidence that Billy was a passing woman, namely, Mike Brandon's wife, Joann. Shortly after Mike bought the Sobol agency, they ran into Billy at an auto show for which the agency had booked entertainment. Joann had been hearing about Billy for years from Mike, but when she looked at Billy, "My take was, that's a *dyke!*" Joann was a nurse, observant about people. Moreover, as she explained, she had grown up in Los Angeles and worked in Hollywood for a while before her marriage, so Billy was a social type she thought she recognized. But as her relationship to Billy developed, the insight faded. "My relationship to Billy was a relationship to a man," she said. "Even though I saw him as the caregiver in the family, certainly with William, his mannerisms, his way of interacting with me and others, were all those of a man."

Joann discussed her surmise with Mike, and he dismissed it.

When we first heard the news, after Billy's death, my wife said, "What did I tell you?" I wasn't shocked, exactly — more like sur-

KIN

DEATH DISCLOSES BILLY TIPTON'S STRANGE SECRET: HE WAS A SHE

From the 1950s, when the fair-haired, baby-faced Tipton, above, center, led a jazz trio, to her final years, right, no one saw through her sexual masquerade.

To his fans in Spokane, Wash., Billy Tipton was a jazzman extraordinaire, a gifted pianist and saxophonist who had played with such luminaries as Jack Teagarden and Russ Carlyle before forming his own popular trio in the 1950s. To friends and neighbors he was a true family man, a loving husband and devoted father of three adopted sons. "A perfect gentleman" is how Dave Sobol, his longtime friend and agent, remembers him. But after the aged and ailing Tipton died at home late last month of bleeding ulcers, he was found to be not quite the perfect gentleman. In fact, he was a woman.

The revelation left Tipton's children both bereaved and, to put it mildly, bewildered. Neither Jon Clark, 26, nor his brothers, Scott, also 26, and Billy Jr., 19, had ever suspected their father was female. The news also stunned most residents of the quiet northwestern city. "I couldn't sleep for two days," says Sobol. "For 40 years I knew Billy as a man, and now he's a woman." Meantime, the one woman who could shed light on the mystery—Kitty Oakes, 60ish, the woman Tip-

The elderly Billy with a saxophone

prised, and it did answer some questions. Then I felt kind of as though something had been taken away from me, because of all the conversations Billy and I had shared. Here, obviously, was an aspect of his life that he felt very strongly about. It was as though he'd had some religious beliefs I never found out about. We'd talked about religion, we'd talked about politics, we talked in depth about music, about morality, all kinds of things. Why not this? Was he threatened by me, or did he feel I couldn't handle it? Or that I would tell? I felt, not hurt, but in that direction — something taken away.

One of Billy's female clients, a pianist named Shirley Lent, felt much the same way. "I wish Billy had let me help him out when he was needy," she said. "He sure went to bat for me when I needed him. I talked to Billy several times a year, even after I quit show business. He called every so often just to say hello, but never let on he was having any problems. And you know, I had worked with a lot of gay entertainers. I thought I was so sophisticated! But if anybody had told me Billy was passing, I'd have said they were lying. You know why I never wondered about him? Because he was a caretaker, and I was very, very self-centered, probably just like all his other clients."

One person who did penetrate Billy's disguise and confront him before his death was his former wife Maryann. Back in December 1961, when Billy had been stealthily removing his possessions from their home in the valley and moving in with Kitty, Maryann had inspected the boxes he was packing. "I'm a rather snoopy person," she explained. "I didn't want any of my things to go with him, so I went through the boxes and found a birth certificate with the name Dorothy Tipton on it." At the time, she wasn't sure this was Billy's; it might have belonged to a relative. Maybe a sister he had never mentioned. In any case, she removed it and hung on to it.

Then, during one of her visits to Spokane after the boys had moved out, Billy brought up the subject of living together again.

> I hadn't doubted him for all those years, but that night, driving me to my girlfriend's, he's saying, "Why don't you come on back and stay?" And then it dawned on me. I confronted him about it, threw it up at him. Said, "Why don't you just come out with the truth? Why would you want me when you're a woman?" And then I came out with it. "Your name is Dorothy. Isn't it?" He didn't say a word. He just gave me a terrible look.
>
> And then I went in and told my girlfriend. I needed to talk to somebody about it. But I never told another soul until after Billy's death. I think I was the only one who knew, out of all the crowd that knew him.
>
> A while later, when he was getting sick, I said, "This is the kind of secret nobody keeps. If you ever need help, it will come out." I wanted him to come stay with me and let me take care of him. But that was the end of his asking me to move in.

Why *didn't* Maryann talk to some of their mutual acquaintances about what she had discovered? "Billy was a good person. We all do things that are wrong, you know, someplace along the line. I would like to have things right for Billy now. Just because he cross-dressed like he did and went the way he did doesn't make him a bad person. It doesn't agree with society, that's all." Indeed, she said, the subject never came up between them again. They talked on the phone as they always had, and she continued to put up food for him in her freezer and take it to him when she visited. "I was worried about him," she said. "He was getting so he couldn't walk across the room without losing his breath. I'm calling Billy 'him.' I just can't think of Billy as a woman."

She paused. "The other day on the radio I heard 'The Nearness of You.' I never realized before what pretty words that song had. Beautiful words. 'I need no soft lights to enchant me, / if you'll only grant me / the right to hold you ever so tight / and to feel in the night / the nearness of you . . .'" That had been the song playing on the jukebox when Billy took her in his arms for the first time and they danced and she thought "Lucky me!" It now brought back the feelings for Billy that had survived every separation, feelings not for a *him* but for a *you.* "I sat there listening, just crying up a storm over my life, you know. That's the kind of music I like, something I can cry over. Makes me feel so good."

The story of Billy's decline invites pathos, but should it? Trying to see Billy from inside out, I think of the role Walter Matthau played in the film of Neil Simon's play *The Sunshine Boys,* an aging vaudeville actor. To the Matthau character, the world is divided between star and stage-hands, himself and everybody else. His anxious nephew shows his devotion by trying to interest the actor in family life and retirement. He doesn't get it. For Matthau's character, acting *is* his life.

In Billy's case, it was the affectionate cousins who were trying to lure their relative into retirement, for the sake of her health. Back in 1983, when Billy first took over the Sobol agency, Cousin Eilene and her husband had passed through Spokane on a trip to western Canada and stayed overnight in a motel. Billy showed them around town, including a stop by the office for a quick tour, since Eilene was interested in the business.

But at the motel, when we had a chance to talk, I asked her if she was ever going to change back. William was still at home, and she said when she got him grown she was going to disappear and change back. But right then she knew she needed a lung x-ray and knew she couldn't get one. Before, when she and I talked on the phone, she had said in the state of Washington they had laws pertaining to transsexuals, cross-dressing or something. She said she couldn't live in the state of Washington and go back — she could be arrested.

As I say, I think Madeline and I were the only two that understood her and loved her. And we didn't care what she did. We respected her, and I know I always admired her, especially when I was getting older. She didn't feel sorry for herself or complain about doing what she had to do. You know, we were the only people she could talk to. Poor Mother couldn't accept it at all, and we had to be very careful. If anybody came or was around we always called her Billy, but among ourselves she was *Dorothy*. Mother never gave up calling her Dorothy, and she said, "It's *silly* for her to do that!" Mother always thought she should change back as soon as she got a job and could change back. But I think she was talented and good-looking and had a great personality, and once the ball started rolling, I don't think there was any turning back for her.

Billy had conducted an equally frank discussion with her cousin Madeline Byrd later that same summer, in 1983. Madeline and her husband arrived in mid-August and stayed with Billy in the trailer. Madeline remembered vividly that Billy was in top form, joking and ebullient, just like the Dorothy she remembered from the old days, when they had slept on the floor of the one-room apartment in Muskogee and Dorothy had turned herself into Billy for the first time. "Normally she couldn't talk to anybody openly. She and I went off into the bedroom and talked all night. We both wished we could see more of each other, but she wouldn't leave her boys." Madeline had an agenda on that visit. The Byrds were on their way south to visit their daughter Pat, who lived in Berkeley. Billy could drive down with them, stay with Pat, and anonymously get medical attention for what she was afraid was emphysema. Billy put Madeline off, saying she was short of money, but Madeline knew she was just being cautious. "You don't know what fear she lived under that she'd be found out," Madeline commented. But Billy told Madeline that she was content. "She was *determined* to be happy. That was the night she told me, 'Some people might think I'm a freak or a hermaphrodite. I'm not. I'm a normal person. This has been my choice.'"

Yet Billy wanted to keep the secret from her boys. On that visit, Billy asked Madeline to promise that if she got sick, Madeline would come and get her, take her away from Spokane to die. "Then, after I die, you

have my body cremated so I'll just disappear." And Madeline agreed
that she would.

In the fall of 1988, Billy caught a cold that lingered. His usual hacking
smoker's cough grew deeper and more wrenching. He told a friend that
he thought the problem was phlebitis. One of his old sidemen, Ben
Tessensohn, ran into him at a supermarket and noticed that he was
unwell. "I said, 'Hi, Billy, how you doin'?' and he said, 'Oh, fine,' but he
was looking really thin and tired. We talked for a minute, then I went
on my way with the shopping cart. I was doing my own thing when I
noticed he was behind me again. Looked away when he saw I had
noticed him, but every time I turned around, he was following me.
After Billy died, I told Dave Sobol about it and he said, 'That's it. You're
a good friend and he wanted to tell you but didn't know how to do it.' I
think he did want to tell me something, following me."

Billy kept up the act as long as he could, but by December he was
starting to miss work. This was so unusual that all his friends began
to worry. Mike Brandon began asking him to see a doctor, but Billy
claimed there was only one doctor in the whole of Spokane he would
see and that doctor was out of town. Billy gave the name, and Joann
Brandon did a little research. He was a general practitioner with an
office nearby in the Spokane Valley, but he was in fact out of town, and
Billy was adamant that he would go to no one else.

Friends rallied around Billy. Barron Stringfellow offered to cover
Billy's bookings. Without work that produced commissions, Billy
would have no income. The head of the musicians' union, Jimmy
Nixon, was frequently in touch by phone, and Thomas Lipsanski, an-
other agent, tried to bundle Billy into a car and take him to a hospital.
Billy wouldn't cooperate.

The holidays came and went, and Billy's health continued to deterio-
rate. William remembered that he had no appetite and lost a lot of
weight during those weeks, and that it was very cold in the trailer. Yet
Billy didn't seem to understand how ill he was. For company and
warmth, he had that rack of 78 rpm records and the big black Labrador,
Sam, whom William had left behind when he moved away. Jazz and a
dog were the consorts in Billy's life that outlasted every wife and all the
children. To Sam, I fancy, Billy spoke easily of what could not be said to
anyone else. Long ago, in a love letter, Billy had told Kitty that while

Billy's last driver's license

she was away he always kept their dog beside him to confide in: "He's the sweetest little fellow. He and I eat and sleep together. I try to love him all I can while I'm at home. He even comes in the bathroom with me while I take my bath . . . He cocks his head from side to side, just like he understands. And sometimes I think he does."

Despite his obvious illness and weakness, Billy seemed in reasonably good spirits to the people who visited. Nor is there evidence that she was preparing to make the getaway she had envisioned with her cousins. In holiday letters to Madeline and Eilene, Billy made no plea for rescue from the possibility of helplessness and disclosure. "I have been getting your cards from various places you and Madeline travel," she wrote to Eilene. "I think it's great. Lord knows I've done my share and I wouldn't take anything for the memories. Of course, I didn't go to Europe, but I've had fun. I always wanted to go to Hawaii but guess I'll never make it. Oh well, I don't look good in a hula skirt anyway."

To Madeline, Billy mentioned her upcoming birthday. Only the cousins knew about those five years Billy had sheared from the official record.

I'm still at the same old stand — booking bands and acts. I am not as active as I used to be. My health is not too good so I conserve myself as much as possible. After all I will be 74 years old the 29th. The day after Aunt Cora's birthday. My body feels fine. I just haven't any wind. It is a chore for me to walk across the floor. And my situation being what it is I can't get medical help — so I tough it out.

Scott's wife is expecting a baby in January. John is still single and [William] just moved into his first apartment. My dog and I have the mobile home to ourselves. Of course the boys check in practically every day — to raid the refrigerator, etc. I am sure you have been thru that!

Write me all the news. Have a wonderful Holiday Season and take care of yourselves.

Love,
Billy

These were the last letters Billy wrote, and in them she reminded the two women who had shared her childhood and adolescence that she was one and the same Billy they had always loved. Did she know death was approaching when she wrote these breezy holiday letters? When he died, Billy was wearing no bindings or genital gear, nor were they to be found anywhere among his possessions. This was the only sign that Billy was anticipating discovery. But she did not ask Madeline and Eilene to rescue her and keep the secret intact. Until death arrived, Billy swung as easily as ever in the hammock s/he had strung between those double pillars of identity, those pronouns that sort the world into opposites and complements. "My body feels fine": no deathbed conversion to gender fundamentalism for this veteran trouper. Early in the new year, on the brink of a new decade and on the threshold of a new century, Billy looked up from his son's arms to see a figure beckoning from the darkened wings. Billy knew who it was. Lifting her face as death removed the mask, Billy breathed a long, deep sigh, while out beyond the footlights rose the first stirring of the sound she had lived for, a murmur and a rustle, then the outburst of applause.

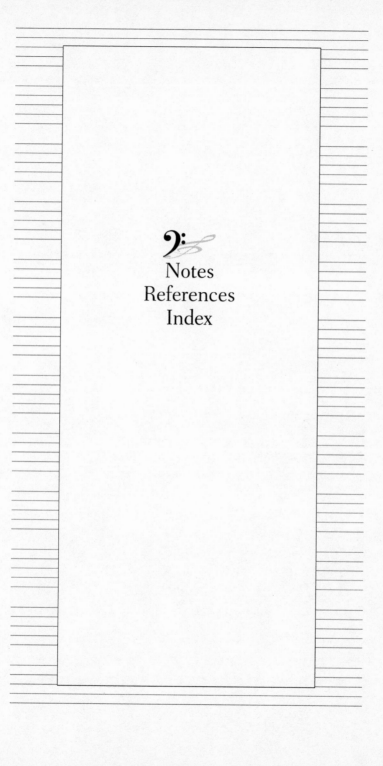

Notes
References
Index

Notes

1. Born Naked

PAGE

3   "I was in awe": William Alan Tipton, interview with DM, 14 Jan. 1992.
5   The autopsy report: Autopsy number 20-JA-89, performed by George R. Lind-
    holm, M.D., at Holy Family Hospital, Spokane, Washington, 23 Jan. 1989.
    The coroner signed: Richard Merkin, "Billy's Blues," *Vanity Fair*, Aug. 1989,
    p. 56, and Doug Clark, interview with DM, 26 Jan. 1995.
    She contacted: Donald Ball, interviews with DM, 28 Jan. 1995 and 2 Aug.
    1996.
    The wire services: "Musician's Death at 74 Reveals He Was a Woman" (Asso-
    ciated Press); *New York Times*, 2 Feb. 1989, p. A18.
    A tabloid published: Kitty Tipton Oakes, "My Husband Was a Woman and I
    Never Knew," *Star*, 21 Feb. 1989, pp. 6–8, 31.
    "He'll always be": Quoted in *New York Times*, 2 Feb. 1989, p. A18. John
    Thomas Tipton began using the name Clark around 1982, occasionally spell-
    ing his name Jon; Scott Lee Tipton began using the name Scott Miller
    around 1982 also.
6   "Even now": Merkin, "Billy's Blues," p. 60.
    Throughout history: For comments about cross-dressing Civil War soldiers,
    see Livermore, *My Story of the War*, p. 120. On Catalina de Erauso, see Bul-
    lough and Bullough, *Cross Dressing*, pp. 96–97, and de Erauso, *Lieutenant
    Nun*. For a discussion of James Barry, see Bullough and Bullough, pp. 160–61,
    and Garber, *Vested Interests*, pp. 203–5. For information about Barry's contri-
    bution to obstetrical medicine, see *Obstetric and Gynecological Clinics of
    North America*, Vol. 16 (1989), p. 269.
7   Academic researchers: See the discussions of Billy Tipton as a cross-dresser
    in Garber, pp. 67–71, and Bullough and Bullough, p. 159.
    With a lawyer's assistance: Codicil to Last Will and Testament of Billy Lee
    Tipton, dated 23 July 1982.
8   the likes of: Billy Tipton, quoted in "People and Business: Lounges Want
    Neater Talent," *Spokane Daily Chronicle*, 22 Mar. 1974, p. 22.

2. But Who Was *She?*

The account of the Tipton family in this chapter is drawn, unless otherwise indicated, from numerous interviews with Dorothy/Billy's brother and sister-in-law, W.
T. and Doris Tipton, from 1992 to 1997. Information about Dorothy Tipton's maternal family, unless otherwise indicated, came from interviews conducted in 1992
and 1994 with Dorothy's cousins, who have been given the pseudonyms Madeline

Byrd and Eilene Pierce, at their request. Madeline Byrd also permitted me to draw
from her unpublished memoir, which includes her mother's recollections of the
years she and Reggie spent in the orphanage.

Details about the early history of Oklahoma were drawn from the following
sources: Arnold, *Legendary Times and Tales of Second Street*; Chapman, *Okla-
homa City: From Public Land to Private Property*; Debo, *Oklahoma: Foot-Loose and
Fancy-Free*; Edwards, Oliphant, and Ottaway, *The Vanished Splendor: Postcard
Memories of Oklahoma City*; Franklin, *Born Sober: Prohibition in Oklahoma, 1907–
1959*; McGrill, *And Satan Came Also: An Inside Story of a City's Social and Political
History*; Morgan and Morgan, *Oklahoma: A History*; Stein and Hill, *The Culture of
Oklahoma*; and Stewart, *Born Grown: An Oklahoma City History.*

Discussion of early aviation is based on information in Bilstein, *Flight in America: From the Wrights to the Astronauts*; Corn, *The Winged Gospel: America's Romance with Aviation 1900–1950*; and George E. Goodhead, Jr., "Ranger-Coffman
Airplanes," *Sport Aviation*, July 1970, pp. 26–28. Discussion of the Tipton household in the 1920s is drawn from information in Mirken, *The 1927 Edition of the
Sears, Roebuck Catalogue.*

13 The nuns named her: Twelfth Census of the United States, Schedule 1, 1
June 1900: Population. New Orleans, Louisiana, House of the Good Shepherd (signed by Sister Mary of St. Martin McLaughlin). This document lists
as "inmates" "Lindsay [sic] Maud, b June '88, age 11; Cora, b Aug. '92, age 7;
Regina, b July '96 [should be Oct.], age 3."

15 "I carry the burn": Bonnie Spencer, interview with DM, 29 Mar. 1995.

19 G.W. was driving: Ella Bywater Tipton died 4 Aug. 1916. The claim for $10,
brought by Thomas Tipton against the Chicago, Rock Island and Pacific
Railway Company for negligence was settled out of court for the sum of $1
(Case #2885); G.W.'s claim for $10, was settled for $500 (Case #3066).

20 In the spring of 1919: Information about G. W. Tipton's aviation business
comes from a eulogy read at his funeral, one page, typed, unsigned; collection of W. T. Tipton.

Customers would pay: Stewart, *Born Grown*, p. 185.

21 "There was a big pasture": Pauline Lane, telephone interview with DM, 18
Aug. 1994.

She had been named: L. Frank Baum, *The Wonderful Wizard of Oz* (1900),
was also made into a "musical extravaganza" that ran on Broadway for 293
performances in 1903.

25 The cover drawing: "Nigger War Bride Blues," by Mitch Le Blanc and "Jimmie" Marten (Houston: Thomas Goggan and Bro., 1927).

The law confined: The numbers of Negroes (as they were then classified)
tallied in the U.S. Census of 1910 approached twenty percent of the total
population: 6546 out of 37,090. In 1922, the Calvary Baptist Church —
"mother church" of the black Baptist congregation in Oklahoma City — was
built on the corner of East Second and Walnut, cattycorner to the Tipton
home.

"If you were black": L. W. James Brooks ("Doebelly"), interview with Mark Hollars, Oklahoma City, 5 July 1995.

26 As one music historian: Savage, *Singing Cowboys and All That Jazz*, p. 8.

During Dorothy Tipton's childhood: I am indebted to Lawrence Jackson and his unpublished doctoral dissertation, "Ralph Ellison's Early Years, 1913–1941" (Stanford University, 1997), for addresses and details about the Ellison household in Oklahoma City.

"jamming in a shine": Ellison, *Shadow and Act*, p. 208. On Charlie Christian, see p. 235.

After closing time: The jazz pianist Norma Teagarden, raised in Oklahoma City, remembered that "Deep Two," as she called it, was off limits to white women. See Crawford, *Norma Teagarden*, p. 19.

"You know, back then": Wayne Benson, interview with DM, 1 Aug. 1994.

27 It was G.W. who filed: Case #2401D, *Tipton* v. *Tipton*, Petition dated 5 Mar. 1927.

Not four days: See Case #2401D, *Tipton* v. *Tipton*, Answer and Cross Petition, dated 9 Mar. 1927.

28 "When my husband began": "Mrs. Chaplin Gets Alimony, $1500 Month," *Daily Oklahoman*, 30 Apr. 1927, p. 1.

3. Kansas City

The source of information about Dorothy's life in Kansas City, unless otherwise indicated, is Dorothy's brother, W. T. Tipton. Information about Reggie's life in Muskogee comes from Dorothy's cousins Madeline Byrd and Eilene Pierce.

Details about the history of Kansas City were drawn from Brown and Dorsett, *KC: A History of Kansas City, Missouri*; Reddig, *Tom's Town: Kansas City and the Pendergast Legend*; Trillin, *Messages from My Father*; and Worley, *J.C. Nichols and the Shaping of Kansas City*.

Details about jazz in Kansas City while Dorothy lived there, from 1929 to 1932, are taken from Dexter, *The Jazz Story from the '90s to the '60s*; Franklin S. Driggs, "Kansas City and the Southwest," in Hentoff and McCarthy, *Jazz*, pp. 191–230; Hennessey, *From Jazz to Swing: African-American Jazz Musicians and Their Music*; Porter, Ullman, and Hazell, *Jazz: From the Origins to the Present*; Sales, *Jazz: America's Classical Music*; Schuller, *Early Jazz: Its Roots and Musical Development*; and Shapiro and Hentoff, *Hear Me Talkin' to Ya*. The Oklahoma City–Kansas City connection is emphasized in Savage, "Oklahoma City and the Blue Devils," in *Singing Cowboys and All That Jazz*, pp. 18–33. For a provocative discussion of the economic and racial complexities of making jazz popular, see William Howland Kenney, "Historical Context and the Definition of Jazz: Putting More of the History in 'Jazz History,'" in Gabbard, *Jazz Among the Discourses*, pp. 100–116.

32 "When you stand": Heat-Moon, *Blue Highways*, p. 131.

The country club district was: Worley, *J. C. Nichols and the Shaping of Kansas City*, pp. 124–30.

33 The Coffeys personally: Reddig, *Tom's Town*, pp. 165–66.

33 George Coffey became known: Obituary for George W. Coffey in the *Kansas City Times*, 9 June 1936, p. 14.

34 He and Dorothy: Dorothy's registration card shows that she enrolled in E. C. White School at Forty-eighth and Main Street, a block from their home, on 21 Jan. 1929.

37 In surrounding blocks: Brown and Dorsett, *KC*, pp. 194–95.

38 "the girl you've all": *Kansas City Star*, 1 May 1932.
    The month *Grand Hotel:* The *Kansas City Star* serialized a celebrity profile of Joan Crawford (John C. Moffitt, "The Rise of Joan Crawford," 8–20 May 1932). For details about Crawford's nickname, see Guiles, *Joan Crawford*, p. 24.

39 Enrolled in Kansas City's elite: Report cards show that Dorothy Tipton took four years of English, two years of Latin, algebra, geometry, biology, physics, history, and quite a lot of public speaking, or "expression." Photocopy of record book from Connors State College High School, courtesy of W. T. Tipton.
    Some of the sheet music: Dorothy's copy of "Moonlight on the River," by Bud Green (1932), is inscribed with the nickname "Tippy Tipton." Her little brother was given the same nickname in high school after he started playing the trumpet and formed a band he called Billy Tipton's Swing Orchestra. W. T. Tipton, interview with DM, 30 Jan. 1993.
    "I remember seeing": Quoted in Dahl, *Stormy Weather*, p. 26. An earlier version of this story had a less feminist spin; see "Mary Lou Williams," an entry developed from a 1954 interview in the British journal *Melody Maker*, in Gottlieb, *Reading Jazz*, p. 88.

40 "because Julia Lee": Dorothy Dreher to DM, 4 Feb. 1994.
    "Kansas City, Missouri, wasn't": Quoted in "Mary Lou Williams," in Gottlieb, *Reading Jazz*, p. 99.

41 "a heavenly city": Ibid., p. 97.
    "Pete [Johnson]": Quoted in Shapiro and Hentoff, *Hear Me Talkin' to Ya*, p. 292.
    On local stations: Dexter notes that local stations carried Bennie Moten live and lists the sax players active in Kansas City during Dorothy's years there; see *Jazz Story*, pp. 81–83. Sales mentions that Basie was broadcast remote from a club in Kansas City; see *Jazz*, p. 114.
    "They don't think": Quoted in Dahl, *Stormy Weather*, p. 67.

42 "Clubs like the Masqueraders": Mrs. Justin Hoy, telephone interview with DM, 27 Feb. 1994.

43 Charlie, she claimed: Documents in the case of *Reginald Tipton Herr, Plaintiff v. Charles L. Herr, Defendant*, filed 25 Aug. 1933.
    She returned: *Tipton v. Tipton*, case #2401.
    G.W. had recently: "Speed Plane Repaired for Race after Crackup, *Daily Oklahoman*, 17 July 1930, p. 1.

44 Reggie won: *Tipton v. Tipton*, case #2401, documents #1759–63.

45 She stayed for one: Kansas City Board of Education records show a transfer of Dorothy Tipton's credits to Central High School in Muskogee (probably in

Sept. 1932) and to Connors State College High School (probably in Jan. 1933).

45 She got a job: Document #1801: Plaintiff found guilty of contempt and fined $100 and ordered to pay sum in arrears. Dated 24 May 1933.

When her divorce: *Reginald Tipton Herr, Plaintiff,* v. *Charles L. Herr, Defendant,* 25 Aug. 1933.

4. The "In" Sex

The discussion of Depression-era Oklahoma City is drawn from information found in Edwards, Oliphant, and Ottaway, *The Vanished Splendor;* McGrill, *And Satan Came Also;* and Morgan, *Rising in the West.*

Speculation about Reggie's life in Oklahoma City is based on Benson, *Counter Cultures: Saleswomen, Managers, and Customers in American Department Stores, 1890–1940,* especially pp. 177–226. Department store saleswomen made relatively good incomes in comparison to other women workers, but during the Depression stores cut costs by deploying part-time workers in split shifts during the busiest time of the day. The status of saleswomen was also higher than that of other unskilled workers, such as domestics, needleworkers, and factory laborers. Benefits for full-time workers often included medical attention onsite, discounts on purchases, subsidized food and recreation, and, for long-term employees, paid vacations, but we do not know whether Reggie's work was part-time or full-time.

Information about the Teagardens comes from radio, print, and personal interviews with Norma Teagarden, conducted by various people between 1988 and 1993; and from Whitney Balliett, "Big T (Jack Teagarden)" in *American Musicians II;* Crawford, *Norma Teagarden;* Feather, *The Encyclopedia of Jazz;* Charles Edward Smith, "Jack Teagarden," in Gottlieb, *Reading Jazz;* and Smith and Guttridge, *Jack Teagarden: The Story of a Jazz Maverick.*

Contemporary scholarship proposes that cross-dressing is not "perverse" (in the psychoanalytic sense of a defensive posture or mechanism) but normal, given the way oppositional notions of sex difference function in culture. Three works that are useful in thinking about Tipton's cross-dressing are Bullough and Bullough, *Cross Dressing, Sex, and Gender;* Garber, *Vested Interests: Cross-Dressing and Cultural Anxiety;* and Orgel, *Impersonations: The Performance of Gender in Shakespeare's England.* For a discussion of psychological issues that might apply to the relationship between Tipton's cross-dressing and her creativity, see Young-Breuhl, *Creative Characters.*

For commentary on Greta Garbo's trouser role in *Queen Christina,* see Terry Castle, "A Polemical Introduction, or, The Ghost of Greta Garbo," in *The Apparitional Lesbian,* pp. 2–20, and Betsy Erkkila, "Greta Garbo: Sailing Beyond the Frame," *Critical Inquiry* 11, no. 4 (June 1995): 595–619.

49 Everybody had a story: One citizen whose family arrived during the Run of '89 recalled the excitement when the well blew: "We lived five miles away but the side of our house and our car were coated with oil and had to be repainted."

She also remembered that Mary Sudick, owner of the property, bought a Maytag washing machine with her first profits. Hazel Craddock, telephone conversation with DM, 14 Feb. 1997.

50 Dorothy and Reggie would share: "The hassle for that one bath was unbelievable! People lined up in the hall with towels over shoulders awaiting their turn." Nadine Myers Thiel to DM, 24 Feb. 1997.
Playing music: Lucille Rice, telephone interview with DM, 1 Mar. 1997.
Reggie was downright phobic: W. T. Tipton and Doris Tipton, interviews with DM, 30 Jan. 1993 and 10 Feb. 1996.

51 Reggie hated the food: Hearsay about Reggie's eating habits was passed on by Cora to her daughters and to DM in interviews with Madeline and Eilene.
She was calling: *Polk's City Directory* for 1935 lists Mrs. Reginald Tipton as a clerk at Kerr Dry Goods Co., residing at the Cadillac Hotel, 204 NW Third.
Dorothy, who was already: Lucille Rice, telephone interview with DM, 1 Mar. 1997.

52 Prohibition was not lifted: Morgan and Morgan, *Oklahoma: A History*, p.116.
"Why, anybody": Clarence Cagle, interview with DM, 28 Jan. 1994.
Musicians were also: Norma Teagarden, interview with DM, 11 Feb. 1993.

53 "I was about thirteen": Clarence Cagle, interview with DM, 28 Jan. 1994.

54 "Now, the Missourians": Jerry Seaton, interview with DM, 22 Apr. 1995.
"an older lady": Paul Jensen, interviews with DM by telephone, 11 Feb. 1994 and 17 Jan. 1996.

55 "in dire straits": Eilene Price, interview with DM, 3 Oct. 1992.
"That's what I admired": Madeline Byrd, interview with DM, 1 Oct. 1992.

57 "Aunt Bess": W. T. Tipton, interview with DM, 29 Jan. 1993.
"My darling": Reggie Fullenwider to B. L. Tipton, 22 Mar. 1961.
"True acting": Peter Hall, "Behind the Mask," program notes for the Oedipus plays, produced at the National Theatre, London, 1996.

60 "normal person": Madeline Byrd, interview with DM, 1 Oct. 1992.

5. Graduation

For a historical overview of endurance contests, see Calabria, *Dance of the Sleepwalkers: The Dance Marathon Fad*; for closer looks, see the actress June Havoc's memoirs *Early Havoc* and *More Havoc* and her play *Marathon '33*, as well as the jazz vocalist Anita O'Day's memoir, *High Times, Hard Times*. The subject has also been dramatized in *They Shoot Horses, Don't They?*, a 1969 film directed by Sydney Pollock, based on the novel by Horace McCoy (1935), and in *Steel Pier*, a Broadway musical by John Kander and Fred Ebb (1997).

The sexual style of the 1920s and 1930s, as the scholar Terry Castle has noted in *Noel Coward and Radclyffe Hall: Kindred Spirits* (p. 27), "often turned upon an implicitly 'homosexual' confounding of sex roles." On changing views of women's sexuality in particular, see D'Emilio and Freedman, *Intimate Matters: A History of Sexuality in America*, and Katz, *Gay American History*. For an overview of lesbian historiography, see Martha Vicinus, "'They Wonder to Which Sex I Belong': The Historical Roots of Modern Lesbian Identity," in Abelove et al., *Lesbian and Gay*

Studies Reader, pp. 432–52. For a discussion of the emergence of working-class lesbian consciousness, see Kennedy and Davis, *Boots of Leather, Slippers of Gold: The History of a Lesbian Community* (1993), and for research into the life of women who lived discreetly as the sexual intimates of other women, see Kennedy's article, "'But We Would Never Talk About It': The Structures of Lesbian Discretion in South Dakota, 1928–1933," in Lewin, *Inventing Lesbian Cultures in America.* For an early study of lesbian women's sexuality, see "Sex Variant Women," 1930s, case studies by Robert Latou Dickinson, in Duberman, *About Time: Exploring the Gay Past,* pp. 112–21.

62 "My dad had": Clarence Cagle, interview with DM, 28 Jan. 1994.

63 Billy, dressed: Helen P. Rhoden, telephone conversation with DM, 14 Feb. 1997.
   After greeting her son: Smith and Guttridge, *Jack Teagarden,* p. 84.

64 "We never had music": Quoted from interviews with Norma Teagarden in Jeff Kaliss, "The Greening of Teagarden," *San Francisco Examiner Datebook,* 27 Aug. 1989, p. 39, and on *Marian McPartland's Piano Jazz,* National Public Radio, 4 Sept. 1984.

65 "Billy was very outgoing": Helen P. Rhoden, telephone conversation with DM, 14 Feb. 1997.
   "I met Billy": Norma Teagarden, interview with DM, 11 Feb. 1993.

66 Later, when Billy had acquired: Ron Kilde, interview with DM, 28 Apr. 1995.
   "I wore a suit": Norma Teagarden, interview with DM, 11 Feb. 1993.
   During World War II: Crawford, *Norma Teagarden,* p. 60.
   "beautiful long evening gowns": Norma Teagarden, interview with DM, 11 Feb. 1993.
   "my high school buddies": Hentoff, *Listen to the Stories,* pp. 25–26.

67 Woody Herman also hired: Herman and Troup, *The Woodchoppers Ball,* p. 73; and Jerry Ney (a.k.a. Jeri Brown, who was given her stage name by Woody Herman), interview with DM, 16 Nov. 1995.
   "I did things": Quoted in Kaliss, "The Greening of Teagarden," p. 39.
   "Billy lived, roomed": Norma Teagarden, interview with DM, 11 Feb. 1993.
   "Non Earl just followed": Thelma Whitt, interview with DM, 29 July 1994.

68 "We were starved": Havoc, *More Havoc,* p. 41.

69 Non Earl's partner: Court document (no case number), filed by Attorney Wayne Wheeling on behalf of Mitchell Thayer requesting attachment of property of Defendants Charles Hayden and Vern Kirk, no date (circa 15 Feburary 1932).
   The Baptists won: "Walkathon Is Ended as Arrests Are Threatened," *Oklahoma City Times,* 16 Feb. 1932, p. 6.
   "My folks": Non Earl Hancock (Non Earl Harrell's namesake), telephone interviews with DM, 22 Aug. 1994 and 30 Mar. 1995. She added, "Some way my mother told Non Earl [Harrell] about naming the baby after her. She came to visit us when I was about six months old and told my folks, 'The only thing I ever had named after me before is a pig!'" Non Earl, who had no living children, apparently took an interest in her namesake and kept in touch off

and on; she gave Non Earl Hancock, among other gifts, an oil painting of herself.

70 "looked after Billy": Clarence Cagle, interview with DM, 28 Jan. 1994.

71 "striding swiftly": *World Telegram,* 17 Jan. 1932, quoted in Faderman, *Odd Girls and Twilight Lovers,* p. 125.

72 "Colored women": L. W. James Brooks ("Doebelly"), interview with Mark Hollars, 5 July 1995.
    "liberal interpretation": Edwards, Oliphant, and Ottaway, *The Vanished Splendor,* Vol. III, card 492.
    "that reputedly had gays": Lela Lowell, interview with DM, 3 Aug. 1994.

73 "We always thought": Paul Jensen, interview with DM, 25 Apr. 1995.
    "That such a relation": Douglas C. McMurtie, "A Legend of Lesbian Love Among the North American Indians," excerpted in Katz, *Gay American History,* p. 322.

74 "Non Earl was her first": W. T. Tipton, interviews with DM, 29 and 31 Jan. 1993.
    Billy's attraction: Information provided by Norma Teagarden's cousins Helen Rhoden and Lucille Rice, telephone interviews with DM, 14 Feb. and 1 Mar. 1997.
    "Well, I would": Wayne Benson, interview with DM, 1 Aug. 1994; Sara Murphy, interview with DM, 31 July 1994.

6. The Playboy

Information about Billy's involvement with the Banner Cavaliers comes from interviews conducted during 1994 and 1997 with W. L. "Son" Wallin. Clarence Cagle provided details about Billy's band at the Swing Time during interviews in 1994 and 1997.

The material about Bob Wills is drawn from Savage, *Singing Cowboys and All That Jazz,* and from biographies by Ruth Sheldon (*Hubbin' It: The Life of Bob Wills*) and Charles R. Townsend (*San Antonio Rose: The Life and Music of Bob Wills*).

For an evocative look at the jazz scene in the black district of Oklahoma City during the 1930s, see Rudi Blesh's "Flying Home," a memoir of Charlie Christian, in Gottlieb, *Reading Jazz,* and Ellison's *Shadow and Act.*

77 Saturday night: Details about Oklahoma nightclubs provided by Lew Raines, telephone conversation with DM, 17 Feb. 1997.

79 "show-type person": Clarence Cagle, interview with DM, 28 Jan. 1994.

80 "the miles of dirt": "Mary Lou Williams," in Gottlieb, *Reading Jazz,* p. 96.
    By 1935: Allen, *Voices on the Wind,* pp. 53, 57–58.

81 Farmers would haul: "Bob Wills' Famous Sound Will Resound at Tulsa Festival," *Sunday Oklahoman,* travel and entertainment section, 25 Feb. 1996, p. 5.
    "and never miss": Leon McAuliffe, guitarist for the Texas Playboys, quoted in Townsend, *San Antonio Rose,* p. 73.

83 Guitar and banjo players: Townsend, *San Antonio Rose,* pp. 133–34.

84 "considered the new studios": Allen, *Voices on the Wind,* p. 64.

85 "Not a bit pretty": Dorothy Sessions, telephone interview with DM, 14 Aug. 1994.
"thick bottle glasses": Sara Murphy, interview with DM, 31 July 1994.
"got so she looked": Alice Holmes, telephone interview with DM, 27 July 1994.
"One night": Dorothy Sessions, telephone interview with DM, 14 Aug. 1994.
"couldn't sing": Ellen Reynolds, telephone interview with DM, 28 July 1994.
"She was very crude": Ibid.
The broadcasting studio: Gene Allen, in his history of radio in Oklahoma, tells about the young oil millionaire E. H. Rollestone, who planned to put the town of Bristow on the map by investing in a powerful transmitter and up-to-date facilities and programming. After station KFRU went on the air in Jan. 1925, "crowds filled the . . . lobby to watch the broadcasts." One young man "hitchhiked all the way from his home near Pawnee just to watch one of the broadcasts. Rollestone had designed the studio with large windows on all sides so visitors could see as well as hear the performances." Allen, *Voices on the Wind*, pp. 31–32.

86 "People said Buck": Ellen Reynolds, telephone interview with DM, 28 July 1994.
"The only time": Source wishes not to be identified. Telephone interview with DM, 27 July 1994.
"'He-she' was": Dorothy Sessions, telephone interview with DM, 14 Aug. 1994.
"Back in the days": Source wishes not to be identified. Telephone interview with DM, 27 July 1994.
The band's regular appearances: *Polk's City Directory* gives another address for the Swing Time: 1317 SE Twenty-ninth. Wallin may have conflated the Swing Time with the Garden of Allah, later Louie's 29 Club.
Since Hickman's services: *Polk's City Directory* for 1936 lists a residence in Oklahoma City for Wm. Tipton, musician, at the Combs Hotel, 217 N Broadway. Non Earl is not listed as his wife, but people remember that she lived with him that year.

88 "a *wild* place": Tommy Perkins, recalling stories he heard from older members of his family, interview with DM, 23 Jan. 1994.

89 Nonetheless, the application: Social Security Application for account number 444–09–5067, 9 Feb. 1937.

90 In 1938, Buck's father: Allen, *Voices on the Wind*, p. 65.

91 A promotional postcard: The other side of the postcard contains a printed message: "Dear Friend: You are cordially invited to be a guest of Louvenie at KTOK, Monday through Friday, 4:15–4:45 P.M. Saturdays 5:30–6:00 P.M."
Buck, out of work: Case #13678, County of Oklahoma. In 1939 Buck was charged with forgery for signing a ten-dollar check with her father's name. She was sentenced to spend one year at the state penitentiary, "concurrently with sentence in case #13677" [file missing], plus to pay costs of prosecution, $47.95. The information about Mary Louise Thomason's subsequent occupations comes from listings in *Polk's City Directory*, 1932–1982.

92 "It was common knowledge": Wayne Benson, interview with DM, 1 Aug. 1994.
93 "Buck and her girlfriend": Sara Murphy, interview with DM, 3 Aug. 1994.

7. Reggie's Daughter

Information about Dorothy's family life is drawn from interviews with W. T. Tipton conducted from 1993 to 1997.

Background and lore about the jazz bands that played small clubs during the 1930s is taken from Crow, *Jazz Anecdotes*; Hentoff, liner notes, *Little Club Jazz: Small Groups in the '30s*; Shapiro and Hentoff, *Hear Me Talkin' to Ya*; and Lees, *Cats of Any Color: Jazz Black & White* and *Meet Me at Jim & Andy's*.

96 Photos taken: Reggie's warmth toward Non Earl apparently outlasted the liaison with Billy, for her letters go on mentioning contacts with "Nonie" long after Billy moved on to other territory, with other female companions. For example, "I tried to call Nonie, but phone disconnected," Reggie Fullenwider to B. L. Tipton, 19 Oct. 1956, and "Talk to Nonie Earl once in a while, but haven't seen her as neither of us have a car to drive," 2 July 1957.
97 "for its undermining": *Sylvia Scarlett* (1935), directed by George Cukor, starred Katharine Hepburn, Edmund Gwenn, and Cary Grant and is credited as the film "which first picks up the thread of androgyny that runs through Hepburn's career, [and] was a ground-breaking film for its undermining of socially constructed norms of femininity and masculinity." Monaco, *Encyclopedia of Film*, p. 253.
    "better looking": "Cinema," *Time*, 13 Jan. 1936, p. 43.
100 "You could hear": Wilson et al., *Teddy Wilson Talks Jazz*, p. 7.
    By the mid-1930s: As early as 1934, Billy could have heard Wilson's solo on "Moonglow," performed at the only recording session of a Goodman band that Wilson shared with Jack and Charlie Teagarden.
101 "Western swing was not": Tommy Perkins, interview with DM, 23 Jan. 1994.
102 "kind of a chunk": Rose Marie Moore, telephone interview with DM, 28 July 1994.
    "When Tiny was around": Thelma Whitt, interview with DM, 28 July 1994.
    Autry was a loyal: Edwards, Oliphant, and Ottaway, *The Vanished Splendor*, Vol. 3, card 500.
    The brother offered: Thelma Whitt, interview with DM, 29 July 1994.
    "little bit funny": Source wishes not to be identified. Telephone interview with DM, 28 July 1994.
    "You know, when": Paul Jensen, interview with Gerry Everding, 20 Nov. 1996.
    "Tiny said to me": Wayne Benson, interview with DM, 1 Aug. 1994.
103 Singing "Red Sails": Rose Marie Moore, telephone interview with DM, 28 July 1994.
    In his first movie: Information about Wayne Whitt's movie career comes from undated and unidentified newspaper clippings, courtesy of his relative Patty Cunningham.

"I used to walk": Lew Raines, interviews with DM, 5 Apr. and 21 Apr. 1995.

104 "Dear Mom": Billy Tipton to Mrs. Lynn Fullenwider, 24 Dec. 1940.

105 The Gladstone was: "Sale of Gladstone Hotel Is Scheduled on Dec. 11," unidentified news clipping dated 30 Nov. 1969, and "Built in 1924, Gladstone Was the Social Center," undated newspaper clipping, both in Frances Seely Webb Collection, Casper College Library, Casper, Wyoming. The Broadmoor Country Club was later renamed the Aviation Country Club; "Broadmoor Club Falls to Air Age," *Rocky Mountain News*, 17 Apr. 1949, p. 20.

He and Non Earl: *Polk's City Directory* for Joplin, 1942, lists "Tipton, Wm (Nona), musician, r 105 N. Moffet Ave."

The distinction: Marjorie Garber elaborates this point in her commentary on Dustin Hoffman's role as Dorothy in the film *Tootsie:* "If it is not a critique of gender roles, that may be because it is a critique of gender itself as a category." *Vested Interests*, p. 9.

8. Self-Made Man

Details about Cab Calloway's career are based on Calloway's memoir (written with Bryant Rollins), *Of Minnie the Moocher and Me,* and on Haskins, *The Cotton Club,* which became the basis of a film by Francis Ford Coppola (1984).

For the career of Teddy Wilson, see his autobiography, *Teddy Wilson Talks Jazz.* An account of the 1938 night at Carnegie Hall that marked (for the media) the transformation of jazz into the popular form called "swing" appears in "Benny Goodman," in Balliett, *American Musicians II: Seventy-two Portraits in Jazz,* pp. 158–65. For details about Goodman's small-group combos and the composition of "Flying Home," see the account by Rudi Blesh in *Reading Jazz,* pp. 516–36. On playing dance music for a living, see Albert Murray, "The Blues as Dance Music," in Gottlieb, *Reading Jazz,* pp. 992–96.

Several publications are helpful on the tradition of male impersonation as popular entertainment: Bell-Metereau, *Hollywood Androgyny*; Sue-Ellen Case, "Towards a Butch-Femme Aesthetic," in Hart, *Making Spectacle,* pp. 282–99; Ferris, *Crossing the Stage: Controversies on Cross-Dressing*; Maitland, *Vesta Tilley*; Slide, *The Vaudevillians* and *Great Pretenders: A History of Female & Male Impersonation in the Performing Arts*; and Tomalin, *Mrs. Jordan's Profession.*

109 On Friday the Fourth: "Spend the 4th at the air-cooled Cotton Club/George Mayer and His Orchestra playing two all-night dances." Ad in the *Joplin Globe,* 1 July 1941. An undated clipping in Billy's 1952–1953 scrapbook indicates that the Cotton Club was built in 1933 and went out of business in 1950. Other details about Joplin's Cotton Club come from interviews with Paul Jensen, Lee McKee, and Bill Pierson.

110 "wasn't well done": Paul Jensen, interview with DM, 11 Feb. 1994.

111 "Billy's voice": Marvin Richter, interview with DM, 22 Nov. 1995.

Its sound is: A session of the George Mayer Sophisticated Swing Trio with Billy Tipton was recorded at the Shalimar Room, Roseburg [Oregon], 1949 [n.d.]. Two sessions of the Billy Tipton Trio at the Ranch Inn, Elko [Nevada] Broadcasting Co. were made in Dec. 1955.

111 Billy Tipton had probably: In a letter written shortly after Billy's death, Mayer recalled meeting Billy "in the late 1930s in Oklahoma City. At that time, Billy and I formed a quartet . . . we wound up in Joplin, Missouri, with a bigger band: eight men!" George Mayer to Unistar International Pictures, 15 June 1989.

Mayer had grown up: Details about Mayer's family background are drawn from Spencer Pearson, "Pendulum Swings with Trumpet's Aid," *Corpus Christi Caller-Times*, 13 Jan. 1970; Hilary Hylton, "California Rose — She Sang, Remembered," *Corpus Christi Caller-Times*, 4 Aug. 1977, section C, pp. 1–2; and Jeannette Jones, "Paralyzed Arm Doesn't Stop Popular Trumpeter: Meet George Mayer," *Corpus Christi Caller-Times*, 24 Apr. 1980.

112 Mayer was in his: George Mayer routinely gave inconsistent information about his age. His obituary said he was sixty-two at the time of his death, that is born in 1927; his social security record showed that he was born 18 April 1917.

Feature-length films: By 1941, Calloway had appeared in *The Big Broadcast of 1932*, *Old Man of the Mountain* (1933), *Cab Calloway's Jitterbug Party* (1935), *Singing Kid* with Al Jolson (1936), *Manhattan Merry-Go-Round* (1937), and *Meet the Maestros* (1938); in 1943 he appeared in *Stormy Weather* with Lena Horne. George Gershwin wrote the part of Sportin' Life in *Porgy and Bess* with Calloway in mind.

"cool as an ice cube": Calloway et al., *Of Minnie the Moocher and Me*, p. 72.

"he was all motion": Haskins, *Cotton Club*, p. 64.

Nobody recalled: George Mayer's parents are identified in Pearson, "Pendulum Swings."

One of his wives: Marigold Hill, interview with DM, 24 Apr. 1997.

113 "George Mayer was dark-complected": Paul Jensen, interview with DM, 22 Apr. 1995.

114 Another source recalled: Charles Boeckman, telephone interview with DM, 11 Mar. 1997.

"George was Castilian": Bill Pierson, interview with DM, 22 Apr. 1995.

George's aunt: Mayer's aunt Rose Fitchett (stage name, California Rose) said in a newspaper article that her father, George's grandfather, was a world-famous Italian violinist named Rinaldo Rabogliatte and that her grandmother was the opera star Adelina Patte; Alarcon was the name of a stepfather. Hylton, "California Rose," pp. 1–2. Mayer's daughter Kathleen Mayer Grandmain said that her father would never talk about his ancestry and that de Castro was his stepfather's name; neither she nor her mother knew his birth father's family name. Telephone conversations with DM, 16 and 29 Mar. 1997.

George, impersonating: Details about Mayer's routines are drawn from audiotapes of radio broadcasts from the Shalimar Room in Roseburg, Oregon, 1949, and from Jeannette Jones, "Paralyzed Arm Doesn't Stop Popular Trumpeter: Meet George Mayer," *Corpus Christi Caller-Times*, 24 Apr. 1980.

"was a nut": Bill Pierson, interview with DM, 22 Apr. 1995.

"He'd sing this thing": Ibid.

115 "particularly suitable": Newton, *Mother Camp*, p. 7.

One of his wives: Marigold Hill, interview with DM, 24 Apr. 1997.

116 "It was the middle": Clarence Cagle, interview with DM, 28 Jan. 1994.

"Somebody started calling": Bill Pierson, interview with DM, 22 Apr. 1995.

He told George: Kenny and Dolly Richards remembered that George Mayer told them this story in the 1960s. Interview with DM, 14 Nov. 1995.

117 "Musicians I worked with": Clarence Cagle, interview with DM, 28 Jan. 1994.

"Now, when you're born": Lew Raines, interview with DM, 21 Apr. 1995.

"I'll tell you why": Bill Pierson, interview with DM, 22 Apr. 1995.

"We noticed that": Paul Jensen, interview with DM, 22 Apr. 1995; Roy Ferguson, interview with Gerry Everding, 21 Nov. 1996. Ferguson identified the spy as one of the reed men; he also claimed that the musicians talked among themselves about the rumor that Billy was a woman.

"if you were stopped": Robert Oakes, interview with DM, 29 Jan. 1995.

During the war: Kirkman and Stinnett, *Joplin*, p. 121.

"got a doctor": Paul Jensen, interview with DM, 22 Apr. 1995.

George Mayer was classified: George Mayer to Unistar International Pictures, 15 June 1989.

118 "I was put": Paul Jensen, interview with DM, 22 Apr. 1995.

"I was playing": Bill Pierson, interview with DM, 22 Apr. 1995.

During this period: Billy's story about his physical condition seemed to have evolved over time. Raines glimpsed the bindings in Joplin during the 1940s. Billy's wife Betty felt a rib poking out like a knuckle but didn't feel the pelvic cup. His wife Maryann felt the pressure of the hard device on the pelvis, but Billy didn't say it was a surgical cup. His wife Kitty was told that the pelvis had been crushed.

119 "George Mayer, the music": Bill Pierson, interview with DM, 22 Apr. 1995.

"wasn't cute": Roberta Ellis Brower, interview with DM, 11 June 1995.

121 "There was a moviehouse": Bill Pierson, interview with DM, 22 Apr. 1995.

"He took a caring": Roberta Ellis Brower, interview with DM, 11 June 1995.

122 "That stuck": Bill Pierson, interview with DM, 22 Apr. 1995.

After Billy's death: Marigold Hill, interview with DM, 24 Apr. 1997.

123 "He told me": Roberta Ellis Brower, interview with DM, 11 June 1995.

124 "Billy was such": Ibid.

In 1943, Non Earl: *Polk's City Directory* shows Earl Harrell cohabiting with Winnie during the 1940s. The historian Lillian Faderman describes as fairly common in the 1930s "the 'bisexual' compromise of women who maintained marriages and long-term lesbian liaisons at the same time." *Odd Girls and Twilight Lovers*, pp. 94–99.

Non Earl and Earl: Joan Salathiel remembered that the Harrells were her landlords in 1954–1955 and that Non Earl raised parakeets in their part of the house, "thousands of them"; the tenant upstairs ran whiskey. Telephone interview with DM, 15 Aug. 1994.

125 "Nonie was just": Donna Brown, telephone interview with DM, 30 July 1994.

125 "Billy talked about": Roy Ferguson, interview with Gerry Everding, 9 Sept. 1997.

9. Swinging

I designed June's outfit based on information drawn from Hollander, *Sex and Suits*; McDowell, *Forties Fashion and the New Look*; and Olian, *Everyday Fashions of the Forties as Pictured in Sears Catalogues*.

Sources on Joplin history were Stinnett, *Joplin: A Pictorial History*; Renner, *Joplin: From Mining Town to Urban Center*; and Van Gilder, *Jasper County, The First Two Hundred Years*.

Descriptions of the Joplin nightclub scene were provided by Billy Pierson, Lew Raines, and Clark Stewart. For descriptions of lesbian bar cultures, see Faderman, *Odd Girls and Twilight Lovers*.

For the suggestion that Billy's facial hair and body contours may have been symptomatic of androgen insensitivity syndrome or polycystic ovary syndrome (PCOS), I am grateful to Louann Brizendine, Ph.D. For a review of current clinical views on PCOS, see Franks, "Polycystic Ovary Syndrome." Occurrence of this disease appears to be high among females who identify their gender as masculine, a topic discussed in issues of the newsletter of the organization Female to Male International; see, for example, Kirk, "Polycystic Ovarian Syndrome," and Green, "PCOS Again." Androgen insensitivity syndrome, an X-limited recessive trait in males, is caused by mutations of the androgen receptor that lead to defective virilization of the external genitalia; genital ambiguity ranges from completely female to unequivocally male. See Hiort et. al., "Clinical and Molecular Spectrum," and Patterson et. al., "Androgen Insensitivity Syndrome."

126 The street is crowded: In the fall of 1942, 155 members of the 43rd Headquarters Company of the new Women's Army Auxiliary Corps arrived for service at Camp Crowder. Van Gilder, *Jasper County*, p. 266.
    Is that why: Clark Stewart, interview with Gerry Everding, 14 Mar. 1997.
    This is Billy: "Talented Pianist Brightens Shows . . . Youthful Veteran Added to KWTO Musical Staff," *The Dial* (Springfield, Mo.), Mar. 1944, p. 3.
    "oh so hip": Bill Pierson, interview with DM, 23 Oct. 1995.

127 "tiny": Betty Cox, interview with DM, 2 Feb. 1994; Christine Jones, interview with Gerry Everding, 8 Mar. 1997; Verda Lippitt, interview with Gerry Everding, 10 Mar. 1997.
    "June could sing": Lew Raines, interview with DM, 21 Apr. 1995.
    "a gorgeous, beautiful": Christine Jones, interview with DM, 21 Sept. 1997.
    "just skip across": Clark Stewart, interview with Gerry Everding, 14 Mar. 1997. In *Jesse James*, Wayne Whitt plays a postal worker whose boxcar is looted in the James brothers' first big train robbery.

128 "had a red-light": Lee McKee, interview with Gerry Everding, 8 Mar. 1997. Harry Guinn, a former fireman in Joplin, added that twenty-seven houses were taken down in the red-light district in the 1960s and City Hall stands on that spot today.

"For years, gambling": Lee McKee, interview with Gerry Everding, 8 Mar. 1997.

Widowed young: Wally Kennedy, "Former Joplin Restaurateur Dies," *Joplin Globe*, 14 Jan. 1995.

"had all kinds of games": Clark Stewart, interview with Gerry Everding, 14 Mar. 1997.

"was not a rough crowd": Lee McKee, interview with Gerry Everding, 8 Mar. 1997.

129 "would go out": Betty Patrick, a "longtime patron," quoted in Kennedy, "Former Joplin Restaurateur Dies."

Billy rented a cabin: Christine Jones said, "We knew of him a long time before he met June; he lived out there before he met June, might have lived there before he started working here [at Gladys's]." Interview with Gerry Everding, 8 Mar. 1997.

"it looked like": Bill Pierson, interview with DM, 22 Apr. 1995.

130 "sometimes she'd be doing": Lee McKee, interview with Gerry Everding, 8 Mar. 1997.

When she died: Lew Raines, interview with DM, 21 Apr. 1995.

"a lot of Gladys's": Harry Guinn, interview with Gerry Everding, 18 Mar. 1997.

131 "was a beehive": Lee McKee, interview with Gerry Everding, 8 Mar. 1997.

"Billy dressed": Clark Stewart, interview with Gerry Everding, 14 Mar. 1997.

"spoiled her to death": Christine Jones, interview with Gerry Everding, 8 Mar. 1997.

"Why, we all played": Jerry Seaton, interview with DM, 22 Apr. 1995.

132 The town: During any training cycle, over forty thousand troops were quartered at Camp Crowder, according to Stinnett, *Joplin*, p. 120.

"real polite": Virgil Phillips, interview with Gerry Everding, 4 May 1997.

"Bill is the new": "Talented Pianist Brightens Shows," p. 3. W. T. Tipton embarked for service in Europe on 1 Mar. 1944, with the rank of second lieutenant in the U.S. Army Cavalry. Telephone conversation with DM, 18 Sept. 1997.

133 "backed him up": Virgil Phillips, interview with Gerry Everding, 4 May 1997.

134 "Corpus Christi Texas": George Mayer to Unistar International Pictures, 15 June 1989.

One of Mayer's: "The Palmero was a nice place where couples came to listen to the music and dance. No fistfights, no chicken wire . . . I would be willing to make a large wager that George saw the movie [*The Blues Brothers*] and it gave him inspiration for a touch of drama to add to the letter he wrote [to Unistar International Pictures]." Charles Boeckman to DM, 2 Apr. 1997.

In fact, Billy and June: Social security records show Billy employed at the Palmero Grill in Corpus Christi from mid-1944 into the first quarter of 1946.

135 "Now this woman": Source wishes not to be identified. Telephone interview with DM, 11 Feb. 1994.

136 One contemporary biologist: Anne Fausto-Sterling, "The Five Sexes," *Sciences*, Mar./Apr. 1993, pp. 20–24.

"Each of these categories": Ibid., p. 21.

137 "The body habitus": Autopsy number 20-JA-89; pathologist, George R. Lindholm, M.D., of Pathology Associates Inc., P.S., Spokane, Wash.
140 "I hope": Lynn Fullenwider to B. Tipton, 24 June 1961.

10. The Son-in-Law

Speculation about Billy's experience of intimacy with Betty was stimulated and
informed by Bright, *Sexual State of the Union*; Chernin, *My Life as a Boy*; Nestle,
The Persistent Desire: A Femme-Butch Reader; Leslie Feinberg's autobiographical
novel, *Stone Butch Blues*; and Minnie Bruce Pratt, *S/HE*, a first-person account of
living with Leslie Feinberg.

Background on the recording ban and the postwar fortunes of the big bands was
drawn from Merod, *Boundary 2, special issue: Jazz as a Cultural Archive*; Sales, *Jazz:
America's Classical Music*; and Schuller, *The Swing Era*.

141 "in a little bitty": Betty Cox, interview with DM, 2 Feb. 1994.
146 Lula Mae counseled: Lula Mae Meier, interview with DM, 2 Feb. 1994.
147 "You just never": Maryann Cattanach, interview with DM, 23 Apr. 1994.
"He was short": Betty Cox, interview with DM, 2 Feb. 1994.
148 "He and Betty": Source wishes not to be identified. Letter to Dave and Rubye
Sobol, postmarked 1989, and telephone interview [with Robert Basil], 11
Sept. 1995.
149 In a poll: Chafe, *The Unfinished Journey*, p. 125.
"It was pretty": Betty Cox, interview with DM, 2 Feb. 1994.
150 "the owner's wife": Lew Raines, interview with DM, 25 Apr. 1995.
151 "silly little act": Loretta Crews, undated holograph letter/memoir.
The only surviving: Billy Tipton Quartet, recorded at station KFSB in Joplin,
Mo., 28 Mar. 1949 (twelve-inch transcription disc labeled Sound Craft. Side
one: "Flying Home"; side two: "Yesterdays").
"He would come": Terry Wilson, interview with DM, 2 Feb. 1994.
"The minute Billy": Russ Carlyle, interview with DM, 13 Feb. 1996.
152 "the compulsion": Jim Merod to DM, 9 Nov. 1997.
154 "You see, Billy's love": Lew Raines, telephone interview with DM, 5 Apr. 1995.
155 George's beautiful: Marigold Hill (formerly Margaret Strange, whom everyone called Margo), interview with DM, 24 Apr. 1997.
All he needed: The third member of the trio was sometimes a bass player,
sometimes a drummer. The bass player is unidentified in the trio's recordings; the drummer who worked with Mayer and Tipton on and off, George
"Ronny" Ronconi, declined to be interviewed for this book.

11. Mobility

The jazz historian Ted Gioia summarizes the constraints on the development of
jazz in California as both geographical (all those wide-open spaces) and cultural,
noting especially the absence of newspaper coverage of western jazz musicians; his
observations pertain to California but apply to the Pacific Northwest as well.

Information about jazz in the 1950s is drawn from Gioia, "Final Considerations," in *West Coast Jazz: Modern Jazz in California, 1945–1960.*

Details of life on the road with Billy Tipton come from interviews with Betty Cox, her mother, Lula Mae Meier, and her sister Juanita Jama; with Marigold Hill, the former Mrs. George Mayer; and with former members of the Billy Tipton Trio: Kenny Richards, whose memories were augmented by those of his wife, Dolly, and by a typescript of a memoir written for his children, dated Dec. 1994; and Dick O'Neil, who shared both his memories and his voluminous scrapbooks. Betty Cox's sister Loretta Crews permitted me to use the unpublished letter/memoir she wrote shortly after hearing about Billy Tipton's death.

160 But if George said: Anderson-Walker Attractions, based in Portland, was the booking agency that handled the George Mayer Sophisticated Swing Trio from 1949 to 1952.
"That La Salle was": Juanita Jama, interview with DM, 2 Feb. 1994.
"Well," Betty recalled: Betty Cox, interview with DM, 2 Feb. 1994.
"It comes down": W. T. Tipton, interview with DM, 31 Jan. 1993.

161 "Made it okay": in a souvenir folder of postcards of Salt Lake City, Utah, Billy Tipton to Mr. and Mrs. Lynn Fullenwider, 2 Aug. 1949.
"I'm just": Betty Cox, interview with DM, 2 Feb. 1994.

162 Until Billy arrived: Pencil notes on transcription disks do not identify the third member of the trios.
"not the kind of place": Jane Clark, telephone interview with DM, 10 Apr. 1997.

163 "Whenever I think": Quoted by Whitney Balliett, "The Key of D Is Daffodil Yellow," in *American Musicians II*, p. 360.
"Why, that sounds great!": Norma Teagarden, interview with DM, 11 Feb. 1993.
"turkey circuit": George Mayer to Unistar International Pictures, 15 June 1989.
"way *up* there": Betty Cox, interview with DM, 2 Feb. 1994.

164 "He was a local": Marigold Hill, interview with DM, 24 Apr. 1997.

165 "Shown in the act": "Popular," undated clipping from Billy Tipton's scrapbook.
"I thought I was *in!*": Marigold Hill, interview with DM, 24 Apr. 1997. In *Gilda* (1946), Rita Hayworth, wearing glamorous clothes, fakes a striptease while singing "Put the Blame on Mame." George Mayer and Margaret Strange did eventually appear in a feature film, *Hooked,* shot in Wichita Falls, Texas, in 1954, and released nationally.

166 "I had a gambling": Composite of interviews with Dave Sobol, 31 Jan. 1993 and 2 May 1995.

167 "We were — or": Marigold Hill, interview with DM, 24 Apr. 1997.

170 "without a single": Betty Cox, interview with DM, 2 Feb. 1994.

171 Billy experimented: Kenny Richards recalled that an excellent clarinet player named Glenn Dickover worked with the trio for several months but didn't want to quit his day job to travel, so Billy replaced him. A drummer named

John Paul Jones also worked with Billy in Longview. Kenny Richards, interview with DM, 15 Nov. 1995.

"Dick was a drummer": Ron Kilde, interview with DM, 29 Apr. 1995.

"I hardly knew": Dick O'Neil, interview with DM, 30 Jan. 1995.

172 BILLY: Hey, Dick: Folder of comedy routines, no title, circa 1955–1960.

"Billy could have gone": Dick O'Neil, interview with DM, 30 Jan. 1995.

"As I was unloading": "Kenny Richards," unpublished ms., no date.

173 "Ned kept": Kenny Richards, interview with DM, 14 Nov. 1995.

In the aftermath: Loretta Crews, letter/memoir, undated.

174 "I would almost": Dick O'Neil, quoted in "Musician's Death at 74 Reveals He Was a Woman," *New York Times,* 2 Feb. 1989.

175 "I really wish": Dolly and Kenny Richards, interview with DM, 14 Nov. 1995.

"I cannot in my wildest": Betty Cox, notes to DM, 1993.

177 "We woodshedded": Kenny and Dolly Richards, interview with DM, 14 Nov. 1995.

178 big box of sanitary pads: Source wishes not to be identified. Telephone interview with DM, 5 Jan. 1996.

"We'd often": Betty Cox, interview with DM, 2 Feb. 1994.

"To get back": Kenny Richards, interview with DM, 14 Nov. 1995.

179 Billy's old Joplin chum: Bill Pierson, interview with DM, 22 Apr. 1995.

"Maybe we made": Betty Cox, interview with DM, 2 Feb. 1994.

"Now Betty was": Dave Sobol, interview with DM, 31 Jan. 1993.

"Betty was a cute": Source wishes not to be identified. Letter to Dave and Rubye Sobol, postmarked 1989, and telephone interview, 11 Sept. 1995.

"didn't care": Lew Raines, telephone interview with DM, 5 Apr. 1995.

180 "We had so much": Betty Cox, interview with DM, 2 Feb. 1994.

12. Making It

Scrapbooks are a major source of information in this chapter. Unannotated, they remained difficult to decipher until I read *But Beautiful: A Book about Jazz,* by Geoff Dyer. In this novel, improvisatory jazz portraits are threaded into a fictional narrative that carries Duke Ellington and Harry Carney through a night and part of a day on the road. "My purpose was to present the musicians not as they were but as they appear to me," Dyer explains (p. viii). *But Beautiful* is the epitome of bringing jazz culture — "a community of audiences and performers" (p. 184) — alive in words.

182 The Duke Ellington Orchestra: Billy Tipton saved snapshots of two occasions when his trio's path crossed Ellington's: a performance of the Ellington Orchestra in a gymnasium at Fort Lewis, Washington, 20 Apr. 1952, with Betty Rocket as vocalist, and the birthday party on 29 Apr. 1954 in Albany, Oregon.

184 "Many people forget": Mary Lou Williams, quoted in Gottlieb, *Reading Jazz,* p. 115.

186 "We had stayed": Kenny Richards, interview with DM, 14 Nov. 1995.

"I had a day": Ron Kilde, interview with DM, 28 Apr. 1995.

188 "Musical nonsense": Billy Tipton quoted in Dick Larsen, "Omak Is Climbing into Saddle for 22nd Annual Stampede," *Wenatchee Daily World*, 11 Aug. 1955, p. 1.

"rubber-faced antics": *Let's Go!*, 17 Mar. 1958.

189 KILDE: You've seen: Ron Kilde, interview with DM, 29 Apr. 1995, and Dick O'Neil, interview with DM, 30 Jan. 1995 (blended comments).

STRAIGHT MAN: Do you have: Billy Tipton, "Gee Quiz," circa 1955.

191 "Looming on the spotlight": scrapbook item dated 31 Mar. 1956.

192 The intonations: A documentary film about Chet Baker, *Let's Get Lost*, opens with a voice-over by Baker, whose speaking voice sounds exactly like Billy Tipton's.

she was the first: "Finally, Recognition for a Pioneer," *Los Angeles Times*, 23 Feb. 1993, Part F, p. 1.

"The gays weren't": Hadda Brooks, interview with Robert Basil, 15 Sept. 1995.

193 The trio's first recording: *Sweet Georgia Brown*, featuring the Billy Tipton Trio [L1522/TOPS, $1.49]. Side one: "What Is This Thing Called Love," "Sweet Georgia Brown," "Don't Blame Me," "Begin the Beguine," "Sit Right Down and Write Myself a Letter," "September in the Rain." Side two: "Bernie's Tune," "Take the 'A' Train," "Under a Blanket of Blue," "The Man I Love," "Perdido," "Willow Weep for Me."

"a gal who": Ron Kilde, interview with DM, 28 Apr. 1995.

Carl Doshay liked: Notarized "Recording Contract & Agreement," signed 6 Aug. 1956 by Billy L. Tipton.

"I believe": Carl Doshay to Billy Tipton, 13 July 1956.

195 "Tipton has worked": "Comes from 'show me' state," clipping, no date [circa 30 July 1952].

"had mentioned": Ron Kilde, interview with DM, 28 Apr. 1995.

Billy Tipton is: Back cover, *Billy Tipton Plays Hi-Fi on Piano* [L1534/TOPS]. Side one: "Can't Help Lovin' Dat Man," "Marie," "Delilah," "These Foolish Things," "What'll I Do," "The World Is Waiting for the Sunrise." Side two: "You Go to My Head," "Christopher Columbus," "Begin the Beguine," "If I Had You," "Blue Skies," "Stars Fell on Alabama."

197 "My how you have": Reggie Fullenwider to B. L. Tipton, 19 Oct. 1956.

"With Billy": Maryann Cattanach, interview with DM, 23 Apr. 1993.

199 "a classy one": Dick O'Neil, interview with DM, 30 Jan. 1995.

"Yes, it was right": Kenny and Dolly Richards, interview with DM, 14 Nov. 1995.

"Five stones": Maryann Cattanach, interview with DM, 23 Apr. 1993.

"Because he had": Maryann Cattanach interviews with DM, 23 and 24 Apr. 1993.

201 Or perhaps Billy's: Money, *Gay, Straight and In-Between*, pp. 136–38.

"Just, his habit": Maryann Cattanach, interview with DM, 23 Apr. 1993.

"primarily for the exploitation": Carl Doshay to Billy Tipton, 3 Oct. 1956.

202 According to the only: Tops Music Enterprises to Billy Tipton, 24 Feb. 1958.

203 "A poster on an easel": Lew Raines, interview with DM, 21 Apr. 1995.

"Billy seemed": Bill Pierson, interview with DM, 22 Apr. 1995.
204 "Well, I'm from California": Source wishes not to be identified. Telephone interview with DM, 5 Jan. 1996.
"I met Billy": Shannon Handler, interview with DM, 12 Feb. 1996.
"I saw Billy": Larry Martin, telephone interview with DM, 13 Mar. 1996.

13. Man's World

Success in passing as a man in daily life places Billy Tipton in a venerable tradition that is currently receiving attention from historians and theorists of gender. One contemporary analysis focuses on the psychology of the "transgendered" person, one whose gender identity is not congruent with biological sex. For exhaustive social scientific and literary research on distinctions between "trans" identity and homosexual identity, see Prosser, *Second Skins: The Body Narratives of Transsexuality.* Prosser provides a historical genealogy for the idea of transgendered identity, tracing it from the concept of "inversion," hypothesized by Krafft-Ebbing and Freud, which from 1900 was subsumed under the category of homosexuality, to its reemergence as a diagnosable medical condition — gender identity disorder — in the 1940s and 1950s. Prosser's work builds on theoretical arguments pertaining to gender as a performance, a perspective developed influentially in the work of Butler, *Gender Trouble: Feminism and the Subversion of Identity,* and in Kaplan, *Female Perversions.*

"Gender blender" is the term for "trans" identity preferred by the feminist sociologist Holly Devor in her presentation of interviews with fifteen women who were often mistaken for men; see *Gender Blending: Confronting the Limits of Duality.* For other accounts of "trans" consciousness, see Leslie Feinberg's compendium of historical examples in *Transgender Warriors: Making History from Joan of Arc to RuPaul,* and the first-person account in Green, "Meaning to Change."

The material on Alberta/Alan Hart in these pages is a composite of details taken from Katz, *Gay American History: Lesbians and Gay Men in the USA,* pp. 258–79, and Katz, *Gay/Lesbian Almanac: A New Documentary,* pp. 516–22. Katz's primary source was J. Allen Gilbert, "Homosexuality and Its Treatment," *Journal of Nervous and Mental Disease* 52, no. 4 (Oct. 1920): 297–332.

My discussion of the entertainer Stormé DeLarverié draws on an interview, (6 Dec. 1996), on a documentary film by Michele Parkerson (*Stormé: The Lady in the Jewel Box,* 1987), and on commentary by Elizabeth Drorbaugh, "Sliding Scales: Notes on Stormé DeLarverié and the Jewel Box Revue, the cross-dressed woman on the contemporary stage, and the invert," in Ferris, *Crossing the Stage: Controversies on Cross-Dressing,* pp. 120–43.

Works consulted about the life of a burlesque dancer included Corio, *This Was Burlesque;* Meiselas, *Carnival Strippers;* and Paris, *Queen of Burlesque: The Autobiography of Yvette Paris.*

210 "One year we were lucky": Maryann Cattanach, interview with DM, 23 Apr. 1993.
211 Built in 1914: Henry Matthews, "A Decade of Hopes and Fears: The Preserva-

tion of Spokane's Davenport Hotel," *Arcade,* Feb./Mar. 1991, pp. 10–13.

212 The Sobol agency represented: Dave Sobol, interview with DM, 20 Sept. 1993, and Ed Costello, "Agile Dave Sobol Beats the Odds," *Spokesman-Review,* 10 July 1960, p. 15.

"I saw that he": Dave Sobol, interview with DM, 31 Jan. 1993.

Working on commission: Dave Sobol's estimate, not reflected in social security records, where Billy designates himself as self-employed. Interview with DM, 20 Sept. 1993.

213 "a two-bedroom": Maryann Cattanach, interview with DM, 23 Apr. 1993.

"I used to spend": Source wishes not to be identified. Interview with DM, 4 May 1995.

"after the war": Robert Oakes, interview with DM, 29 Jan. 1995. Police corruption in Spokane is the basis of Timothy Egan's true crime narrative *Breaking Blue.*

214 "Boys' Night": Gerald Johnson, interview with DM, 2 May 1995.

215 "There wasn't much": Source wishes not to be identified. Interview with DM 4, May 1995.

216 "fully cognizant": Gilbert, quoted in Katz, *Gay American History,* p. 277.

In addition to: Alan L. Hart, *These Mysterious Rays* (New York: Harper, 1946).

"Whether or not": *New York Times,* 31 Mar. 1935, p. 17.

217 For her role: Stormé DeLarverié, interview with DM, 6 Dec. 1996.

"Some say sir": Stormé DeLarverié to Michele Parkerson, in the documentary film *Stormé.*

218 "family entertainment": Drorbaugh, "Sliding Scales," p. 129.

STRAIGHT MAN: Who was: Quoted from a folder of comedy routines, no title, circa 1955–1960.

219 "that kind of thing": Gilbert Keithly, telephone interview with DM, 20 Sept. 1997.

"Before I met Billy": Don Eagle, interview with DM, 3 May 1995.

"One of Billy's": Ron Kilde, interview with DM, 28 Apr. 1995.

"Musicians can be": Marvin Richter, interview with DM, 22 Nov. 1995.

Ironically, he kept: Kitty Oakes, interview with DM, 12 Jan. 1992.

220 "Oh, I went": Maryann Cattanach, interview with DM, 23 Apr. 1993.

"guys would try": Marvin Richter, interview with DM, 22 Nov. 1995.

221 "a mouth on her": Dick O'Neil, interview with DM, 30 Jan. 1995.

"a pretty good dancer": Kyle Pugh, interview with DM, 26 Jan. 1995.

222 "Billy had given": Kitty Oakes, interview with DM, 12 Jan. 1992.

"He said that": Kitty Oakes, interview with DM, 15 Jan. 1995.

she had had a hysterectomy: Summary of clinical data on Stella (Kitty) Tipton, patient of Thomas J. Osten, M.D., opened 2 June 1975, gives the year of the hysterectomy as 1960.

One band member recalled: According to Ron Kilde, "They had a motel they were meeting in for quite a while. I know this gal came to see me from Portland, and had worked there at Allen's Tin Pan Alley, that's where I met her. Billy suggested that if I wanted to get together, we could use their room. Kitty was right in on it too, said, 'Joy can come stay with me and you guys can

use my room, our room.'" Interview with DM, 28 Apr. 1993. Kitty Oakes
vehemently disputed the accuracy of this memory in an interview with DM,
18 Nov. 1995.

223 "My typewriter": Billy Tipton to Kitty Kelly, 18 Nov. 1960.
"Deep in the valley": Typescript, "Composed by Billy Tipton," dated 15 Dec.
1960.
The following June: Painting signed "S. Jeffreys, 6/61."
"A woman's breasts": Kitty Oakes, interview with DM, 12 Jan. 1992.
"One night": Kitty Oakes, interview with DM, 13 Jan. 1992.

224 During this courtship: Billy wrote to Kitty about the possibility that one of the
trio would leak the rumor. "Dick [O'Neil] said he had seen this coming for
some time, so it didn't surprise him. If he says anything to Mary, I'll tell her
the truth, that's all." BT to Kitty Kelly, 29 Aug. 1961.
"Why didn't you": Maryann Cattanach, interview with DM, 24 Apr. 1993.
"I have never had": Kitty Oakes, interview with DM, 12 Jan. 1992.

226 "The morning after": Kitty Oakes, interview with DM, 15 Jan. 1995.
"Passion!": Kitty Oakes, interview with DM, 15 Jan. 1995.

227 "I do like privacy": Billy Tipton to Kitty Kelly, 11 Sept. 1961.
"We could make": Billy Tipton to Kitty Kelly, 22 Aug. 1961.
"Ouch!": Billy Tipton to Kitty Kelly, postmarked 24 Aug. 1961.
"Hortense — cum home!": Billy Tipton to Kitty Kelly, 20 Sept. 1961.
"I got a call": Billy Tipton to Kitty Kelly, 24 Aug. 1961.
"I have been behaving": Billy Tipton to Kitty Kelly, 25 Aug. 1961.
"Billy's sense of humor": Kitty Oakes, interview with DM, 27 Jan. 1995.

228 "To me you are": Billy Tipton to Kitty Kelly, 28 Aug. 1961.
"Tell those salesmen": Billy Tipton to Kitty Kelly, 11 Dec. 1961.
"your old dad": Billy Tipton to Kitty Kelly, 13 Sept. 1961.
"Maybe some guys": Billy Tipton to Kitty Kelly, 29 Aug. 1961.
"You know that I worship": Billy Tipton to Kitty Kelly, 30 Aug. 1961.
"Oh my darling": Billy Tipton to Kitty Kelly, 14 Sept. 1961.
"When the snows fall": Billy Tipton to Kitty Kelly, 18 Sept. 1961.
"I don't know how": Billy Tipton to Kitty Kelly, 14 Sept. 1961.

14. Family Man

229 Billy and Kitty exchanged: "Stella Marie Kathleen Flaherty" was the name
the bride entered on the documentation of their wedding. Born Stella Marie
Banks, Kitty frequently used her stepfather's name, Flaherty, for official purposes. "Kitty" was her childhood nickname; "Kitty Kelly" was her stage name.
"Kathleen" was a name Billy gave her. The gold rings are referred to in a
newspaper article written two months after Billy's death: "In 1962 the couple
was wearing wedding bands, each inscribed with the year and KT-BT in fine,
cursive script." Kit Boss, "No Rest in Peace," *Seattle Times/Seattle Post-Intel-
ligencer*, 19 Mar. 1989, section L, p. 6.
Or so it says: "A Keepsake of Your Wedding," printed by Buzza-Cardozo,

Hollywood USA, 6 pp. Photos in the album Kitty kept show her in bed with
their dogs the next morning at the Garden Motel and posed outside the door
of the motel later — the first mementos of her life as Mrs. Tipton.

230   "consummated with a full": My italics. Title 32, I.S. §308, *Idaho Code* (New
York: Bobbs-Merrill,1963).

"Everything is going": Billy Tipton to Carrie Flaherty, inscription in a card
postmarked 9 May 1962.

"I fell in love": Billy Tipton to Kitty Kelly, 15 Sept. 1961.

"If I spoil you": Billy Tipton to Kitty Kelly, 13 Dec. 1961.

232   "The operation": Billy Tipton to Carrie Flaherty, 30 May 1962.

"We slept in": Kitty Oakes, interview with DM, 12 Jan. 1992.

"He's a pretty good": Billy Tipton to Kitty Kelly, 11 Dec. 1961.

"My Darling": Billy Tipton to Mrs. Billy L. Tipton, postmarked 20 Dec. 1968.

233   "Billy's age": Kitty Oakes, interviews with DM, 13 Jan. 1992 and 27 Jan. 1995.
Kitty Oakes withheld the names of the mothers and intermediaries in these
adoptions.

The baby, a boy: Kitty and Billy sent Carrie a birth announcement: "I wasn't
'expected' — I was 'selected.'" Kitty signed it, "Your loving daughter and son,
Kitty and Billy."

"Billy walked in": Kitty Oakes, interview with DM, 13 Jan. 1992.

235   It took many months: Kitty Oakes, annotations on appointment calendar,
July-Oct. 1966.

236   "My two kids": Kitty Oakes, interview with DM, 15 Jan. 1995.

"I would like": Robert Calicoat to Spokane Chamber of Commerce, 1967
Inland Empire "Mother of the Year" contest, no date [1967].

238   "Out of behemoth": Asher, *Notes from a Battered Grand*, p. 278.

Billy experienced: The musician in Billy disliked rock music, but Billy the
agent put the best face on "the musical revolution of the 1960s," as he called
it in a newspaper interview in 1974. "Things have settled down from those
wild days when the young people sort of broke out and started doing their
own thing . . . You have to be a little flamboyant to please the audience.
That's show business." "People and Business: Lounges Want Neater Talent,"
Spokane Daily Chronicle, 22 Mar. 1974, p. 22.

"things we do": Ben Tessensohn, interview with DM, 28 Jan. 1995.

"Billy was a creative": Kyle Pugh, interview with DM, 26 Jan. 1995.

"Often we didn't": Ben Tessensohn, interview with DM, 28 Jan. 1995.

"Normally when we were": Marvin Richter, interview with DM, 22 Nov. 1995,
and Ben Tessensohn, interview with DM, 28 Jan. 1995.

240   "I talked to my attorney": Billy Tipton to Kitty Kelly, 14 Sept. 1961.

"If I said": Dave Sobol, interview with DM, 28 Jan. 1995.

241   She contacted Billy: Certificate of Live Birth #031019, Vital Statistics Section, State Board of Health, State of Oregon.

"I slept": Kitty Oakes, interview with DM, 18 Mar. 1992.

242   Shortly after William's: Carrie C. Flaherty's name appears on the quit claim
deed of the house at S. 2403 Manito Blvd., dated 4 May 1971.

"Each of us had": Carrie Flaherty, interview with DM, 13 Jan. 1992. No clear chronology could be derived from Mrs. Flaherty's account of her marriages, moves, and employment.

244 Succeeding letters inquire: In one letter, Reggie asks Billy to thank Maryann for the afghan she knitted and sent as a gift. Reggie Fullenwider to B. L. Tipton, 19 Oct. 1956.

"My Darling": Reggie Fullenwider to B. L. Tipton, 18 Dec. 1956.

245 "Hope Kitty": Reggie Fullenwider to B. L. Tipton, 17 Dec. 1965.

"Mother [Dorothy's Aunt Cora]": Eilene Pierce, interview with DM, 4 Oct. 1992.

246 Dorothy alone: Doris and W. T. Tipton, interview with DM, 30 Jan. 1993.

After a brief service: Eilene Pierce, interview with DM, 3 Oct. 1992.

247 "You could have taken": Doris and W. T. Tipton, interview with DM, 29 Jan. 1993.

"I now know": Kitty Oakes, interview with DM, 19 Mar. 1992.

248 She never met: Information about legacies is drawn from W. T. Tipton to Billy Tipton, 23 Dec. 1975, and from W. T. Tipton, interview with DM, 12 Feb. 1996.

"seemed perfectly": Madeline Byrd, interview with DM, 1 Oct. 1992.

They talked about: G. W. Tipton died at age eighty-three on 11 Aug. 1975 in Fayetteville, Arkansas.

"She said that she": Eilene Pierce and Madeline Byrd, interviews with DM, 1–3 Oct. 1992.

250 "When he got dressed up": Kitty Oakes, interview with DM, 19 Mar. 1992. Billy performed "All I Want for Christmas" on a tape the family made for Carrie at Christmas in 1974.

William remembered: William Alan Tipton, interview with DM, 19 Mar. 1992. A typed manuscript of lyrics and pencil notation of instrumentation exists for "Red Hair and Green Eyes," by Billy Tipton, 1965; in 1996 a version of the song was recorded by the ensemble East Wind on an audiotape "Remembering Billy Tipton," commissioned by Oakes-Tipton Inc.

251 "We were so *normal*": Kitty Oakes, interview with DM, 19 Mar. 1992.

"while the rest": Greg Mason, interview with DM, 21 Nov. 1995.

Scads of photos: "Scouts Honor Six with Top Awards," *Spokesman-Review*, 3 Feb. 1980, p. B5.

252 A big glossy: Northwestern National Life Insurance Company to Kitty Tipton, regarding 1978 Company Calendar: a painting by Billy titled "Let It Snow" was submitted by Elaine Lippert, teacher at the Hutton School, 8 May 1977.

"The kids looked forward": Kitty Oakes, interview with DM, 19 Mar. 1992.

"They were the first": Denise Numbers, interview with DM, 17 Nov. 1995. One episode of troublemaking is well documented. For several days in Sept. 1977, someone pelted the Tiptons' house with a shower of stones and pebbles, breaking glass in the upper windows. Suspicion settled on Scott and John, and the parents agreed to a polygraph test. Eventually the boys were charged with obstructing a public officer. Spokane Police report #7743023.

253 "The kids started": Kitty Oakes, interview with DM, 12 Jan. 1992.

254 "a battle of boys": Carrie Flaherty, interview with DM, 13 Jan. 1992.

One of the boys: In an interview two months after Billy's death, Scott (Tipton) Miller acknowledged some of his most serious transgressions: "Miller says he was arrested as a juvenile for taking a pistol to school and stealing a car." Boss, "No Rest in Peace," section L, p. 6.

The family fell apart: Billy's two older sons gave accounts of the end of family life that differ significantly from Kitty's version and each other's. John said that Kitty had become "abusive" and that he and Scott walked out in 1977, when they were fourteen years old; John (Tipton) Clark, interview with DM, 20 Nov. 1995. Scott said, "My brother John and I left home when we were fifteen because Mom became increasingly overpowering. Two months after we left home, Dad couldn't stand it either. He walked out, left the big house and everything he owned to her"; quoted in *National Enquirer,* 13 Feb. 1989, p. 24.

255 "I started yelling": Kitty Oakes, interview with DM, 12 Jan. 1992.

15. Out and Down

257 "Billy came by": Dave Sobol, interviews with DM, 31 Jan. 1993 and 2 May 1995.

"Nobody could explain": William Alan Tipton, interview with DM, 14 Jan. 1992.

258 "I missed my mother": William Alan Tipton, interview with DM, 20 Mar. 1992.

"Scott would crank up": William Alan Tipton, interviews with DM, 14 Jan. 1992 and 18 Mar. 1992.

"skittish and apprehensive": William Alan Tipton, interview with DM, 14 Jan. 1992.

"I was a sounding board": Carrie Flaherty, interview with DM, 13 Jan. 1992.

"Dad wanted our love": William Alan Tipton, interview with DM, 14 Jan. 1992.

259 "I'll try harder": Kitty Oakes, interview with DM, 19 Mar. 1992.

One of his friends: Barron Stringfellow, interview with DM, 4 Apr. 1997.

260 "I stayed mad": Maryann Cattanach, interview with DM, 23 Apr. 1994.

"He'd never even mentioned": William Alan Tipton, interview with DM, 14 Jan. 1992.

"I would want grass": Maryann Cattanach to Billy Tipton, 21 June 1982.

"I couldn't take": Maryann Cattanach to Billy Tipton, 11 June 1983.

261 "You know honey": Maryann Cattanach to Billy Tipton, 30 Sept. 1983.

"Billy and I would": Maryann Cattanach, interview with DM, 23 Apr. 1994.

262 "I said to Billy": Dave Sobol, interview with DM, 14 Jan. 1993.

"Most people want": David Sutton, "'Whatever the people want . . .' That's Show Biz, Claims Agent," *Spokane Valley Herald,* 28 Dec. 1983, p. 6.

263 Cousin Eilene: Eilene Pierce to Billy Tipton, 3 Jan. 1983, and interview with DM, 3 Oct. 1992.

"My satisfaction": "People and Business: Lounges Want Neater Talent," *Spokane Daily Chronicle,* 22 Mar. 1974, p. 22.

"I'll never forget": Barron Stringfellow, telephone interview with DM, 4 Apr. 1997.

264   "The day I first": Mike Brandon, interview with DM, 31 Jan. 1995.
      "the boys took advantage": Carrie Flaherty, interview with DM, 13 Jan. 1992.
265   "A group would be booked": Marvin Richter, interview with DM, 22 Nov.
      1995.
      "Billy knew absolutely": Mike Brandon, interview with DM, 31 Jan. 1995.
266   "I said, Go ahead": Dave Sobol, interview with DM, 14 Jan. 1993.
      "I was kind of": Mike Brandon, interview with DM, 31 Jan. 1995.
267   "an unvarying routine": William Alan Tipton, interview with DM, 14 Jan.
      1992.
      "He had arthritis": William Alan Tipton, interview with DM, 19 Mar. 1992.
268   "Every day we lived": William Alan Tipton, interviews with DM, 14 Jan. 1992
      and 18 Mar. 1992.

16. The End

270   "I'm talking about things": Mike Brandon, interview with DM, 31 Jan. 1995.
271   "Dad was so sentimental": William Alan Tipton, interview with DM, 19 Mar.
      1992.
272   "My dad had": Doug Brock, interview with DM, 31 Jan. 1995.
273   "I told him": Mike Brandon, interview with DM, 31 Jan. 1995.
      "Yes," he remembered: Barron Stringfellow, interview with DM, 4 Apr. 1997.
274   "He didn't have": Mike Brandon, interview with DM, 31 Jan. 1995.
      "a lot of the musicians": Doug Brock, interview with DM, 31 Jan. 1995.
      "My take was": Joann Brandon, telephone interview with DM, 26 July 1996.
      "When we first heard": Mike Brandon, interview with DM, 31 Jan. 1995.
275   "I wish Billy": Shirley Lent, interview with DM, 25 Jan. 1993.
276   "I'm a rather snoopy": Maryann Cattanach, telephone interview with DM, 22
      Feb. 1993.
      "Billy was a good person": Maryann Cattanach, interview with DM, 23 Apr.
      1993.
277   "But at the motel": Eilene Pierce, interview with DM, 3 Oct. 1992.
278   "Normally she couldn't": Madeline Byrd, interview with DM, 1 Oct. 1992.
279   He told a friend: Jimmy B. Nixon, interview with DM, 31 Jan. 1995.
      "I said, 'Hi, Billy'": Ben Tessonsohn, interview with DM, 28 Jan. 1995.
      For company and warmth: Newspaper articles written a few months after
      Billy's death enumerate his possessions. Kit Boss, "No Rest in Peace," *Seattle
      Times/Seattle Post-Intelligencer,* 19 Mar. 1989, section L, p. 1, lists "old suits
      still in their dry-cleaning bags, a rack of 78rpm records, a Golden Home and
      High School encyclopedia set, a diamond ring, a 1978 Dodge Diplomat, a
      12-by-60-foot mobile home and alto and soprano saxophones." Ann Japenga,
      "A Jazz Pianist's Ultimate Improvisation," *Los Angeles Times,* 13 Feb. 1989,
      Part V, p. 1, notes that "Mr. T's possessions included books on Elvis Presley,
      an ivory money clip and a row of men's shoes, each with a lift in the heel."
280   "He's the sweetest": Billy Tipton to Kitty Kelly, 13 Dec. 1961.
      "I have been getting": Billy Tipton to Eilene Pierce, 9 Dec. 1988.
      "I'm still at the same": Billy Tipton to Madeline Byrd, 12 Dec. 1988.

References

Abelove, Henry, Michèle Aina Barale, and David M. Halperin. *Lesbian and Gay Studies Reader.* New York: Routledge, 1993.

Allen, Gene. *Voices on the Wind: Early Radio in Oklahoma.* Oklahoma City: Oklahoma Heritage Association, 1993.

Arnold, Anita G. *Legendary Times and Tales of Second Street.* Oklahoma City: Black Liberated Arts Center, 1995.

Asher, Don. *Notes from a Battered Grand.* New York: Harcourt, 1992.

Balliett, Whitney. *American Musicians II: Seventy-two Portraits in Jazz.* New York: Oxford University Press, 1996.

Bell-Metereau, Rebecca. *Hollywood Androgyny.* New York: Columbia University Press, 1985.

Benson, Susan Porter. *Counter Cultures: Saleswomen, Managers, and Customers in American Department Stores, 1890–1940.* Urbana and Chicago: Illinois University Press, 1986.

Bilstein, Roger F. *Flight in America: From the Wrights to the Astronauts.* Baltimore: Johns Hopkins University Press, 1984.

Bright, Susie. *Sexual State of the Union.* New York: Simon & Schuster, 1997.

Brown, Theodore and Lyle Dorsett. *KC: A History of Kansas City, Missouri.* Boulder, Colo.: Pruett, 1978.

Bullough, Vern L., and Bonnie Bullough. *Cross Dressing, Sex, and Gender.* Philadelphia: University of Pennsylvania Press, 1993.

Butler, Judith. *Gender Trouble: Feminism and the Subversion of Sexual Identity.* New York: Routledge, 1990.

Calabria, Frank M. *Dance of the Sleepwalkers: The Dance Marathon Fad.* Bowling Green, Ky.: Bowling Green State University Press, 1993.

Calloway, Cab, and Bryant Rollins. *Of Minnie the Moocher and Me.* New York: Crowell, 1976.

Case, Sue-Ellen. *Feminism and Theatre.* London: Macmillan, 1988.

Castle, Terry. *The Apparitional Lesbian.* New York: Columbia University Press, 1993.

———. *Noel Coward and Radclyffe Hall: Kindred Spirits.* New York: Columbia University Press, 1996.

Chafe, William H. *The Unfinished Journey: America Since World War II.* 3d ed. New York: Oxford University Press, 1995.

Chapman, Berlin B. *Oklahoma City: From Public Land to Private Property.* Oklahoma City: Oklahoma Historical Society, 1960.

Chernin, Kim. *My Life as a Boy.* Chapel Hill, N.C.: Algonquin, 1997.

Corio, Ann, with Joseph DiMona. *This Was Burlesque.* New York: Grosset, 1968.

Corn, Joseph. *The Winged Gospel: America's Romance with Aviation 1900–1950.* New York: Oxford University Press, 1983.

Crawford, Caroline. *Norma Teagarden: Grand Lady of Piano Jazz,* an oral history conducted in 1992–1994 by Regional Oral History Office, Bancroft Library, University of California, Berkeley, 1994.

Crow, Bill. *Jazz Anecdotes.* New York: Oxford University Press, 1990.

Dahl, Linda. *Stormy Weather: The Music and Lives of a Century of Jazzwomen.* New York: Limelight, 1992.

Debo, Angie. *Oklahoma: Foot-Loose and Fancy-Free.* Norman: University of Oklahoma Press, 1949.

de Erauso, Catalina. *Lieutenant Nun: Memoir of a Basque Transvestite in the New World.* Boston: Beacon, 1996.

D'Emilio, John, and Estelle B. Freedman. *Intimate Matters: A History of Sexuality in America.* New York: Harper, 1988.

Devor, Holly. *Gender Blending: Confronting the Limits of Duality.* Bloomington: Indiana University Press, 1989.

Dexter, Dave, Jr. *The Jazz Story from the '90s to the '60s.* Englewood Cliffs, N.J.: Prentice Hall, 1964.

Duberman, Martin Bauml. *About Time: Exploring the Gay Past.* New York: Sea Horse, 1986.

———, Martha Vicinus, and George Chauncey, Jr., eds. *Hidden from History: Reclaiming the Gay and Lesbian Past.* New York: New American Library, 1989.

Dyer, Geoff. *But Beautiful: A Book about Jazz.* New York: North Point, 1996.

Edwards, Jim, Mitchell Oliphant, and Hal Ottaway. *The Vanished Splendor: Postcard Memories of Oklahoma City.* 3 vols. Oklahoma City: Abalanche Book Shop Publishing, 1982, 1983, 1985.

Egan, Timothy. *Breaking Blue.* New York: Berkeley, 1993.

Ellison, Ralph. *Shadow and Act.* New York: Random House, 1995.

Faderman, Lillian. *Odd Girls and Twilight Lovers: A History of Lesbian Life in Twentieth Century America.* New York: Columbia University Press, 1991.

Fausto-Sterling, Anne. *Myths of Gender: Biological Theories about Women and Men.* New York: Basic, 1992.

———. "The Five Sexes: Why Male and Female Are Not Enough." *Sciences* (March–April 1992): 20–25.

Feather, Leonard. *The Encyclopedia of Jazz.* New York: Da Capo, 1960.

Feinberg, Leslie. *Stone Butch Blues: A Novel.* Ithaca: Firebrand, 1993.

———. *Transgender Warriors: Making History from Joan of Arc to RuPaul.* Boston: Beacon, 1996.

Ferris, Lesley. *Crossing the Stage: Controversies on Cross-Dressing.* London: Routledge, 1993.

Franklin, Jimmie Lewis. *Born Sober: Prohibition in Oklahoma, 1907–1959.* Norman: University of Oklahoma Press, 1971.

Franks, Stephen, M.D. "Polycystic Ovary Syndrome." *New England Journal of Medicine* 333, no. 13 (Sept. 28, 1995): 853–60.

Frazier, Ian. *Great Plains.* New York: Farrar, Straus and Giroux, 1989.

FTM International Newsletter. Issues 1–38 (Sept. 1987–Aug. 1997). Oakland, Calif.: FTM International.

Gabbard, Krin, ed. *Jazz Among the Discourses.* Durham, N.C.: Duke University Press, 1995.

Garber, Marjorie. *Vested Interests: Cross-Dressing and Cultural Anxiety.* New York: Routledge, 1991.

Gioia, Ted. *The Imperfect Art: Reflections on Jazz and Modern Culture.* New York: Oxford University Press, 1988.

———. *West Coast Jazz: Modern Jazz in California, 1945–1960.* New York: Oxford University Press, 1992.

Gottlieb, Robert, ed. *Reading Jazz: A Gathering of Autobiography, Reportage and Criticism from 1919 to Now.* New York: Pantheon, 1996.

Green, James. "The De Nijs Prosthesis." *FTM International Newsletter.* Issue 27 (Apr. 1994): 5.

———. "Meaning to Change." *Anything That Moves* (Summer 1991): 56–57.

———. "PCOS Again." *FTM International Newsletter.* Issue 38 (Aug. 1997): 4.

Guiles, Fred Lawrence. *Joan Crawford: The Last Word.* London: Pavilion, 1995.

Hajdu, David. *Lush Life: A Biography of Billy Strayhorn.* New York: Farrar, Straus and Giroux, 1996.

Hamm, Charles. *Yesterdays: Popular Song in America.* New York: Norton, 1979.

Hart, Lynda, ed. *Making Spectacle: Feminist Essays on Contemporary Women's Theatre.* Ann Arbor: University of Michigan Press, 1989.

Haskins, Jim. *The Cotton Club.* New York: Random House, 1977.

Havoc, June. *Early Havoc.* New York: Simon & Schuster, 1959.

———. *Marathon '33.* New York: Dramatists Play Service, 1969.

———. *More Havoc.* New York: Harper, 1980.

Heat-Moon, William Least. *Blue Highways: A Journey into America.* Boston: Atlantic/Little, Brown, 1982.

Hennessey, Thomas J. *From Jazz to Swing: African-American Jazz Musicians and Their Music.* Detroit: Wayne State University Press, 1994.

Hentoff, Nat. Liner notes, *Little Club Jazz: Small Groups in the '30s.* New World Records: NW 250, 1976.

———. *Listen to the Stories.* New York: HarperCollins, 1995.

———, and Albert J. McCarthy, eds. *Jazz.* New York: Da Capo, 1975.

Herman, Woody, and Stuart Troup, *The Woodchoppers Ball: The Autobiography of Woody Herman.* New York: Limelight Editions, 1994.

Hiort, O., et al. "The Clinical and Molecular Spectrum of Androgen Insensitivity Syndromes." *American Journal of Medical Genetics* 63, no. 1 (3 May 1996): 218–22.

Hollander, Anne. *Sex and Suits: The Evolution of Modern Dress.* New York: Knopf, 1994.

Joyce, Davis D., ed. *"An Oklahoma I Had Never Seen Before": Alternative Views of Oklahoma History.* Norman: University of Oklahoma Press, 1994.

Kaliss, Jeff. "The Greening of Teagarden." *San Francisco Examiner Datebook,* 27 Aug. 1989, pp. 39–40.

314 · *References*

Kaplan, Louise J. *Female Perversions: The Temptations of Emma Bovary.* New York: Anchor, 1991.

Katz, Jonathan. *Gay American History.* New York: Crowell, 1976.

———. *Gay/Lesbian Almanac: A New Documentary.* New York: Harper, 1983.

Kehoe, Monika. *Lesbians over 60 Speak for Themselves.* London: Haworth, 1989.

Kennedy, Elizabeth Lapovsky, and Madeline D. Davis. *Boots of Leather, Slippers of Gold.* New York: Routledge, 1993.

Kirk, Sheila. "Polycystic Ovarian Syndrome." *FTM International Newsletter.* Issue 36 (March 1997): 5.

Kruse, Holly. "Early Audio Technology and Domestic Space," in Anahid Kassabian, ed. *Music in the Age of Interdisciplinarity* (special issue of *Stanford Humanities Review*) 3, no. 2 (Autumn 1993): 1–13.

Lackmann, Ron. *Remember Radio.* New York: Putnam, 1970.

Lees, Gene. *Cats of Any Color: Jazz Black & White.* New York: Oxford University Press, 1994.

———. *Meet Me at Jim & Andy's.* New York: Oxford University Press, 1988.

Lewin, Ellen, ed. *Inventing Lesbian Cultures in America.* Boston: Beacon, 1996.

Livermore, Mary. *My Story of the War.* Hartford, Conn.: A. D. Worthington, 1876.

McCoy, Horace. *They Shoot Horses, Don't They?* New York: Avon, 1935.

McDowell, Colin. *Forties Fashion and the New Look.* London: Bloomsbury, 1997.

McGrill, Albert. *And Satan Came Also: An Inside Story of a City's Social and Political History.* Oklahoma City: Britton, 1955.

McReynolds, Edwin C. *Oklahoma: A History of the Sooner State.* Norman: Oklahoma State University Press, 1964.

Maitland, Sara. *Vesta Tilley.* London: Virago, 1986.

Meiselas, Susan. *Carnival Strippers.* New York: Farrar, Straus, 1976.

Merod, Jim, ed. *Boundary 2, special issue: Jazz as a Cultural Archive* 22, no. 2 (Summer 1995).

Mirken, Alan, ed. *The 1927 Edition of the Sears, Roebuck Catalogue.* New York: Crown, 1970.

Monaco, James. *The Encyclopedia of Film.* New York: Perigee, 1991.

Money, John. *Gay, Straight and In-Between: The Sexology of Erotic Orientation.* New York: Oxford University Press, 1988.

Morgan, Dan. *Rising in the West.* New York: Knopf, 1992.

Morgan, H. Wayne, and Anne Hodges Morgan. *Oklahoma: A History.* New York: Norton, 1984.

Nestle, Joan, ed. *The Persistent Desire: A Femme-Butch Reader.* Boston: Alyson, 1992.

Newton, Esther. *Mother Camp: Female Impersonation in America.* Chicago: University of Chicago Press, 1979.

O'Day, Anita, with George Eells. *High Times, Hard Times.* New York: Putnam, 1981.

Olian, JoAnne. *Everyday Fashions of the Forties as Pictured in Sears Catalogues.* New York: Dover, 1992.

Orgel, Stephen. *Impersonations: The Performance of Gender in Shakespeare's England.* Cambridge: Cambridge University Press, 1996.

Paris, Yvette. *Queen of Burlesque: The Autobiography of Yvette Paris*. Buffalo, N.Y.: Prometheus, 1990.

Patterson, M.N., et al. "Androgen Insensitivity Syndrome." *Baillieres Clinical Endrocrinology and Metabolism* 2 (8 April 1994): 379–404.

Porter, Lewis, Michael Ullman, and Ed Hazell. *Jazz: From the Origins to the Present*. Englewood Cliffs, N.J.: Prentice-Hall, 1993.

Pratt, Minnie Bruce. *S/HE*. Ithaca: Firebrand, 1995.

Prosser, Jay. *Second Skins: The Body Narratives of Transsexuality*. New York: Columbia University Press, forthcoming.

Raban, Jonathan. *Bad Land: An American Romance*. New York: Pantheon, 1996.

Reddig, William M. *Tom's Town: Kansas City and the Pendergast Legend*. Philadelphia: Lippincott, 1947.

Renner, G. K. *Joplin from Mining Town to Urban Center*. Northridge, Calif.: Windsor, 1985.

RuPaul. *Lettin' It All Hang Out: An Autobiography*. New York: Hyperion, 1995.

Sales, Grover. *Jazz: America's Classical Music*. New York: Da Capo, 1992.

Savage, William W. *Singing Cowboys and All That Jazz: A Short History of Popular Music in Oklahoma*. Norman: University of Oklahoma Press, 1983.

Schuller, Gunther. *Early Jazz: Its Roots and Musical Development*. New York: Oxford University Press, 1968.

———. *The Swing Era: The Development of Jazz, 1930–1945*. New York: Oxford University Press, 1989.

Shapiro, Nat, and Nat Hentoff, eds. *Hear Me Talkin' to Ya*. New York: Dover, 1966.

Sheldon, Ruth. *Hubbin' It: The Life of Bob Wills*. Privately published, 1938.

Slide, Anthony. *The Encyclopedia of Vaudeville*. Westport, Conn.: Greenwood, 1994.

———. *Great Pretenders: A History of Female & Male Impersonation in the Performing Arts*. Lombard, Ill.: Wallace-Homestead, 1986.

———. *The Vaudevillians*. Westport, Conn.: Greenwood, 1981.

Smith, Jay D., and Len Guttridge. *Jack Teagarden: The Story of a Jazz Maverick*. New York: Da Capo, 1988.

Stein, Howard F., and Robert F. Hill, eds. *The Culture of Oklahoma*. Norman: University of Oklahoma Press, 1993.

Stewart, Roy P. *Born Grown: An Oklahoma City History*. Oklahoma City: Fidelity Bank National Association, 1974.

Stinnett, Roger. *Joplin: A Pictorial History*. Virginia Beach, Va.: Donning, 1981.

Tomalin, Claire. *Mrs. Jordan's Profession*. London: Viking, 1994.

Townsend, Charles R. *San Antonio Rose: The Life and Music of Bob Wills*. Urbana: University of Illinois Press, 1976.

Trillin, Calvin. *Messages from My Father*. New York: Farrar, Straus and Giroux, 1996.

Van Gilder, Marvin L. *Jasper County, The First Two Hundred Years*. Joplin, Mo.: Marvin L. Van Gilder and the Jasper County Commission, 1995.

Wilder, Alec. *American Popular Song: The Great Innovators, 1900–1950*, ed. and with an introduction by James T. Maher. New York: Oxford University Press, 1972.

INDEX

"Valse Melodic" (song), 39

Walkathons, 68–69, 70
Waller, Fats, 100
Wallin, Son, 80–86 *passim*, 89
"Wall Street Broker" (comedy
    routine), 77
"The Way You Look Tonight" (song),
    184
Webster, Ben, 41
Weill, Kurt, 6
Western Swingbillies, 91, 103
Whiteman, Paul, 63
"Whispering," (song), 110
Whitt, Wayne "Tiny," 102–3, 105
Williams, Mary Lou, 39, 40, 41, 80, 184

Wills, Bob, 77, 80–81, 84, 88, 101, 272
Wilson, George, 133
Wilson, Norm and Terry, 151
Wilson, Slim, 54
Wilson, Teddy, 8, 9, 89, 100, 110–11
Women in jazz field. *See* Jazz
Wonderful Wizard of Oz, The (Baum),
    21, 117
"The World Is Waiting for the Sunrise"
    (song), 194
Wynn, "Big Anne," 18

"Yesterdays" (song), 151
Young, Gig, 69
Young, Lester, 26, 41
Young Man with a Horn (movie), 194